STARTING A NEW DESIGN FIRM

STARTING A NEW DESIGN FIRM, OR RISKING IT ALL!

FRANK A. STASIOWSKI, A.I.A.
with JULIA WILLARD

JOHN WILEY & SONS, INC.
New York / Chichester / Brisbane / Toronto / Singapore

This text is printed on acid-free paper.

This publication is designed to provide accurate and
authoritative information in regard to the subject
matter covered. It is sold with the understanding that
the publisher is not engaged in rendering legal, accounting,
or other professional services. If legal advice or other
expert assistance is required, the services of a competent
professional person should be sought.

Library of Congress Cataloging in Publication Data:

Stasiowski, Frank, 1948–
    Starting a new design firm / Frank A. Stasiowski with Julia Willard.
        p.   cm.
    ISBN 0-471-58576-9 (cloth)
    1. Architectural firms—United States—Management.   2. Small
business—United States—Management.   I. Willard, Julia, 1962– .
NA1996.S748   1994
729'.068—dc20   93-40912

Printed in the United States of America

10 9 8 7 6 5 4 3

PREFACE

Why Start a Business in the 1990s?

The purpose of this book is to acquaint the reader with the general concerns in setting up a new design practice, and also to inspire the aspiring entrepreneur. Most of the firm owners I interviewed, if not all of them, relayed a resounding "Yes!" when I posed the question: "Has it all been worthwhile?"

Servicing the client, creating designs that produce unique solutions to the problems and the buildings and the structures that house our workplaces and our lives, these are the true inspirations and true goals in setting up a business. For the firms interviewed here, the primary objective has been to create viable design work, while generally making a "comfortable" living. Most owners have accomplished at least that, if not more.

Many would wonder about the viability of setting up a design practice in 1994—coming off the end of perhaps the worst white collar recession in a fifty year span. However, a post-recessionary period is the best time to start a business, for several reasons.

First of all, we're psychologically geared toward cutting corners and cutting costs. Starting a new business, when you may have to live on apprentice's wages for a year or so, isn't so bad when you're just coming out of a recessionary period, a period when there hasn't been a lot of "big spending."

Second, it's easier to ride the crest of a wave than it is to ride the trough of a wave. In starting up a business at the "beginning" of a new economic period, you will be "riding the wave" as it is developing. You will have the advantage.

Third, the world and the workplace are changing. Thousands are cutting the cord from traditional work arrangements and traditional jobs, and setting up jobs to fit their lifestyles—whether that be at home or in a small office. Most likely, if you are starting out small, you will be one of these people.

Finally, it's easier to get work. Why? There are fewer companies out there, the cost of help is down, office rents are lowered, and the general cost of doing business is down. If you are willing to invest the time and provide service beyond the norm, you can only do well.

Literally what we see coming out of this recession is a way of developing several different new markets. If you can hop onto one of these new waves, you can ride it for five years! Then you will have time to prepare and plan for the next recession: the next anticipated "down" business cycle.

This book was written to inspire, motivate, and instruct you in setting up your own design practice, and to instill in you the belief that with the proper process of goal setting and planning, your vision will come to fruition. The tough part is it requires participation—foresight and endless hours of grueling work. But for the entrepreneurs interviewed for this book, the hours and work have been worthwhile, since they have been the price of freedom and economic security. Most design professionals agree that they could have made more money in other professions, but not one expressed an ounce of regret. Most, in fact, wouldn't have had it any other way. I hope that's the way your experience goes as well.

Best of luck.

Frank A. Stasiowski

Newton, Massachusetts
1994

CONTENTS

INTRODUCTION

"You are selling to one of the most sophisticated groups of clients in history, and you too must equal their level of expertise if you plan to stay competitive." —*Frank Stasiowski*

Why start a new design firm? Design entrepreneurs generally begin their enterprise because they crave more artistic control, they have an interest in a particular building type or service, or they take on a small commission that does not interest the parent company. You may have identified a particular niche in the design world in which you are sure you will excel. At any rate, the jump to start a new firm most often results from the combination of a high degree of self-confidence and an equally high degree of frustration.

However a firm begins, it must learn to sustain itself. Establishing the firm's initial identity has great influence over its final success or demise. So in setting up your office you must ask yourself: What is your vision? Your mission? Your goals? And who will be your clients?

The pages of this book are devoted to helping you define those questions, and to instilling within you a sense of purpose about your work. Down the line, the vision you determine today will dictate all decisions, from office space and furniture, to clientele, to market research, to whom you wish to hire, to what you will do should the work dwindle. If the book seems to be repetitive in stating the importance of your initial decisions, it is meant to be. The seed you plant today turns into a sapling tomorrow and the next day it's a fully grown tree—and it is difficult, at best, to replant a 20 foot tree.

Remember that you are selling to one of the most sophisticated groups of clients in history, and you too must equal their level of expertise if you plan to stay competitive. Today's clients are looking for experts: What is your expertise? What do you have to sell? Why would anyone buy your services? How much will they pay you to perform? How much can you produce? How many hours do you want to work? How little money are you wiling to live on until the firm gets a secure foothold in the market?

These questions are hard, but inevitable. And they must all be considered in starting a design practice, now more than at any other time in history.

A few words of caution about breaking away: Most established principals are not offended by a young architect or engineer who leaves to start his or her own firm. After all, that is the ultimate goal in professional practice. The trouble begins when clients are at stake. Ethically it is best not to solicit your former clients. If they come to you because they want to, then so be it. But let it be their move, not yours. You never know when you might need to go back to the old firm, set up a joint venture or partnering agreement, or negotiate a subcontract. You can't get back home again if there are no bridges to cross. Don't burn them. In the long run, it's not worthwhile.

SHOULD YOU HAVE A PARTNER?

For the past ten years, I've cautioned design firm owners to reduce the numbers of partners in design firms. Yet by their nature, all of the design firms I've consulted for, sat on roundtables with, and helped with planning have had partners. Design firms are, by definition, top heavy. But I keep telling them to reduce partners because of the decreasing profitability of design firms, and the increasing use of CADD for drafting. Honestly, having lots of partners to start up a firm not only spreads the profits very thin, but also wastes valuable time. When there are more than three partners (and three is generally too many when starting up a firm!), all decisions become unwieldy. Think of the billables wasted when four partners sit down to meet every Monday morning for four hours!

The choice to go it alone or to go with a partner really depends on your personality, your abilities, and your willingness to risk it all. The work volume you expect and your financial situation are also factors. The bottom line is that if you do choose a partner (or partners), you must both (or all) be able to share ability and wealth, each shouldering an equitable workload.

Partnerships work best when the partners complement each other by function or discipline, according to a recent article in *Architecture* magazine ("Starting Your Own Firm," by Nancy Solomon, June 1992). Solomon notes that male/female partnerships are becoming a popular way to secure commissions as well. Each partner has a different approach, and the more variety you offer in terms of getting along with different clients, the better.

WHY FIRMS FAIL

Start-up design firms fail most often because they lack sufficient capital to get them through the slow periods. As a general rule, you should have four months' to one year's earnings in the bank when you start, or have three ongoing projects to ensure adequate cash flow. This book will emphasize the importance of maintaining cash flow, getting paid on time, and starting off on the right foot.

NEW IDEAS?

You may note that this book takes a new turn, and some of the ideas set down here may appear to be contrary to those I set down in *Staying Small Successfully* or *Value Pricing for Design Professionals*. Those books were written for design firms that already existed, and therefore the focus here is entirely different.

In starting a design firm, and in this book, you must focus on the kinds of design problems you would like to be solving, the client base you wish to serve, and then build your profit and payment strategy from there. In all my books I hold strategic vision above profit and financing because strategic vision comes first, and it's what will carry you through in the long term. That still holds true here. If you don't know where you are going or why you want to get there, then you won't get there!

A well planned, well executed business plan, financial plan, and profit strategy naturally follow the development of your vision and your mission.

Each and every year my firm holds a week long seminar in

Beaver Creek, Colorado. Some of the attendees return year after year, as a chance to get away and to rethink their firms, once each year. One year my topic was marketing, and for the first eight hours of the seminar I talked about mission. All the attendees rethought their company missions, and at the end of that first day, they felt they were done. The second day, I came in, and informed them that we would be spending the morning rewriting their missions. Their minds hit the roof and their pencils hit the ceiling. But after that second day, the attendees had the most focused vision and mission statements they had ever produced.

The point is, take the time to truly think out, in advance, the kind of firm you'd like to be. Write down the vision, write out the mission, and then build the plan from there.

DEFINING TRUE LEADERSHIP

1 WHY LEADERSHIP IS IMPORTANT

> "Leadership and leading are indispensable to each other."
> —*Remarks prepared for delivery at the Trade Mart*
> *in Dallas, Nov. 22, 1963*

An entrepreneur is, by nature, a risk taker. The entrepreneur sees the benefits and the possibilities, rather than getting hung up on how things might not work out. If you do not have that element of risk taking in your makeup, then I don't recommend that you start up a firm. However, entrepreneurs and good leadership do not automatically go hand in hand. The mark of a successful entrepreneur is great leadership as well. For without a captain, a ship doesn't sail, and the crew has no point of direction. If the captain did not have navigating equipment, where would the ship be? As the leader of a design firm, your navigating equipment starts with your leadership qualities and finishes with your business plan. Without this equipment, you'll be stuck in a dinghy getting nowhere fast. With good, solid leadership and a well conceived business plan, you'll develop your firm and it will travel to successes your never anticipated. So your first task in striking out on your own is to develop leadership qualities within yourself, and then learn how to coach others to greatness.

An avid fan of management books, I've always had an insatiable need to verify my beliefs on the true qualities of a leader, mostly because these qualities can be so intangible. Recently I picked up a copy of *On Becoming a Leader,* by Warren Bemis, to review it for the readers of the professional journal my company publishes. I thought it important to pass Bemis' thoughts on leadership along. According to Bemis, there are three reasons why the leader is important, paraphrased here:

1. The leader is responsible for the effectiveness of the organization—its success or failure depends on the perceived quality of the leader
2. Changes in past years have left an empty seat—people in our society need leaders
3. People are looking for integrity in their role models: they like to have a leader with integrity

"A dreamless sleep is death," Bemis says. You, as the leader of your new firm, are the carrier and the executor of the dream. Design work in itself is the fulfillment of a particular client's dream, the selling of a vision to a client. As a design entrepreneur, you are extending that dream creation one step further. As the head of your firm, you must manage the dream. You alone:

- Communicate the vision.
- Recruit the personnel to carry it out.
- Reward them adequately to keep motivation high.
- Retrain them so they stay the best in their field.
- Organize your firm to stay ahead of the game.

The bottom line isn't everything—it's a lot—but don't neglect to think through entirely all the consequences of your vision. The choices you make in setting up the fulfillment of your dream—your firm's size, your market, your goals—must all adhere to the vision you set down. "A leader without some vision of where he wants to take his organization is not a leader," Bemis says. In formulating that vision, beware of the hazards of short-term thinking: "Our addiction to the short term gave us freeze-frame shots of a changing world, preventing us from seeing that it was shrinking, heating up, growing rancorous and ambitious—not just socially but economically."

In our time we have come to expect neat, simple answers. Nothing is simple. Answers are long term; they are complex. Understand this complexity and communicate its meaning through your work. Your judgement and character will be communicated in your vision, and it will manifest itself inevitably.

Take a look at the vision statement provided in Figure 1.1 by Gresham, Smith and Partners. This is a combined vision and mission statement that gets to the heart of the belief systems of the owner, and to the core aspects behind the business. It specifically names geographic area and markets, but

GRESHAM, SMITH AND PARTNERS

Mission/Vision

Gresham, Smith and Partners accepts the challenge to improve the environment and the community in which it exists. In order to successfully perform its objectives the organization must:

- Respond with excellence specifically to the issues, requirements, and desires of our clients
- Provide all employees the opportunity for professional challenge, development, advancement, and incentives

Gresham, Smith and Partners' challenge is to provide quality architectural, engineering, interior design, and landscape architectural services.

Gresham, Smith and Partners focuses on Southeastern United States market with operating offices in Nashville, Birmingham, Huntsville and Jacksonville and other locations as deemed appropriate. Growth shall not occur at the expense of the quality of service provided to existing clients.

Excellence is the provision of innovative, effective, and valuable solutions to our clients' specific needs, worthy of special recognition by our peers, clients, and public. In order to respond to the client, the firm is internally organizing to reflect specific market segments. Our market segments are health care, corporate/commercial, governmental, industrial, institutional; and others requiring building systems and non-building engineering services. Each client is associated with a principal with an expertise in their specific market area. We will anticipate changes in client and market needs and respond appropriately.

Gresham, Smith and Partners respects the dignity and rights of the individual. People are provided with responsibility and opportunity to participate and contribute, to be innovative and accountable, to grow professionally and personally through education and experience, and to participate in the financial success of the organization.

Profitability requirements include the ability to fund incentive compensation, ownership return, growth, retirement planning and capital investment. Innovation, research, and extraordinary professional services are only possible within the profitable organization.

Figure 1.1

also states how the firm's principals view their employees ("People are provided with responsibility and opportunity to participate and contribute, to be innovative and accountable ..."). It is obvious from this vision/mission statement that the owners of Gresham, Smith and Partners have developed leadership qualities in themselves, and have thought out how they will pass on their inspiration to their employees.

HOW DO YOU DEFINE YOUR VISION?

In later chapters you will explore how to develop your firm's vision. Here you must understand how to uncover your true instinct. If your instinct says you are going down the wrong path or if you are uncomfortable, feel shaky, don't believe in what you're doing, then rethink your position. If your partner believes one thing and you can't truly be sold on it, then perhaps you should part ways. Another solution is to concentrate on separate areas of business. When your gut reaction tells you "no," there's a self-fulfilling element that will hold back. And when your gut reaction tells you "no" it is usually right!

A true leader knows how to follow his or her inner voice. Do you view your every day as a constant reinvention of yourself and your firm's career? In order to let yourself emerge and find out what your true needs and instincts are, you must recognize and delight in your own uniqueness. Listen to those impulsive voices inside, but weigh their messages. In all of your efforts, seek to express; don't try to prove. What's every angle, every perspective? What is the heart of the issue, the core?

A true leader has developed the following qualities, according to Bemis, and I think they are worth stating here:

Curiosity.

Broadness of knowledge base.

Belief in teamwork.

Willingness to take risks.

Devotion to the long term rather than the short term.

Commitment to excellence.

Virtue.

Vision.

The ability to view mistakes as a part of life, not as a failure.

Think about your priorities. Most companies are started because owners want to create the most suitable work environment possible for themselves. In essence, in starting your own firm you are setting your own priorities. Be sure you understand what they are. Is your priority profit, or progress? What are your long- and short-term goals? What social problem would you truly like to address in your work? What contributions is your firm going to make to design as a whole?

How much money do you want to make? How much can you make?

You may not have the answers to all of these questions, but certainly consider them and think about what you are planning to accomplish in your lifetime as head of this firm.

If you are in the position of rethinking your present design practice, then you will be reshaping your original vision, or perhaps you will be testing whether or not you still adhere to its principles. For example, I recently consulted with a firm in Brookline, Massachusetts—Parencorp. Parencorp is run by two dynamic individuals who balance each other out symmetrically: Gordon Hurwitz is the thinker and main designer, while Merrill Diamond is the risk taker, the marketer, the entrepreneur.

Back in the 1980s, Parencorp's vision was to develop and/or renovate high priced housing. The duo received wide acclaim, awards, and high commissions for such work as The Grand, which was the renovation of a hospital the company purchased from the Lahey Medical Clinic, and Dream Wold, an estate that had gone into disrepair until Parencorp purchased and developed it. They renovated the mansion into seven units and built a village of new units that were architecturally in keeping with the turn-of-the-century styling set by the mansion.

The duo had met in college, had gone their separate ways, and ended up several years later working in the same architectural firm. It was then that the pair decided to make their break. As was evident by their unprecedented success and six figure incomes, Parencorp was a profitable enterprise, and their incomes were higher, by far, than the average architect (see Figure 1.2 for a chart on the income of the average architect and the average engineer). The 1990s hit them over the heads with a resounding whump! Work in development nearly came to a standstill. After two years of headscratching, they finally came up with a new vision for their firm, a new focus. Rather than defining their vision as "developers," they are going back to being "architects." They are setting up a plan to work on smaller high priced housing projects, and are going back to defining themselves as architects. When we last spoke, their business was picking up again, and they are off on a new start.

There are times when a company outgrows its dreams, and other times when a company gets swayed away from them. What have been your overriding priorities, from the beginning? Have they changed over the past few years?

COMPENSATION PER TOTAL STAFF

Dollars	Compensation per Total Staff			
	25th	Median	Mean	75th
Overall	32,569	38,361	38,919	43,857
Staff Size:				
1-5	22,666	31,500	33,689	38,800
6-10	27,126	36,333	37,249	40,642
11-15	32,308	37,141	39,363	44,636
16-25	30,964	36,867	36,963	42,165
26-50	33,358	39,627	39,710	43,909
51-100	31,760	36,549	38,050	39,924
101-150	34,247	39,006	43,642	42,205
151-250	36,439	42,388	41,912	44,890
251-500	32,457	35,719	37,687	40,940
Over 500	39,150	43,705	43,921	45,019
Architectural	33,659	39,000	40,052	42,450
Architectural/Interiors	34,883	37,933	37,907	41,005
Landscape Architect	28,166	28,333	40,394	36,873
Engineering (Prime)	32,316	39,153	39,289	44,643
Engineering (Subconsultant)	30,000	36,304	37,961	44,812
Engineering (Survey)	32,363	35,777	38,621	38,541
Mapping	16,193	29,120	27,981	30,311
A/E	32,015	38,410	39,057	42,234
A/E/P	33,648	39,178	40,819	43,566
All U. S.	35,115	42,774	41,567	45,345
Northeast	31,998	39,580	39,135	41,957
South	32,330	37,680	36,585	40,385
Midwest	30,405	35,493	35,166	38,149
Southwest	29,971	33,166	35,256	36,585
Mountain	30,891	33,588	36,492	38,727
West	37,051	42,437	42,619	49,412
All Canada	40,122	45,045	49,106	52,389
Eastern Canada	NR	39,740	39,740	NR
Central Canada	35,854	46,680	50,455	51,262
Western Canada	38,880	40,833	50,227	47,500
Private	32,316	38,800	39,545	44,681
Government	31,890	37,052	38,093	42,370
Mixed	33,033	38,361	38,891	43,199
Transportation	33,549	36,533	39,532	43,147
Government Buildings	33,848	40,500	39,858	44,509
Environmental	31,450	38,331	39,025	42,762
Industrial	32,342	35,500	39,124	39,443
Energy	28,722	30,928	34,228	36,427
Commercial Users	36,712	40,390	41,156	43,725
Commercial Developers	28,862	35,376	40,859	44,394
Housing	29,090	40,939	40,482	44,633
Health Care	35,518	36,333	37,216	39,812
No Specialty	31,998	37,052	38,314	42,787

Figure 1.2

DON'T HIRE "YES PEOPLE"

A true leader doesn't surround himself or herself with "yes people." A true leader is not afraid to hire other leaders. You will be instructed later on to formulate a human relations plan for the firm. Remember in so doing to hire people who will challenge you, not people who agree with you. Don't feed your ego and fall into the trap of having to be the only top gun on the block. The reason for Parencorp's success and continuance through the 1990s is the interplay between the partners. One has big ideas and broad principles about their image, but these are always reviewed carefully by the other.

Your job as orchestrator is to pull the excellence out of your orchestra. Pull excellence from the excellent. Hire people who will not let you go off on the wrong tangent, who will challenge you even when you do not want to hear it. "When we forego our own thoughts and opinions, they end up coming back to us from the mouths of others." (Norman Lear, quoted in Bemis's *On Becoming a Leader*).

SET OUT INSTRUCTIVE GOALS

Finally, a true leader sets realistic, albeit instructive and ambitious expectations for people. If the goals you set are too high or too low, then your organization will lack initiative. But if they are specifically designed to instruct and grow with an individual year by year, then you will have an inspired and continually growing workforce ... something that is, in all honesty, difficult to find in most design firms today.

WHICH KIND OF LEADER ARE YOU?

Leadership style depends on many factors. In general there are two basic types of leaders: hierarchical leaders and roving leaders. Hierarchical leaders generally rule the subordinates; roving leaders are part of the team. Roving leaders are those individuals who take charge automatically, who are there when you need them. Which type of leader are you?

It is often difficult for hierarchical leaders to break "custom" and allow their subordinates to take the lead. In certain situations, however, the hierarchical leader must identify the roving leader, allow him or her to take charge, and exhibit grace enough to enable the roving leader to lead.

In setting up your firm's culture, you must decide whether other employees, technical people, or principals are to share in the ownership of problems, and to take possession of a situation. To allow roving leadership its fullest potential is true delegation.

Measure your qualities against the following items to test whether or not you are a good leader.

Do you do more than manage numbers? Do you go beyond taking care of day-to-day business, and pressuring employees for immediate results?

Do you strike a balance between management and leadership? Do you pay as much attention to doing the right thing as you do to doing things right?

Do you place a high value on doing what is necessary to make the firm prosper over the long term? This includes making investments in areas that do not provide immediate returns.

Do you provide direction? Do you then make sure that it's communicated throughout the organization?

Do you articulate a vision? Do you enlist support and involvement for a common cause, and cement relationships that make people pull toward a common goal?

Do you enable, empower, and entrust your managers?

Do you serve as a role model? This is done by making sure that your behavior and actions are consistent with your stated goals.

Do you motivate employees? Do you help them grow personally as well as professionally?

Do you place a high value on employee education and training?

Do you not only communicate well, but also listen attentively?

Do you handle mistakes professionally?

Do you praise in public? Do you reprimand in private?

Do you show legitimate interest and appreciation? Do you express these in a timely manner?

Do you reward outstanding performance?

Have you ever changed someone's performance by improving it?

Have you built a corporate environment in which everyone feels they're a part of the team?

In short, leadership begins with self-definition. Where are you at? Where are you going? Where do you want to be, from the heart? In setting up your firm, corny as it may sound, that's where it all begins—with you.

2 MASTERING YOURSELF

"I wish I'd done a better job of communicating with GM people.
I'd do that differently a second time around and make sure that
they understood and shared my vision for the company."
—*Roger Smith, former CEO, General Motors*

Norman Lear once said, "It is very hard to be who we are, because it doesn't seem to be what anyone wants." You've experienced it, the squabbles and scrambles of your ego against
another's. It can be frustrating to try to express yourself. And
yet defining that ego can be the most important factor in your
life: What is it that drives you, that truly inspires you to do
your best work?

Again, to quote Warren Bemis (author of *On Becoming a
Leader*), there are four steps to true success:

1. Becoming self-expressive.
2. Listening to the inner voice.
3. Learning from the right mentors.
4. Giving oneself over to a guiding vision.

Your vision should equal your self-belief. If you believe that
your design firm is going to handle 12 projects per year, and
5 out of those new projects will be hospital projects, then
you will find a way to make that happen. If you have no con-
ception of where you want to take your work, you won't get
anywhere. How far can a boat get without navigation? You run
the risk of driving yourself in circles.

Mastering yourself is the process of mastering your context: Are you where you want to be? Do you enjoy the ride?
Waiting for the big successes is not worthwhile—they may
never come. And they may not provide you with all the
money and all the gratification you believe they will reap. You

have to enjoy the journey. Don't do what you think you're supposed to do; *do what you want to do!*

To successfully build your own vision, you must:

Back yourself.

Trust yourself.

Inspire yourself.

Inspire others through your trust in them.

Your firm will then become the ultimate manifestation of your beliefs, once again pointing out the importance of understanding what those underlying motivations are for you. Take, for example, the Herman Miller Company, which is a model of leadership, and which was written about in Max De Pree's *Leadership is an Art.*

De Pree writes about the company from firsthand knowledge—he is chairman and CEO. The famed furniture maker was named one of *Fortune* magazine's ten "best managed" companies, and was chosen as one of the hundred best companies to work for in America. De Pree characterizes the leader as the "servant" of his or her followers in that it is the leader's job to remove the obstacles that prevent the followers from doing their jobs. In short, the true leader enables his or her followers to realize their full potential, "In the most effective and humane way possible." This requires some very clear thinking on your part—clear, mostly, on your own beliefs.

For you cannot encourage others to give you their contrary opinions, to abandon themselves to the strengths of others, until you have the self-confidence and self-knowledge to let go of what you think may be the only way, and to try to listen to and understand what might be a better way.

If you master the art of self-management, you will be able to teach your employees self-management as well. There is a spirit of self-management in every great company.

Take the time to discover your true motives and desires. Experience your own limitations, and look for ways to change them, to outgrow them, to move yourself to a higher plane. As De Pree himself says, "Leadership is an art, something to be learned over time, not simply by reading books. Leadership is more tribal than scientific, more a weaving of relationships than an amassing of information." Try parachuting, ski challenging mountains, take a risk—it'll change your perspective immeasurably.

How do you manage yourself, how do you master the context in which you work and in which you live? Take five minutes to answer the following questions for your firm:

1. What kind of work do you see yourself doing in five years?
2. What are your goals for company profits for the next year?
3. What are your profit goals five years from now?
4. Who are you? What does your gut instinct tell you about yourself and your abilities?
5. What firm would you most like to own, if you could own any design firm you choose?
6. Why? What are the characteristics of that design firm? Why are they so appealing?
7. How would you change that firm?
8. How would you fit in, design-wise, to that firm?
9. What major objective would you like to accomplish in your work over the next year (aside from making money)?
10. How much effort would it take to achieve that objective?
11. Define the context in which you live and work today.
12. How would you change that context to make it work better for you?

Psychologist Abraham Maslow delineated a hierarchy of needs that drive your motivation. These are shown in the pyramid illustration in Figure 2.1. The motivational implications of the hierarchy of needs are shown in Figure 2.2. The main thrust of Maslow's hierarchy is that, "A need satisfied no longer motivates." This means a person will not be motivated by factors below his or her position on the hierarchy. You must realize every individual is motivated by a different set of factors. For example, a draftsman who has been laid off three or four times in the last three years is motivated by security. On the other hand, a senior architect or engineer will be more motivated by recognition for excellence in his or her field.

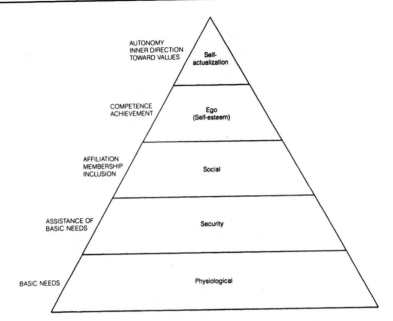

Figure 2.1 Maslow's hierarchy of needs.

What is your motivating factor? What are your needs? Which level of satisfaction are you looking for? How will you go about getting there?

Figure 2.3 is a blank form that you should photocopy and work out to evaluate your needs. For each level on the form, write in the kind of satisfaction you are seeking. For example, on the ego level, what would be most rewarding to you right now? How dependent are you on others, on exterior things, on a firm or a set of circumstances to make that happen?

Hierarchy Level	Reward and Punishment	Dependency	Information Required to Motivate Person
Self-actualization	Working toward one's own goals and standards	High degree of autonomy	High degree of knowledge and expertise about persons, goals, values, cognitive needs, and like barriers to goals
Ego	Respect Achievement General feeling of confidence Ability to do and know Respectability	High degree of interdependence, with self related to others for psycho-social rewards; identification with and respect from others critical	Substantive, knowledge and responsive around: 1. Feelings of competences, belongingness, dependence 2. Desire for control 3. Current existential (here and now) problems
Social	Acceptance Warmth Concern Rejection Exclusion Coldness Hostility Indifference	High degree of dependence on others for external material rewards; often subject to coercion from others	
Security	Projection from danger, threat, and deprivation		Security, physio-logical knowledge of state of depriva-tion and external needs; adequate subservience and overcompliance is usually overt behavior
Physiological	Food, rest, exercise		

Figure 2.2 Implications of Maslow's hierarchy. From *Motivation and Personality* by Abraham H. Maslow (New York: Harper & Row, 1954).

Hierarchy Level	Reward	Degree of Dependency	Information Required to Motivate You
Self-actualization			
Ego			
Social			
Security			
Physiological			

Figure 2.3

3 THE MOTIVATING FACTORS

"The only sacred cow in an organization should be its basic philosophy of doing business." — *Thomas Watson, Jr., founder of IBM*

Learning to be a great leader involves not just your own effort, but the inspiration you provide to your staff, whether that be a staff of one or one hundred. Veteran CADD manager Bill Mihalik shares his insights on a basic principal of leadership: "Take care of your people and your people will take care of you."

Motivation. The greatest motivators are the rewards associated with doing a good job. These can take the form of being assigned greater responsibilities on future projects, a possible promotion, or an increase in salary. If you use bonuses, make sure they are for short time periods.

Recognition. One of the greatest motivators in the workplace is simple recognition. Most workers are motivated by a sense of pride and accomplishment in a job well done, and by receiving recognition for themselves, their group, and their firm. Make sure that they receive this recognition. Institute an "employee of the month" award; post a notice on the bulletin board complimenting an employee for a job well done; give tickets to a baseball game or other sporting event. A little recognition can go a long way.

Involvement. Involve your staff in various aspects of a project, other than production. Seek their opinion on time estimates and processes. Involve them with client contact. Let them know what you are researching, what market niches you plan to develop down the road. Involvement helps you avoid obvious mistakes by bouncing your ideas off another person in the firm, and it pays dividends tenfold in the form of worker pride.

Here are eight additional ways to motivate your future staff:

1. *Redefine the mundane.* Treat your staff as if they were your clients. Get out from behind your desk and visit them in their environment. Ask how things are going. If you don't know what they're working on, ask. You may be surprised at some of the answers.

2. *Provide business cards.* Everyone interfacing with clients should have cards. This is a relatively inexpensive way to motivate employees, gives them an official title, and sends a signal of professionalism to your client.

3. *Make a big deal out of customer satisfaction.* Commit your client service beliefs to writing, read them aloud to the entire staff, and then frame and hang them on a wall near the workers' spaces, not the front office. Publish your client service statement in every issue of your internal and external communication, whether that be newsletters or brochures.

4. *"Top gun" an employee.* Pull one or two out of the trenches and give them to a client for a day to participate in the work from the client's side. It's a win–win experience for everyone.

5. *Empower your staff.* Give staff access to the materials and tools they need to do their job.

6. *Train them.* Training is another tool that is often overlooked. It costs you money, but has two consequences: not only does it make people feel good, it also makes them more productive and effective. Find the time and resources any way you can. There are many ways to skin a cat.

7. *Listen, listen, listen, then measure reactions.* Listen not only to your employees, but also to your clients. If you keep hearing that something's broken, now's the time to fix it.

8. *Say "thank you."* A thank you can take many forms, ranging from a telephone call or personal visit to hand-written and hand-delivered notes to picnics and outings to an evening at the theater or even a trip to Disney World. Case in point: 1991 was a particularly hard year for my staff; we went through the same kinds of difficulties and turmoil as everyone else, trying to determine where the marbles would fall after the turbulent recession hit the construction industry. In June of 1991, I asked my employees to hold on for another year. We were crunching budgets and bonuses like crazy. Most of my employees have been with me for the good part of a decade or more. They stuck by me. As a reward, in June of 1992 I flew everyone in the firm to Disney World in Orlando, Florida. We all stayed at the Swan Hotel inside Disney World. Now that was some reward.

PUTTING THE PLAN IN PLACE

4

SETTING YOUR YARDSTICK FOR GROWTH

> "Cash is like blood or oxygen; without it, you die. And growth eats cash. This is why roughly half of all bankruptcies occur after a year of record sales."
> —*James C. Collins and William C. Lazier,* Beyond Entrepreneurship

There are distinct advantages both to growing into a very large firm, and to staying very small, just as there are risks associated with setting your goals too high or too low. Stagnation occurs when you set growth goals too low. Demotivation sets in when goals are too high and are never reachable. Therefore when setting your strategic goals, consider how fast you want your fledgling firm to grow, and to what size. In defining your needs, your personal goals, and what motivates you, it is important to consider the issue of growth.

Growth is perhaps one of the least understood phenomena of building a business, and the most dangerous. That's why expected growth rate needs to be studied and set during preliminary strategic planning sessions. Where do you want to lead your firm in two years? In five years? In ten years?

Beware of plans for rapid growth. How many companies have you heard about in the last two years who opened a larger shop out of a thriving small business, only to fold crashing, booming down? Remember that rapid growth should never be an ultimate goal. The question is, how many people do I need to hire, how many projects do I need to sustain, in order to obtain the highest profitability possible?

One design firm I've worked with has overall annual receipts of only $350,000, but they employ just two principals and one secretary—very little overhead and lots of room for profit. So in measuring or setting growth goals, don't assume that bigger is naturally better—what's best for your own personal profitability?

RISKS OF RAPID GROWTH

I'm not saying that rapid growth doesn't occur, or that everyone doesn't enjoy the *Inc.* magazine stories of the firm owner who grew his $100,000 a year business into a $3 million business in three short years. But there are hazards to growth that you should be aware of. For instance, growth can blur your vision. When you grow too fast, you lose sight of the firm's original purpose. You also risk cash flow problems—growth costs money. And if your firm did not expect rapid growth and is now experiencing it, all your cash can get tied up in overhead and salaries, with disastrous results.

The most appropriate way to handle growth is to build a flexible growth plan—with contingencies, such as hiring temporary employees (even if temps include year-long design subcontractors!), that can easily be let go at the end of each design project. These temps are subcontractors who can perform the work either at home or at the office, with just a base meeting once or twice a week. And with so many layoffs in the industry, there are scores of candidates out there setting up home offices and working out of their basements. Generally these are individuals who enjoy the freedom of working on their own, and are more than happy to enter into long- or short-term contracts.

James C. Collins and William C. Lazier, in their book, *Beyond Entrepreneurship*, list the following downsides to rapid growth, paraphrased here. In drawing up your growth objectives, keep these in mind:

- Rapid growth can hide gross inefficiencies that do not show up until the growth slows.
- Rapid growth stretches a company's infrastructure, often past the breaking point.
- A rapid growth strategy can pressure your salesforce to commit to prices that severely cut your margins.

- There is a tremendous human cost—the stress and strain on people during a rapid growth phase can be extreme.
- Rapid growth leads to increased organizational complexity and reduced communications.
- Large companies tend to be less fun, and rapid growth just brings about that largeness sooner.
- Rapid growth can quickly dilute the culture of your company, making it very difficult to develop management and reinforce your values.

Mainly, rapid growth causes arrogance and a feeling of invulnerability, which inevitably lead to disaster somewhere along the line. Overconfidence has a way of swelling to dangerous proportions, just naturally caused by a period of years of unchallenged success, setting you up for a fall of catastrophic proportions.

Your firm does not need to grow to 50 or 100 employees by next year in order to be profitable; in fact, you are well advised to know your limitations and to stick with them. If growth occurs, then it should be well tracked. If you get to a point where you are regularly putting in 20 hours a week overtime, it might be time to hire another designer. If you are both putting in 15 to 20 hours a week overtime, then it's time to hire a third designer. These are your first employees. Don't mistakenly make them—or anyone—your partner right away.

Develop a set of criteria for hiring each new designer, technician, or related discipline along the way. You might even consider the idea of sharing office space with another fledgling firm in a related but not competing discipline, such as mechanical engineering if you are an electrical engineer. In this way, you can enter joint ventures if they promise to be mutually satisfying, but are not obligated in any way if there is no work for the related discipline.

5 GATHER ALL THE PIECES

"Tis all in pieces, all coherence gone; All just supply, and all relation"—*An Anatomy of the World, 1611*

A strategic plan is like a map: it should spell out specifically when, where, and how each of the items discussed in this chapter will be addressed for the coming year. You cannot put enough thought into how and where you are taking your firm. The final outcome is the strategic plan. This and the next few chapters outline the proper procedures for assembling a strategic plan.

The following is a listing of items needed to conduct a proper strategic planning session. Don't panic if, in starting your own firm, you do not have all of these elements. But if you are rethinking an existing firm and trying to develop a new focus, then gather these data. If you do not have an item, please calculate a tentative pro forma item on which to base your strategic projections. It will only hurt you not to look at each of the following closely:

1. Most recent balance sheet.
2. Most recent income/expense statement.
3. Last fiscal year-end financial statements.
4. Previous fiscal year-end financial statement (up to three years' history).
5. Profit sharing, pension fund, and/or bonus distributions (up to four years' history).
6. Available calculations of project backlog.
7. Current project list.
8. Marketing brochure.
9. Current stockholder "buy/sell agreement."

10. Any "strategic plan" documentation.
11. Current accounts receivable aging list.
12. Any "marketing plan" documentation.
13. Current employee list.
14. Historical list of number of employees at each of the last four fiscal year periods.
15. Organization chart.
16. Sample individual project management report.

Samuels Engineers, Inc. has kindly provided its strategic planning information for your review; it is shown in Figure 5.1. Take a look at the depth of planning here. Note that this firm does not have a formal marketing plan. Why? They may have an established client base or may simply perceive that they "don't need a marketing plan." Sometimes this theory works, but most of the time it is advisable to include some kind of formalized marketing plan. The redeeming qualities of this plan are its simplicity, its superior organization, and its relatively brief length. (See Chapter 10 for a complete marketing plan.)

Ted Samuels, CEO of Samuels Engineers, inherited the firm from his father and grandfather. The firm was established in 1924 by his grandfather and was incorporated 30 years ago by his father. Although Samuels did not found the firm, he shares with us his objectives for the 1990s:

> Our objectives for the 90s are to produce high quality work and to focus on customer satisfaction. We'd like to expand into the federal works market, while holding down expenses and keeping to a size of nine staff persons. We'd like to expand into new engineering markets as well, possibly environmental engineering or landscape architecture.

Samuels feels strongly that opportunities will arise in environmental engineering for those entering the field over the next decade.

Running an engineering firm, for Samuels, has been worthwhile. "I enjoy the work and provide good jobs for all employees. I feel that this profession is not as lucrative as some others, but all in all it's worth it."

Figure 5.1 contains Samuels Engineering's financial plan, billing rates, organizational plan, balance sheet, job descriptions, and company information. At the present time, Samuels does not have a formal marketing plan.

Firm name:	Samuels Engineers, Inc.
Size:	9
Principals:	3
Focus:	General civil engineering, residential, commercial, and government markets
Address:	130 Vine Street Reno, NV

CURRENT MANPOWER
SAMUELS ENGINEERS, INC. - Reno, Nevada
Organization Chart

FIRM	Registered Engineers	Surveyors Technicians	Support Staff	Admin.
Osgood Engineers	2	4	2	1

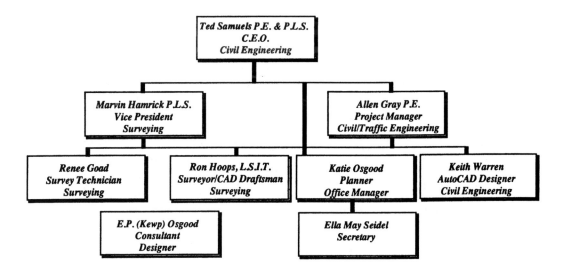

WORKLOAD: Samuels Engineers Is Currently Well Staffed To Handle All Types Of Work. The Current Work Load Would Permit Immediate Response To Any NDOT - On Call Projects.

Figure 5.1

JOB DESCRIPTIONS
for
SAMUELS ENGINEERS

NOVEMBER 10, 1994

Summary

Survey Technician	Part time $ 7.50–11.00 hourly
Executive Secretary	Salary $16,000 to $30,000
Senior Surveyor	Salary $25,000 to $35,000
Associate Engineer	Salary $25,000 to $35,000
CADD Designer	Salary $25,000 to $35,000
Office Manager	Salary $30,000 to $45,000
Project Engineer	Salary $30,000 to $45,000
Principal	Salary $40,000 to $75,000

EXECUTIVE SECRETARY

Ella May Feeney

Reports to the Office Manager, Katie Samuels.

Under the direction of the Office Manager, types all documents, contracts, legal descriptions, proposals, traffic reports, and applications to agencies. Expected to answer the phones. A full bookkeeper with the responsibility to maintain all cash transactions and keep the Accounts Payable and Accounts Receivables books. Produces Payroll twice a month and maintains and completes all Federal forms. Maintains the Job costing books for all jobs tracking employees time and other costs. Produces client billing once a month and on an as needed basis. In charge of purchasing office supplies. Completes all banking transactions. Meets the clients first as both friendly and helpful on any problems. Priority over other tasks should be made on full eight hours in the office to answer phones.

Works a 40 hour week.

Pays $15,000 to $30,000.

Five positions of Executive Secretary from Junior to Executive.

OFFICE MANAGER

Katie Samuels

Reports to the President, Ted Samuels.

Figure 5.1   (Continued.)

Maintains client contacts, keeps the client bills and jobs costs in line with the expected costs. Must work within the budget in the proposal. Creates proposals and cost and time projections to complete work. Expected to be able to keep the work schedule and not to promise work too soon. Coordinates final approvals with agencies. Represents the clients in public meetings. Expected to maintain all computer equipment and software. Expected to work necessary hours. Must keep jobs on track and moving, must be able to troubleshoot when problems and changes come up. Expected to work on gaining new clients and bringing in business.

Office management includes maintaining all financial information for the company, investigating all major purchases and recommending decisions, and reviewing all new advances in related computer equipment. Full Personnel Manager with responsibility for: recruiting new employees, office organization, employee well-being, employee performance review, employee benefit packages, employee salary review. Promotion and marketing with company information and brochures, maximizing company exposure for new work and a good company name. Making the most of the few marketing dollars. Other responsibilities include strategic decision making for the future of the firm. Must work on public image for the Company and work with outside organizations.

Pay range is $30,000 to $45,000.

There are three positions with this description.

PROJECT MANAGER

Allen Winters

- At least four years civil engineering experience.
- Excellent verbal and written communication skills.
- Knowledge of various engineering programs on PCs.
- Control job cost/time schedule.
- Design and draft plans.
- Coordinate with client and government agencies.
- Work necessary hours.
- Prepare cost and quantity estimates.
- Organize project, people, and data collection.
- Willing to do some traveling.

Major Areas of Work. Civil engineering for commercial, residential, and government developments.

Compensation. Competitive salary D.O.Q.; auto allowance; medical-hospitalization plan; profit sharing; bonuses.

Figure 5.1 (Continued.)

Qualifications. Registered Civil Engineer.

As the head of individual projects the responsibilities include: analyze scope of work and propose new work, initiate new client contacts, control job costs and client billing. Maintains client contacts, keeps the client bills and jobs costs in line with the expected costs. Must work within the budget in the proposal. Creates proposals and cost and time projections to complete work. Expected to keep the work schedule for all involved employees and not make unrealistic commitments. Expected to design and draft all types of maps. Coordinates final approvals with agencies. Represents the clients in public meetings. Provides cost and quantity estimates. Expected to have skill running the CADD system. Expected to work necessary hours. Must keep jobs on track and moving, and troubleshoot when problems and changes come up. Expected to work on gaining new clients and bringing in business. Expected to perform job and site inspections.

Complete company management responsibilities include: strategic decision making for the future of the firm; hiring and firing of employees under direct supervision; identifying and reviewing major office purchases. Must work on public image for the company and work with outside organizations. Must be a Professional Engineer. The Project Manager will report to the President or Board of Directors.

PROJECT ENGINEER

Marv Tammend

Reports to the President or Principle Engineer. Responsible for surveyors and technicians. Maintains and schedules all field and office work. At the head of individual projects the responsibilities include: analyzing scope of work and proposing on new work, maintaining client contact, controlling job costs and doing client billing. Maintains client contacts, keeps the client bills and jobs costs in line with the expected costs. Must work within the budget in the proposal. Creates proposals and cost and time projections to complete work. Expected to be able to keep the work schedule for all to be active with work and not to promise work too soon. Expected to design and draft all types of maps. Coordinates final approvals with agencies. Represents the clients in public meetings. Be able to do cost and quantity estimates. Expected to have skill running the CADD system. Expected to work necessary hours. Must keep jobs on track and moving, must be able to troubleshoot when problems and changes come up. Expected to work on gaining new clients and bringing in business. Job and site inspections are expected. Responsible for surveyors and technicians, schedules all field and office work. Must be a skilled Draftsman and a possible RLS or Civil Engineer.

Reports to the President, Ted Samuels.

Pay range is $30,000 to $45,000.

There are five positions with this description.

Figure 5.1 (Continued.)

1994 PROJECTED CASH FLOW   12/7/94

	Income	Expenses	Profit Year to Date	
Jan. (real)	47,489	23,597	23,892	
Feb. (real)	48,310	24,158	48,044	
Mar. (real)	24,013	36,888	35,169	
Apr. (real)	60,854	35,700	60,323	
May (real)	57,751	47,269	70,805	
June (real)	39,649	39,409	71,045	
July (real)	54,905	69,205	56,745	
Aug. (real)	23,227	38,178	41,794	
Sept. (real)	54,971	48,878	47,887	*15K profit share contrib.
Oct. (real)	24,171	58,766	13,292	
Nov. (Est.)	60,683	28,044	45,931	
Dec. (Est.)	10,000	43,000	12,931	
Year Total	506,023	493,092	12,931	
1992 Avg.	42,169	41,091		
1991 Avg.	38,000	33,000		

ACCOUNTS RECEIVABLES 1993

	Nov.	Oct.	Sept.	Aug.	July	June
New billings	49,234	46,405	58,645	43,621	20,151	52,632
30 Days	24,042	20,585	17,388	6,949	9,432	21,304
60 Days	20,103	13,251	5,068	4,065	18,354	18,580
90+ Days	33,726	23,756	21,080	25,331	11,796	12,027
Total	127,105	103,997	102,181	79,966	59,733	104,543

	Income	Growth	Expense	Growth
1992	506,023	12%	493,092	11%
1991	453,000	−56%	445,000	−51%
1990	1,020,670	15%	903,557	4%
1989	890,477	70%	870,675	60%
1988	524,051	4%	545,711	11%
1987	505,128	7%	490,739	12%
1986	471,890	57%	438,799	37%
1985	301,077	6%	319,277	20%
1984	284,751	−16%	265,829	−23%
1983	339,919	63%	347,480	77%
1982	208,029		196,785	

Figure 5.1   (Continued.)

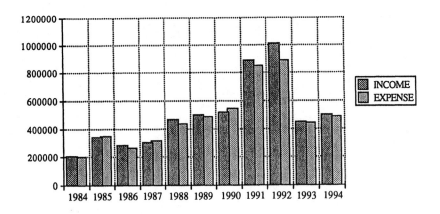

Distribution Plan Year-End/1991			% of Income	
Merit bonus	67%	156,000	18%	23%
Profit plan	23%	53,000	6%	
Operating income	10%	24,000	3%	
	100%	233,000	26%	

Distribution Plan Year-End/1992			% of Income	
Merit bonus	38%	106,007	10%	18%
Profit plan	27%	73,242	7%	
Operating income	35%	97,000	10%	
	100%	276,249	27%	

Distribution Plan Year-End/1993			% of Income	
Merit bonus	0%	0	0%	3%
Profit plan	61%	11,500	3%	
Operating income	39%	7,500	2%	
	100%	19,000	4%	

Distribution Plan Year-End/1994			% of Income	
Merit bonus	35%	15,000	3%	6%
Profit plan	35%	15,000	3%	
Operating income	30%	13,000	3%	
	100%	43,000	8%	

Income: 506,023

Figure 5.1 (Continued.)

BALANCE SHEET

November 30, 1994

Assets		
Current Assets		
Cash in bank—checking	50,539.92	
Savings—MMA—2100000583	58,411.20	
Petty cash	2,134.65	
Cafeteria 125 plan ac#32414	976.07	
Total current assets		112,061.84
Fixed Assets		
Autos	58,110.14	
Automobile depreciation	(53,635.23)	
Field equipment	58,814.13	
Field equipment—depreciation	(48,514.30)	
Furniture, equipments and computer	139,007.00	
Furniture, equipment, and		
computer—depreciation	(107,234.11)	
Computer software	23,584.59	
Computer software depreciation	(20,538.04)	
Total fixed assets		49,594.18
Total Assets		161,656.02
Liabilities		
Current Liabilities		
SIIS deposit	(763.08)	
Accrued federal income tax	(187.00)	
Note payable	9,826.48	
Total current liabilities		8,876.40
Total Liabilities		8,876.40
Capital		
Capital	6,000.00	
Common stock	3,678.00	
Retained earnings	181,513.62	
Additional paid-in capital	16,028.00	
Treasury stock—redemption	(75,000.00)	
Capital stock	8,800.00	
Capital stock	5,500.00	
Capital stock	6,260.00	
Total capital		152,779.62
Total Liabilities and Capital		161,656.02

Figure 5.1 (Continued.)

SCHEDULE OF CHARGES   April 1994

Professional Services

Principal Engineer	80.00 per hour
Project Engineer	75.00 per hour
Senior Engineer	65.00 per hour
Associate Engineer/Surveyor	50.00 per hour
Design Engineer	40.00 per hour
Draftsman/AutoCADD Operator	40.00 per hour
Technician II	40.00 per hour
Technician I	30.00 per hour
Secretary	30.00 per hour

Legal Services

Expert Testimony, Deposition, etc.	150.00 per hour

(A minimum charge of 4 hours will be charged for each day or portion thereof)

Reports or Preparation for Testimony	80.00 per hour

Equipment Charges

CADD Drafting and Computer Computations	35.00 per hour
Electronic Total Stations w/Data Collector	35.00 per hour
Mechanical 24 Hour Traffic Counter	75.00 per day

Expenses and Outside Services

Outside Professional Services	Cost plus 10%
Blueprints In House	1.00 per copy
Outside Services	Cost plus 10%
Photocopies	0.15 per page
Stakes, Monuments, and Material	2.00 per point
Shipping and Special Handling	Cost
Long Distance Communications/Fax	Cost

Out of Town Expenses

Subsistence—Car Rental, Air Fare, Lodging, Meals	Cost
4-Wheel Drive Vehicle	0.50/mile · 8.00/hr
Non-4x4	0.35/mile · 5.00/hr

Travel time will be charged at regular hourly rates, eight hours maximum per day.

Statements will be issued monthly or at the completion of work and are overdue 30 days from the stated billing date. Except as otherwise provided by written agreement, a charge of 1½% per month will be added after 30 days.

Figure 5.1   (Continued.)

STAFF RÉSUMÉS

Founded in 1944—Engineering for Nevadans since 1925

History. Samuels Engineers, Inc. has a long established record in the field of Civil Engineering and Surveying in the Northern Nevada–California area. Edwin P. Samuels, Sr. actually started surveying in the Reno area in the early 1920s. The firm is currently managed by E. P. Samuels, III. With over 60 years of service, Samuels Engineers has established itself as the preeminent engineering firm in the Northern Nevada Area. The professionals on our staff have a combined total of over 140 years experience in Civil Engineering and Land Surveying.

Company Goal. Client satisfaction is our first priority. Samuels Engineers has always strived to maintain a highly ethical, professional, and efficient organization that always puts the client satisfaction first. A common sense approach to engineering provides quality service to our clients and the community.

Experience. Samuels Engineers has been involved in the development of many large commercial and industrial projects. High quality work is a priority. Samuels Engineers is equipped with the latest in computer hardware, software, and surveying equipment. Samuels Engineers' trademark is giving personal attention to projects and making sure they are completed in a timely and efficient manner.

SERVICES OFFERED

PROVIDING OVER 65 YEARS OF SERVICE

Reno's Oldest . . .   Proudest . . .   and Finest . . .

PLANNING   Investigations, Reports, and Comprehensive Planning

- Feasibility studies
- Valuation of existing facilities
- Commercial developments
- Traffic noise and air quality modeling
- Master planning
- Industrial developments
- Traffic impact studies
- Transportation modeling

CIVIL DESIGN   Plans, Specifications, and Construction Management

- Residential subdivisions
- Multifamily developments
- Sewer and storm drain design
- Construction management
- Industrial developments
- Office and commercial developments
- Streets and highways
- Mobile home parks

Figure 5.   (Continued.)

SURVEYING AND MAPPING

- Construction staking
- Boundary surveys
- Topographic surveys
- Building control
- Parcel maps
- ALTA surveys
- Photogrammetry control
- Water right surveys

TRAFFIC AND INTERSECTION DESIGN

- Circulation plans
- Parking management plans
- Intersection design
- Traffic control devices
- Roadway design
- Signal design

PROFESSIONAL STAFF

- Edwin (Ted) P. Osgood III, PE
- Allen Gray, PE
- Marvin Hamrick, PLS
- Edwin P. Osgood Jr., PLS

COMPUTER EQUIPMENT

- AutoCAD® and DCA software, computer for calculations, drafting, and mapping
- Digitizing, computer plotting, and data transfer
- 3-D graphics and computer cut and fill adjustments

SAMUELS ENGINEERS EMPLOYEE MANUAL

This guide is to help and inform employees of Samuels Engineers, Inc. This is not intended as an employee contract and does not constitute one. All items contained in this document are general information and may be changed at any time. Any rules are not intended to be a comprehensive list of all prohibited conduct, but are only examples of the kinds of conduct that may result in discipline.

1. Company Goals and Objectives

Samuels Engineers will work to achieve quality and efficiency and to maintain a great reputation for high ethics and standards. Major emphasis will be on excellent client relations and client satisfaction.

Samuels Engineers very much wants to keep the current client pleased with the work. For every happy client that leaves our office we can count on repeat business and recommendation to others.

We will advance with the latest in technology and expand our capabilities, as required, to stay competitive and look into the future, projecting what services will be needed. Most importantly, we must provide prompt service.

Figure 5.1   (Continued.)

2. Employment

Samuels Engineers is an equal opportunity employer.

Probation Period. All new employees are on probation for three to six months. New employees are given notice either verbally or in an "Offer Letter" of a probation period. Employee evaluation usually takes place after the probation period, at which time the probation period will be removed or extended.

Evaluation. Performance reviews are to be conducted annually with feedback given to the employee. The employee shall be given a review of their work and shall be given the opportunity to review their manager's performance. A meeting will take place to discuss the results and methods of improvements and to set the next year's goals. Salary increases shall be considered by the Board of Directors on an annual basis.

Company Hours. Samuels Engineers is open Monday to Friday, from 8:00 to 5:00. Work load will dictate any extra work. These hours may change at any time.

Payroll. Paychecks are distributed semimonthly as close to the 1st and 15th as possible.

Moonlighting. This policy was added at the request of the liability Insurance Carrier:

The acceptance by employees of outside professional work, sometimes referred to as moonlighting, is strongly discouraged. Our principal commitment is to the efficient and timely delivery of quality professional services to our clients. Working at outside employment can produce fatigue and inattentiveness to detail, which can interfere with meeting our client obligations.

Members of the staff should also be aware that moonlighting can create a conflict of interest, and that it carries serious potential exposure to personal claims of professional liability. This exposure, although not covered by the professional liability insurance carried by the firm, could, nevertheless, require our involvement in the defense of a claim.

For all of the foregoing reasons, our professional liability insurance carrier has required that we prohibit the practice of moonlighting and restrict the use of the firm's name, facilities, and equipment to the conduct of our professional work.

Professional Registration. Employees of the Engineering level will maintain a current Nevada Professional Engineers License. Employees of the Survey Level will maintain a current Nevada Registered Land Surveyors License.

Business Expense. Travel and entertainment that is charged to specific clients with itemized vouchers/receipts can be submitted to Samuels Engineers for reimbursement.

Out-of-Town Work. Any work that requires travel out of town for more than one day will be on a voluntary basis. The travel expenses and subsistence will be reimbursed by Samuels Engineers with a submitted voucher/receipts.

Dress Code. All employees of Samuels Engineers are exposed to the general public. In an effort to promote a business image, please maintain the following

Figure 5.1 (Continued.)

guidelines during business hours, running errands, or in the field: No shorts and no shirtless employees are allowed in the office or in the field.

4. Benefits

Extra Hours / Comp Time. The following is for full-time salaried employees only. If work load is heavy and deadlines are pressing, working later hours and Saturdays is expected. Extra hours are any hours in excess of each eight hour day of the five day work week. Extra hours are voluntary and compensation for the extra hours will be given with time off from work.

Time off may be taken by giving advance notice; Samuels Engineers reserves the right to change time off schedules when necessary. Comp time will not be reimbursed in pay. Comp time expire $1\frac{1}{2} \pm$ years after earning the time. The employee will be given three to six months notice of any comp time at risk of expiring, and if the schedule permits the time should be used before expiring.

Vacation. Employees earn two weeks annually (ten days) of vacation, which does not accumulate to the next year. A new employee can start using earned vacation time after the first year of employment. At the anniversary date an employee cannot have more than 80 hours on the books. If vacation was not used it is lost. Vacation is earned on a monthly basis. Reasonable advance notice of any use of vacation time should be given. Samuels Engineers reserves the right to change vacation schedules when necessary. Vacation will not be reimbursed in pay for unused time.

After five years of service, with the company, three weeks (15 days) of vacation will be available, which does not accumulate, each year.

Sick Leave. Six days per year (6 days annually) are available for sick days. After each additional 5 years of service an additional 3 days are available, up to a maximum of 12 days. The sick days are not accumulated to the next year. Sick leave is earned on a monthly basis. Sick days will not be reimbursed in pay for unused time.

Holidays. Ten Company Holidays are designated and will not be reimbursed in pay. These are Company holidays when the day occurs during the work week:

New Years Day	January 1
Washington's Birthday	Third Monday in February
Memorial Day	Last Monday in May
Fourth of July	July 4
Labor Day	First Monday in September
Nevada Day	October 31
Thanksgiving and day after	3rd week in November
Christmas Eve and Christmas	December 24 and 25

Medical Insurance/Hospitalization. A copy of the medical insurance package is available for your review. Samuels Engineers will pay 100% of the employee's premium. Employee can elect to add family members through payroll deduc-

Figure 5.1 (Continued.)

tions. The medical plan currently is an 80% plan for full-time employees. This plan is subject to change at any time. Any continuation of coverage after termination is the employee's responsibility. Any coverage is terminated at retirement.

Work related accidents are covered by the State as per the State Regulations, NIC (Nevada Industrial Commission) or Workers Compensation.

Company Vehicles. One vehicle will be provided by Samuels Engineers primarily for survey use. If the vehicle is not being used for surveying, then the vehicle may be used for around town business.

Any long mileage placed on a personal vehicle will be submitted for reimbursement by Samuels Engineers and will be billed to the client. The reimbursement rate to the employee for long mileage is 50 cents a mile.

Education. Classes and seminars and books that Samuels Engineers chooses or approves are reimbursed to the employee after supplying proof of successful completion (passing grade, C) and receipt for cost of the class.

Bonuses/Raises. For excellent performance and superior work bonuses may be awarded by the Board of Directors. The Board of Directors will, at their discretion, determine any bonus or raise.

Profit Sharing. A copy of the profit sharing plan is available. Each year Samuels Engineers may contribute to a retirement fund for each employee. Vesting begins after two (2) years of employment. A copy of the plan and specific terms are available for review.

Vesting Schedule:

0–2 years	0%	5–6 years	80%
2–3 years	20%	6+ years	100%
3–4 years	40%	Requires more than 1,000	
4–5 years	60%	hours or work each year	

Because we are a small and dynamic company, the policies and procedures outlined in the document are subject to changes at any time without prior notice, at the discretion of the Board of Directors. This document is intended to be used only as a guideline on company policies and procedures, not in any way an implied contract. Since an employment handbook has been interpreted as an implied contract, the at-will statement is signed by both parties.

Figure 5. (Continued.)

6 OUTLINING THE PROCESS

"Success without a clear sense of direction seems to be short-lived."—*authors of* The Executive Guide to Strategic Planning

Once you've gathered all of the data you need to start your strategic planning, you should divide your effort into six parts. All six basic elements must be addressed in order to properly assess your entire company vision:

1. Vision, mission, and culture statements.
2. Marketing plan and direction.
3. Financial plan.
4. Organizational plan.
5. Human resources plan.
6. Leadership transition plan.

1. VISION, MISSION, AND CULTURE

Vision

The first step in outlining your new firm (or your completely revamped old firm!) is to decide who you are, and where you want to be in 5, 10, and 15 years. Eugene Kohn, Principal of the New York architectural firm Kohn Pederson Fox (KPF), once confided that "Your success will be greatly affected by the work you turn down." KPF had a vision that it wanted to go down in history as being a great architectural firm. As a consequence, the first commissions they chose defined their work from that day forward. The work they chose had to be "significant in moving the firm along."

Your primary task, and perhaps the strongest element you will take away from this book, is the need to define your vision. The greatest leaders in the world are those who defined their vision, and then ate, slept, breathed, and lived their vision each and every minute. Consider the greatest political leaders in the past half century—Winston Churchill, who brought England through World War II, whose motto was "We will fight them on the beaches, we will fight them on the streets, we shall never surrender"; Harry Truman, who determined to carry out the Marshall Plan to reconstruct Europe, and then carried it out; Lyndon Johnson, whose Great Society and legislation for social change were carried out. These leaders believed in their visions to the point of obsession, and carried them out to completion.

How can you live out your vision? What is your true, ultimate goal in starting up your business? A vision statement is a short, one sentence statement defining your purpose.

Sample vision statements include:

To be the largest firm doing international design work out of the United States.

To be the most renowned landscape design firm in the East.

To be the wealthiest engineering firm in the world.

Figure 6.1 is a sample vision statement provided by the Michael Baker Corporation. Although it is longer than the preferred one sentence vision, it is clear and motivational. You will read more about vision statements in later sections, because this is the driving force behind all others.

Mission

The mission is a more specific statement that captures the essence of what you want your business to be. The mission puts into concrete terms the goals you will meet to accomplish your vision. This is a tangible statement, such as "ABC Associates will be hired by six new hospital clients this year," "We will develop seven new housing projects," "To develop three new renovation projects in the next ten month period."

Mission is concrete, whereas vision is a focus, a direction, even a massive wish statement. Vision is the wish, and mission spells out how you will get to that wish.

VISION: MICHAEL BAKER CORPORATION

Our vision for the future of the Michael Baker Corporation embodies the goals that we believe are shared by the clients, shareholders, and employees of the Company. The vision is grounded in fundamentals but unconstrained in consideration of opportunities.

Our vision in turn drives our strategic planning—continually updating our long-range goals and objectives and figuring out what it takes to get there. At Baker, the strategic planning process is characterized by broad participation, representing the best thought and input from every level of the Company. Our visions therefore reflect our mutual goals. The strategic plan is not a voluminous document that looks good on the shelf, but rather an active process and road map that guides our daily decisions in ways both large and small.

The Performance Vision

We see ourselves as a blue chip professional service company—one that sets the standards by which all other similar firms are to be judged. As such, we expect to be rated as a high value, quality investment with good growth prospects. This means a target of 15% growth per year, a return on equity of 20%, and a pretax return on sales of 10%.

The Enabling Vision

We will establish ourselves as the most reliable, most responsive firm in all areas where we compete by relentless, programmed, funded attention to client satisfaction and continued, measured reduction of cycle times and root causes of quality failures. In short, we will: *Do the right thing for our clients, the right way, the first time.*

The Focusing Vision

To achieve our goals, we recognize that we must have a clear understanding of our opportunities in the marketplace and ability to direct our resources to capitalize on those opportunities. This means we will continually strive for a good balance and diversification among planning, design, construction, and operation and maintenance services. It also means that we will be ready to undertake projects of opportunity in all parts of the world, in keeping with our diversification options.

Figure 6.1

Figure 6.2 is the Michael Baker Corporation's mission statement.

Culture

A culture statement may seem irrelevant at this point, but it is important because you need to define the kind of con-

MISSION: MICHAEL BAKER CORPORATION

We believe that as a company our purpose for being is to serve the business needs of our clients. We also believe that our role is to function as members of a partnership with our clients in developing the best solutions to the problems that are presented to us.

We believe that our first responsibility is the constant application of all professional skills and experience to every job, whether large or small, and to strive to produce high-quality, practical, and efficient results in engineering, management, architectural, planning, operations, and technical services. We also believe that it is incumbent upon us to be both objective and innovative in the application of our skills.

As professionals, we recognize it is part of our responsibility to maintain familiarity with, and to make maximum use of, the state-of-the-art technologies that apply to our functions and are available to us.

As members of a company chiefly owned by our fellow employees, it is our responsibility to be mindful of the common good, to work for the success of the organization and to be good stewards of the tools and properties entrusted to our care. We believe that all employees share in the responsibility to ensure that the goals of equal opportunity, recognition of dignity and merit, education and development, and fair compensation are observed and met. As members of the communities in which we live and work, we acknowledge our responsibilities to be good neighbors and good citizens, upholding the standards of public health and safety, and participating in community service on both an individual and company basis.

Our final responsibility is to ourselves as employees and owners, and to the shareholders who have invested in our future, to manage our Company for the realization of a fair profit, to provide a place of stable employment, individual opportunity, and personal security, and to aggressively pursue opportunities for growth by preparing ourselves in every way to be effective competitors.

Figure 6.2

ditions under which you feel most comfortable working. For instance, how important are family, friends, and outside interests? Are they important or will you put them on hold until you develop your firm? How involved do you want to be in the lives of your employees? Do you operate under "strictly business" conditions, or a "family atmosphere." Are you comfortable letting employees manage themselves or do you prefer to be the controller and the eyes for all?

Very few firms take the time to define their culture, but it is one of the most significant signals you will send to the outside world. How would you like to be perceived by your employees? By your clients?

2. MARKETING PLAN AND DIRECTION

The marketing process is outlined in several chapters of this book, however, it is first important to understand the kinds of marketing goals you should strive to reach. A good marketing plan is clear, concise, and measurable. You should target strategies and techniques for attacking a particular market, from a certain number of telephone calls per day to meeting goals for presentation strategies and numbers of proposals submitted. The goals should be based on marketing statistics. Don't set an unrealistic target in your head unless you can back it with statistics.

The average firm wins one in every ten jobs it goes after, so be sure to include funding and time to seek the appropriate number of jobs.

3. FINANCIAL PLAN

Financial planning is another area that should be well researched, and portions of this book will be devoted entirely to developing the financial plan. Here it is important to mention that successful firms have a clear financial plan. The terms and conditions of their financial plan are standardized, so that all reports are the same, all invoices look the same, all change orders have specific forms, all contracts are the same types of contracts (preferably lump sum), and so on.

Standardizing operations from the start simply ensures that projects will run smoothly, that you won't have to go digging around your desk for odd pieces of paper, that you don't waste your time recreating the wheel each time you develop a contract or send out a bill.

Be sure to be clear on employee involvement with your financial plan. If you are going to employ project managers, how are you going to get them to control project costs? How much financial information do you plan to share? What kind of financial reporting system will you use to help them control finances? How will you control job costs and man hours?

Another large component of the financial plan is profit planning. The average operating profit for architectural firms these days is 5%, according to the Professional Services Management Journal's Financial Statistics Survey. Average operating profit for engineering firms is 6%. That does not mean, however, that you must achieve the average profit. You should strive to reach a higher than average profit, and stretch yourself to get there. And do not tolerate staff members who are skeptical of your goals, provided that they are realistic and you can back them with planning and with hard figures.

4. ORGANIZATIONAL PLAN

The type of organizational plan you choose depends mainly on your corporate culture statements. If you decide you want a flat hierarchy because you will be small at first, with all managers on the same decision-making level for projects as yourself, then carefully define the limits of those decisions and the ramifications of the organization.

Firm owners can get hung up on debating the right organizational plan for their firm. Don't waste your time. Make a choice, and stick within its bounds. This is a critical part of your strategic plan, so even if it's you, your draftsman, and your secretary, define the hierarchy and the duties you associate with each role. When it comes time to grow, you'll already know where to go organizationally.

5. HUMAN RESOURCE PLANNING

Human resources is not just the recordkeeping function of sick days, holiday pay, and vacation time. Human resource management is the planning of staffing, recruiting, position planning, career development, performance appraisal, motivation, compensation, rewards, and benefits and employee assistance. You as the firm founder will most likely act as human resource manager for some time, perhaps for the long run. Be sure to address the human resource issues in your strategic plan.

6. LEADERSHIP TRANSITION PLANNING

Every formal strategic plan should include a statement about leadership transition. Of course, when you are just starting out planning your new firm, you probably wouldn't consider it. Simply state in your plan at this point that leadership transition planning has not been addressed.

The questions for leadership transition have long-term effects. Some firms are start-driven, and depend on one leader to carry the firm's vision. Other firms are organizationally-driven, and the choosing a leader is an outgrowth of years of continued stellar performance by one individual.

One important issue to address, particularly in professional service firms, is that of partnership or associate-ship criteria. It is important for your employees to understand how they can move up the ladder, in order to be motivated. Therefore it is advisable to publish in your company manual, your rules of eligibility for becoming an associate. Consider the criteria listed in Figure 6.3 when formulating your rules of eligibility for becoming an associate. Partnerships should be left to your discretion; however, you might set down some specific guidelines to follow should there come a time when you are considering a partner.

The leadership transition plan should have an accounting plan in place in order to finance any kind of partnership agreement. At this point, you should have a simple outline, drawn up with your accountant, on how to detail the legal and financial transactions for bringing future owners into the firm. The more prepared you are now, the better off you'll be down the line.

HOW OFTEN SHOULD YOU ENGAGE IN STRATEGIC PLANNING?

Some recommend that you spend four months per year on strategic planning; other sources recommend you review your strategic plan every six months. Your need will depend on your size, and your workload. Your plan should include, in the very least, six-month and one-year goals, and should include sections addressing both operations and workload. Given the quickly changing economics of the 1990s, it is probably best to plan to look over your strategic goals every six months, and revise them according to the needs of the marketplace.

Rules of Eligibility to be Considered in Becoming an Associate

1. You must have exhibited a willingness to accept responsibility.

2. You must exhibit an attitude of professionalism in the conduct of your responsibilities.

3. You must have exhibited exemplary character, integrity, honesty, fairness, loyalty, dependability, and professional ethics in your working relationships with both those inside as well as outside the company.

4. You must be deemed by the Board of Directors as having gained and maintained the respect of fellow employees.

5. You must have exhibited continued competence in your particular area of expertise. Due to the technical nature of the engineering profession, it is likely that most Associates will be technical employees; however, secretarial, accounting, marketing, business, or other supportive disciplines are not excluded from eligibility.

6. You must be capable of successfully meeting quality, budget, time of completion, and client satisfaction goals on projects in which they are involved.

7. You must have been actively involved in working full time in the engineering/surveying/land planning profession for a minimum of five years.

8. You must have exhibited the ability to be "accepted" by our clients, since those elected to carry the title and exposure which comes with being an Associate are recognized by our clients to be representative of the quality and character of our organization.

9. You must initiate discussion about your intent to become an Associate.

10. Preference will be given to those who have been employees of the company for a minimum of three years.

11. You must be elected by two-thirds of the Board of Directors.

Figure 6.3

III

STRATEGIC PLANNING SESSION

7 STRATEGIC PLANNING

> "You're the symphony conductor. Your staff knows how to play their various instruments; it's your job to make them play together." *—Byron West, AIA*

Many firms operate for years, even decades, without a formal strategic plan. Formalizing a firm's strategic plan gives its goals tremendous value, however, and energizes the organization to make things happen. You cannot implement your plan until you form actual numbers against which performance can be measured. Before getting into the specific elements of the strategic plan outlined in the previous section, take a look at the following ideas on strategic planning in general, and lay the groundwork for your strategic planning session.

HOW OFTEN SHOULD YOU PLAN?

Strategic planning is an ongoing process, in which you draw the line every six months or so, advises architect CEO Byron West. Begin six months in advance of implementation. You must have a structured mission and set of goals before you begin any six-month period. In some firms, planning is ongoing for one to four months per year. The strategic plan then gives you the basis upon which to build your budget. "It's like a tennis game between the CEO and the staff. Obviously, the CEO can't do the plan alone, nor can the staff. Therefore, it becomes a series of vollies back and forth, with a plan emerging by the end of the game," says West. Many design firms put off planning, or avoid it, for fear that what is believed will not be upheld once real numbers are set down. The worst thing to do is nothing at all but worry—instead, take the lead and carry your own torch.

Have you thought out the goals of your plan, not just your personal goals, but specific goals that you can measure? The goals of your strategic plan should be measurable, by the following yardsticks:

1. Increases and decreases in basic numbers, such as gross revenues, number of employees, or number of locations.
2. Changes in the mix of business, measured against target percentages as to type of client and type of work.
3. Skills measurement, including professional registrations and formal courses completed.
4. Marketing indicators that reflect strategic goals, such as the number of proposals, the number of reviews, and the number of wins.
5. Measurement in terms of ownership transition, if there is some sort of statement as to what ownership transition is going to be and how it is going to occur.
6. Revenue per employee. What did you set as a goal? What are you receiving?

Figure 7.1 Goals.

During the strategic planning process, the CEO asks the staff and managers (or you ask yourself if you are a one person firm) for input on where the organization stands, and where it's going. With this information, the CEO identifies where the concerns lie, and from there sets broad goals for the staff and management to reach. The staff then needs to develop the plan necessary to achieve those goals, a formula related to quantifiable goals.

It is the CEO's job to push the staff to meet those goals, publicize the goals, and to get everyone to "buy in" to them. Everyone must understand the firm's mission and goals.

The strategic plan helps you to understand where you are going, what you are thinking, and communicates to the staff the company's plans and goals for the coming period.

See Figure 7.1 for a listing of the kinds of goals to address in your strategic plan.

What are your specific, quantifiable company goals?

DEVELOPING YOUR GOALS

What are your specific company-wide goals? Take a half hour to brainstorm 12 specific goals to set down in order to start the strategic planning process.

1. _____
2. _____
3. _____
4. _____
5. _____
6. _____
7. _____
8. _____
9. _____
10. _____
11. _____
12. _____

GETTING OFF ON THE RIGHT FOOT

Strategic planning is the process whereby the design organization establishes its goals and objectives for the future. So how often do you undergo strategic planning? Normally, you should include specific plans for the next six month to one year period, and also identify broad goals for a three year period.

By arriving at a common understanding and agreement on the future of the firm, the various members of the organization can establish their necessary contributions. The strategic plan gives staff and yourself the opportunity to reconcile personal goals with firm goals. What is your personal goal? Does it match the goals you set out for the firm?

WHO SHOULD PARTICIPATE?

Participants in the strategic planning process should include all equity holders, major functional managers, and perhaps those senior employees who are demonstrably committed to the firm for an extended period. But if you are going to be the only principal, then you alone will actually write your strategic plan. (If others are principals, their input is critical, although one individual should be designated to actually draft the plan.)

OBJECTIVES

Strategic sessions should establish objectives for revenue, profits, employees, markets, disciplines, geographic markets-,branches, clients, ownership, and professional achievement. The objective is to define the firm's strengths and its weaknesses, in order to capitalize on strengths and minimize the importance and the impact of weaknesses.

From these overall objectives, you can then generate specific annual operational plans: business plan, monetary budgets, marketing plan, human resources/personnel plan, and ownership strategy. (These are discussed in separate sections later in the text.)

Design professionals can establish ambitious goals, and, through careful planning, achieve them. Although your decision to start a design practice may be a reaction to your own life situation and needs, do not allow yourself and your firm to simply become a "reactor" to situations and to the economy. You take less risk by careful planning than if you just wait for the next idea to pass through. Be proactive, set up your own market niche, and design!

According to design industry consultant David Rinderer, the following is a list of strategic planning questions to consider. Again, if you really want to define your purpose, set down an answer to each and every one of the following questions. When you are finished, you'll have the outline for your firm's strategic plan.

Firm Strategy

1. What is your definition of growth?
2. What is your mental picture of what your practice should be like in three years?
3. What role will you play in your visionary practice?
4. How many people can you personally manage?
5. What effect does your ownership transition plan have on growth?
6. What talent will you need that is not present now in the firm?
7. Why (and how) is growth important to you?
8. What impact does your management of time have on growth?

9. List three external factors that can help you grow, then list three that will hinder growth.

10. Define change.

11. How do you implement change?

12. What conflicts do you perceive between your visionary firm and the present situation?

13. Why do these conflicts exist?

14. What can you do to resolve these conflicts?

15. Define the kind of leader you are.

16. What impact does your leadership style have on growth?

17. How do your clients perceive the firm?

18. Is their perception in line with goals for your visionary firm?

19. Crystallize your thoughts into a one-statement strategic goal for the firm. Be specific.

Production

1. What utilization ratio do you feel production staff should maintain? (65% is average, but these days, expectations are higher.)

2. What areas of expertise do you feel are lacking?

3. What utilization rate do you feel you personally should maintain?

4. What, in your opinion, constitutes good service to your clients?

5. How important is the quality of computer capabilities to your clients?

6. What constitutes quality work to you?

7. How will you communicate that quality to your future clients?

8. What tools would you make available to your staff to help them excel in their work?

9. Define your project mix as the percentage of jobs with fees below $10,000 and those with fees above $10,000. (Do the same for $50,000 level jobs, if that applies.)

10. Do you feel the same production process should apply to all jobs?

11. Do you feel you need more decision makers? More workers? Both?
12. Rank, in order of importance (for all services):
    a. Meeting or beating schedule.
    b. Profitability.
    c. Quality of plans and specifications.
    d. Satisfaction of user with end product.
    e. Innovation in design.

Marketing

1. What are the three primary strengths of your firm?
2. Do clients perceive these as your strengths?
3. Why do you consider them strengths?
4. List three types of work in which the strengths can be maximized.
5. List three more peripheral markets that you are not now serving that could be entered using your strengths.
6. What kind of work should the firm do, in order of priority?
7. What geographic area should be covered?
8. Who should be responsible for marketing performance in the firm?
9. Define marketing.
10. Define selling.
11. What is the difference?
12. What image do you want your firm to project?
13. What image does the ideal firm, in your opinion, project?
14. How do the images differ?
15. Is there a project too large for the firm?
16. Do you like to sell? List why/why not.
17. Do you have a fear of sales failure?
18. List three things you personally do best.
19. In one paragraph, convince me you are the best.
20. Write a specific marketing goal statement for the firm.

Finance

1. Define profit for your firm.
2. How much money do you need to earn?

3. How much gross income will your firm earn?

4. How does this compare with your earnings today?

5. Where will additional fees come from?

6. How much investment will it take to grow?

7. What is your profit goal for next year? The year after?

8. How does your profit goal tie to your personal income goal?

9. Do you want to communicate the financial status of the firm to the staff?

10. How often do you want to know how well the firm is doing?

11. How much should you spend to get the information you want?

12. Should there be a difference between function and ownership?

13. How much capital do you want to invest in the operations of the firm?

14. Is return on investment important, and, if so, how should it be measured in terms of dollars in light of your goals?

15. List three financial facts affecting growth.

16. What control do you have over each factor?

17. What impact does the economy have on your finances?

18. List three things you can do today to improve the finances of your firm.

19. How can you enlist the support of the entire staff to improve profits?

Human Resources

1. What is your primary goal in life?

2. Where do you want to live?

3. How long do you want to work?

4. What is your favorite hobby?

5. What is your favorite work?

6. If you had all the money in the world, what would you do today?

7. What is your family's goal?

8. Do your spouse's goals meet yours?

9. Do you know the answers to the above eight questions for each of your staff?

10. How do you find out more about each of your people?

11. Define motivation.

12. Define communication.

13. How do you communicate with your staff?

14. How does the staff perceive you?

15. List ten traits you look for in any person you hire. Rank them from one to ten in order of importance.

16. How do the traits compare with what you listed as your three primary strengths?

17. Identify specific skills needed in your firm that you alone do not possess.

18. What traits should people with these skills have?

19. What is the goal of your recruiting effort?

20. How do you reinforce that goal once an individual is hired?

21. List all benefit programs you now provide your staff.

22. Next to each benefit, list how it affects your profit, and how it helps you get more work.

23. How do your benefits compare to those of other firms?

24. Define recognition.

25. List five kinds of recognition you have the power to give each employee.

26. How good a listener are you?

27. In an eight hour day, how much time do you spend listening?

28. How does human resources planning affect market and financial planning?

29. Identify one thing you can do better today to improve the human resources effort in the firm.

THE FORMAL PLAN

When actually writing out your strategic plan, it should generally include the following sections. You are not quite ready to set these into place. However, use this list as a guide after you complete the other exercises in the book, and you'll have a clear, concise plan that conforms to banker's and other financier's requirements.

Here are the sections to include in the strategic plan:

1. *Organizational Mission.* Your firm's purpose, reason for existence. This is where you will include your organizational vision, and the mission you develop out of that vision.

2. *Strategic Analysis.* External and internal factors having the greatest impact on your firm's future. This is also known as the "marketing research" portion of the document.

3. *Marketing Strategy.* Direction of your firm. In this section, you outline how you plan to procure clients, which markets you will "hit" and how. This is your "marketing plan."

4. *Ownership Transition/Issues/Long-Term Objectives.* Results required to carry out your firm's mission and marketing strategy. A one page section (keep it concise and to the point). In this section you are actually envisioning what will happen to your firm when you are gone, where it will be, and so on.

5. *Human Resources/Internal Programs.* In-house programs needed to employ your strategy and accomplish your long-term objectives. Also think out organizational issues and set them down here.

6. *Financial Projections.* Planned financial results and measures of performance.

7. *Executive Summary.* Personalization of plan from the CEO's standpoint. It is very important to keep this to a one page maximum, and to summarize each section and your overall objective.

STRATEGIC PLANNING CHECKLIST

In general if you were writing a strategic plan for an existing company, you would need to compile the following materials for review in order to evaluate your firm before embarking on the strategic planning process. Because you are a start-up firm, you will not have all of these items. However, this is a good checklist of items to look at every six months, and to use as a list of the important reports to monitor in the development of your firm. Each of these items is explained and exemplified in chapter 12.

Financial Data

1. Gross revenues versus net revenues.
2. Revenues generated by client type.
3. Profitability by client type.
4. Revenues generated by project type.
5. Profitability by project type.
6. Bonus structure and disbursement.
7. Pension/profit sharing contributions.
8. Ranking of annual revenues generated by client.

Human Resources

1. Staff turnover rate.
2. Job descriptions for each position.
3. List of staff including position.
4. Corporate and divisional organizational charts.

Operational/Production

1. Size of average projects.
2. Duration of projects for past year.
3. Production capabilities.
4. Project backlog.
5. Changes in technical capabilities.

Marketing

1. List of targeted project types.
2. List of targeted client types.
3. List of services.
4. Geographic area.
5. Market trends for targeted markets.
6. Knowledge of competitors.

EIGHT MORE STRATEGIC PLANNING TIPS

Here are eight no-nonsense tips to apply to your strategic planning session. Post these on the wall next to your desk, land don't forget: HOW ARE YOU GOING TO BETTER SERVICE THE CLIENT? If you do not have an answer, then don't go into business!

- **Focus externally, not internally.** More work always solves more problems than it creates.
- **Focus discussions on strategic issues and topics.** These, not daily operational concerns, are the essence of strategic planning.
- **Involve all key people in planning.** Don't limit yourself to the stockholders.
- **Do your planning away from the office.** Don't involve the spouses. This is an important business activity, not a social event.
- **Use a facilitator.** Without one, you'll waste a lot of time looking back, instead of ahead.
- **Prepare well in advance.** Do a few simple exercises—send out memos with key concerns—to get people thinking strategically, not myopically.
- **Cover all six elements of planning.** They include mission and culture statements, marketing plan and direction, financial plan, organizational plan, human resources plan, and leadership transition.
- **Make staff training in people skills a top priority.**
- **Focus on rapid response to client problems.** Identify ways to break "deadlocked" traditional approaches to practice.
- **Avoid "motherhood and apple pie" discussions, decisions, and statements.** Your plan must relate to the real world.

GET TO IT!

You are now ready to embark on building your firm's strategic plan. Your first task is defining the vision and mission of your firm. The following sections take you through each portion of the strategic planning process. When you've completed all of your steps, you'll have a strategic plan!

8 A VISION TO PURSUE

"Our projects ... have had a direct impact on
literally millions of citizens"—*Freeze & Nichols, Vision Statement*

The physical act of writing down your goals is a powerful motivator toward achieving success. A written vision, both for life and for business, can become the unifying factor that weaves a continuing thread through your life and the firm's destiny. Without vision, without a mission to carry out that vision, all projects, all plans, all acts become situational, not connected, not linked toward a common goal.

An entrepreneurial leader is someone with vision. The definition of entrepreneur in our society is a self-starter, a self-motivator, a person with a drive that forces its way out from within—and the entrepreneurial spirit cannot be taught. It can only be nurtured.

When starting any kind of strategic planning for your firm, you must first develop your vision. Your vision may change next year, but that is of no consequence today. Keep it simple. Mainly, keep it to one sentence.

Figure 8.1 contains a vision statement from Freese & Nichols, Inc. This is a specific vision statement that embodies both the goals and the philosophy of the firm principals. Again, a one sentence vision is most clear, but this is another great motivational example of a firm stating its quest. The entire strategic plan is an outgrowth of this vision.

At a recent seminar I heard several interesting vision statements. One firm said their vision was "To make money." Straightforward. Truthful? Then why design? Design work is one of the most convoluted ways to "make money"! Why put up with the aggravation of clients, contractors, project managers, other architects, and engineers? To create? To create what? Buildings? Hydroelectric plants? Better roads? Alterna-

VISION/MISSION STATEMENT FOR FREESE AND NICHOLS, INC.

Freese and Nichols, Inc. and its predecessor firms have, for nearly 100 years, searched for innovative engineering solutions to improve the quality of life of the people we serve. This tradition began with the firm's founder, John B. Hawley, who was instrumental in developing surface water supplies for Texas cities that had previously relied on underground water, rivers, cisterns, and other less dependable sources. The firm's pioneering efforts have extended to other disciplines as well. Freese and Nichols engineers were involved in the development of some of the first water filtration plants in the nation; the activated sludge process for wastewater treatment; and, more recently, methods for extending the life of landfills through the use of slurry trenches. Projects designed by Freese and Nichols, from the smallest street improvements to major efforts such as the infrastructure development for the Dallas/Fort Worth International Airport, have had a direct impact on literally millions of citizens.

Our vision for Freese and Nichols is to continue and build upon the traditions established during the firm's first 97 years of service. We envision a firm that is known for:

- Developing engineering solutions appropriate to our clients' needs. Both proven solutions and state-of-the-art technology have a place in the engineering world of the 1990s. Freese and Nichols belongs in this world as a center for technical excellence, discovering the type of innovative but practical solutions that best serve our clients and acting as a valuable technical resource to them.
- Placing an unusually strong emphasis on quality in all we do, especially in exceeding our clients' expectations for the quality and timeliness of our services.
- Assembling the very best staff of engineers, scientists, and other professionals in our region. By creating a work environment that responds to their needs, we can enable this group of extremely highly motivated professionals to realize their full potential through their projects and advancement in the firm.
- Conducting our practice in a totally ethical manner in all situations.
- Being a conservatively managed firm that anticipates steady growth consistent with the real growth that will take place in our region over the next decade.

Figure 8.1

tive energy sources? Your vision is a specific statement relating to the kinds of designs you'd like to perform, as if there were no money in the world. If there were no such thing as currency, what would you truly want to do? Now, how can you go about getting to that goal?

Here's a process to follow to develop your own personal vision:

1. Strive for clarity, but don't be afraid to begin with only a foggy notion of what you want.

2. Sit down in a closed room, and fill up the page with your vision for yourself and your firm in five years. Be careful not to edit yourself at this point. No one will read this draft, so don't put a lot of energy into worrying about writing down the "absolute answer" or the "final thing." This is simply a draft. And remember, the values you set for yourself will be directly related to the values you set down for your firm. The environment you create in your life will be reflected in the kind of business you ultimately create.

3. Put away the paper, and take it out in a day or so, or even a week.

4. Take a fresh look at what you've written about your vision. Perhaps it's not accurate, so change it a bit, mark it up with corrections, and be sure to include everything you want to be in five years.

5. Now comes the hard part: take that one page and summarize it into one sentence. That's it. That one sentence must be powerful enough, general enough, yet inspiring enough to motivate you for the next five years.

6. Frame it. Your next task is to have your crack typist or desktop publishing expert (at this point in your business, this may be you!) nicely set the sentence on a 8½×11 inch piece of paper, and then frame it. Purchase an expensive-looking frame, one that you know you can live with for the next five years.

7. Hang the vision statement on the wall, preferably in a space where you and any other employees can see it while working. Hang your vision somewhere where you'll read it every day.

In writing down your vision, don't overwhelm yourself or your co-workers. Be sparing with words. Be conscious of a higher purpose. Be careful of what you want—you may get it.

This is a time to focus on what you'd like to design, what kind of corporate culture you plan to create. Do you want a hard-line, business-only atmosphere? A family culture? A strict 9-to-5 office? Now is the time to make these decisions, so that the office, the employees, and all the other important elements you choose are outgrowths of the original vision— your purpose for being in business.

Maybe you dream of a red Mazarati with a sunroof, but is that what drives you to succeed? It may. Perhaps your vision is "I want to be driving a red Mazarati in five years." Fine.

Now you have to go about planning how to get what you'll need to make that happen. To make your vision happen. With a concise, written vision statement, the task of planning has begun.

Figure 8.2 is an outline of a process for developing a vision for the service firm, originally published in the *Harvard Business Review*. Using the questions as a guide, you can structure your vision to meet your firm's goals and needs. Photocopy this form and fill out the answers for your particular firm, to build the vision you'd like to achieve over the next several years.

TARGET MARKET SEGMENTS

1. What are the common characteristics of the market segments you plan to serve?

   _____

   _____

   _____

2. What dimensions can be used to further segment each market? Demographic? Psychographic? _____

   _____

3. How important are the various segments? _____

   _____

4. What needs does each have? _____

   _____

   _____

5. How well are these needs being served at present in your region? How? By whom?

   _____

   _____

   _____

POSITIONING

1. How does your service concept propose to meet customer needs?

   _____

   _____

2. How do the competitors meet those needs? _____

   _____

3. How is your proposed service differentiated from the competition's?

   _____

   _____

4. How important are these differences? _____

   _____

5. What is good service? _____

   _____

Figure 8.2 Source: Basic and Integrative Elements of a Strategic Service Vision, "Lessons in the Service Sector," by James L. Heskett, March/April 1987, p. 120. Copyright 1987, The Harvard Business Review.

6. Does the proposed service concept provide it? _____

_____

7. What efforts are required to bring customer expectations and service capabilities into alignment? _____

_____

SERVICE CONCEPT

1. What are the important elements of the service to be provided, stated in terms of results produced for customers? _____

_____

2. How are these elements supposed to be perceived by the target market segment? By the market in general? By employees as a whole?

_____

_____

3. How do customers perceive the service concept? _____

_____

4. What efforts does this suggest in terms of the manner in which the service is designed? Delivered? Marketed? _____

_____

VALUE-COST LEVERAGING

1. To what extent are differences perceived between the value and the cost of the services delivered? _____

_____

2. To what extent does this effort create barriers to entry by potential competition? _____

_____

3. What is the difference between your price and theirs?

_____

_____

4. If your price is the same or higher, why should the client choose your firm instead? _____

_____

Figure 8.2   (Continued.)

OPERATING STRATEGY

1. What are important elements of your firm's strategy?

   _____

   _____

2. Where will the most effort be concentrated?

   _____

   _____

3. Where will investment be made?

   _____

   _____

4. To what extent does the coordination of operating strategy and service delivery system ensure:

   High quality? _____

   High productivity? _____

   Low cost? _____

   High morale and loyalty of servers? _____

   _____

5. To what extent does this integration provide barriers to entry by competition?

   _____

   _____

SERVICE DELIVERY SYSTEM

What are important features of the service delivery system, including:

The role of the people? _____

Degree of technology? _____

Equipment? _____

Layout: _____

Procedures? _____

What capacity does it provide? _____

   Normally? _____

   At peak levels? _____

Figure 8.2   (Continued.)

To what extent does it ensure quality standards?

_____

_____

How is it differentiated from the competition? _____

_____

How does this provide barriers to entry by competition?

_____

Figure 8.2   (Continued.)

9 MISSION IMPOSSIBLE?

"I have often thought that the best way to define a man's character would be to seek out the particular mental or moral attitude in which ... he felt most deeply active and alive."

—*The Letters of William James*, 1818

Your next task in building the strategic plan is to translate your vision statement into a firm mission. What are you on a mission to accomplish and how will you get there? This is an elaboration of the who's, what's, when's, where's, why's, and how's of the vision. Vision is a compact statement. Mission can be much larger, but try to account for every element of your purpose.

This is the time to hone your concept and to figure out how you will reach your vision. Mission should be succinct, unique, and tailored to communicate exactly what the firm does for its clients. It should not be generic: "ABC Associates is a unique architectural firm". Instead it should state exactly what the firm is trying to accomplish: "ABC Associates will work for ten hospital clients in the New England region in 1994." Be that specific. It's the only way to ensure success. Again, you need specific numbers against which to measure your goals. The mission statement outlines briefly the specific numbers you intend to reach.

Figure 9.1 is an example of a mission statement from an actual design firm.

MISSIONARY WORK

Most firms have a "mission statement" or a "policy statement," that outlines in rather lofty terms the firm's goals, objectives, and philosophy about their work.

SAMPLE MISSION

Provide quality consulting services to enhance the value of land assets for clients who demonstrate integrity and community responsibility.

(Rodgers & Associates, Rockville, MD)

Figure 9.1

An innovative midwestern design firm takes the use of a mission statement one step further. In addition to including the firm's mission statement in all proposals, the firm includes the mission statement in contracts. The mission statement is accompanied by a project-specific statement that outlines exactly how the firm's mission statement and philosophy will be applied to this particular project, this client, and this scope of work. Everyone is clear on what the firm is working toward, and this facilitates communications in both directions. This practice is not only a good marketing idea, it's an excellent foundation for good and continuing client relations.

MISSION STATEMENTS WITH MEANING

Consider Pepsico's mission statement of several years ago: "Kill Coke." Those two words clearly communicate the company's objective in a way that everyone can understand.

Your mission may be more complex, but should be as powerful, concise, and clear. Effective mission statements include these four elements:

1. *Aggressiveness.* The marketplace is competitive and missions are targets. An effective mission statement should reveal the seriousness of hitting a target or reaching a goal.
2. *Simplicity.* John Kennedy wanted "a man on the moon." That statement became NASA's mission. Mission statements are most effective if they are concise.
3. *Inspiration.* Leaders don't execute missions; followers do. The words in the mission statement must communicate energy and challenge people to meet your goals. (What was Frank Lloyd Wright's mission?)

4. *Focus.* The mission statement should answer the question, "Right now, what are we in business for?"

Review your firm's mission statement and assess whether or not it has meaning. Does it inspire your targeted group — all employees, senior staff, and so on? Is your firm agonizing over semantics? State your objective as simply as possible.

EXERCISE

List your 12 goals on the left-hand side of a sheet of paper, and draw a line down the middle. Now write a sentence next to each goal, explaining how you will reach that goal. (Note: 12 is an arbitrary number! You may have more goals or fewer goals.)

To finalize your mission statement (in one page only!), write a preface to the 12 goals — a short paragraph introducing your plans to turn your vision into reality. Then list the 12 statements on how to reach your goals. The rest of the strategic plan will spell out the tactics and techniques needed to carry forth this mission to completion.

10 DEVELOPING AN EFFECTIVE MARKETING PLAN

"The Golden Age lies before us and not behind us."
—*Edward Bellamy,* Looking Backward, *1888*

Developing an effective marketing strategy for the next year is the most important aspect of strategic planning, especially for a start-up firm. Develop a questionnaire incorporating the questions below to ask yourself and any anticipated partner or staff. These questions will provide the basis upon which you can best use your strengths, and those of your staff, to achieve your marketing goals.

Ask your staff and yourself the following questions:

1. Where would you like the firm to be in three years?
2. What do you think your role could be in achieving that goal?
3. List three external and three internal factors that would help you achieve your vision?
4. What do you think are three of the major strengths of the firm?
5. What do you think are three of the major weaknesses of the firm?
6. What do you think you could do to strengthen your weaknesses?
7. What markets, other than the ones you are currently pursuing, do you think could benefit from the strengths of the firm?
8. What kind of work do you think would bring the most

profitability to the firm and the most satisfaction to the staff?

9. What do you like to do in marketing?

10. What do you *not* like to do in marketing?

11. List three of the most effective marketing techniques you have seen bring in work to a firm.

12. What are your clients' perceptions of you? How will they perceive the firm?

13. How do you think the firm will compare to the competition?

14. What specific suggestions do you have to improve the effectiveness of your firm's marketing?

Compile the responses into a summary report including specific marketing tactics to reach your goals.

MEASURING YOUR STRATEGIC GOALS

Here are some of the quantifiable yardsticks you can use to measure the effectiveness of your performance against the goals of your marketing plan:

Increases or Decreases in Basic Numbers. This refers to numbers such as gross revenues, number of employees, or number of locations.

Changes in the Mix of Business. These can be measured against target percentages as to type of client and type of work.

Skills Measurement. Include professional registrations and formal training courses completed.

Marketing Indicators. These reflect strategic goals, such as the number of proposals, number of interviews, and number of wins.

Measurement in Terms of Ownership Transition. This applies if there is some sort of statement as to what ownership is going to be and how any transition is going to occur.

Revenue per Employee. What did you set as a goal? What are you receiving? (This measure is further explained in Chapter 12.)

Again, going back to the 12 goals you developed earlier, you must now develop 12 separate strategies, one for each goal. Before you do so, you must confirm your beliefs to be sure they are viable. You can do this by performing some simple market research.

MARKET RESEARCH SUPPORTS STRATEGIC PLANNING

Market research is integral to the strategic planning process. A firm cannot make plans for its future if it does not understand the opportunities available in the marketplace and the factors affecting existing and targeted markets. Below is a list of resources to review on a regular basis in order to understand the ever-changing marketplace.

Governmental Agencies

State Economic Development Departments.
State Departments of Commerce.
U.S. Department of Commerce.
County Market Research Departments.
State Departments of Education.

Publications

Fortune and *Forbes* magazines.
Building Design and Construction.
National Real Estate Investor.
Business journal tabloids.
State business magazines.
Urban Land Institute—market profiles.

Real Estate Organizations

Cooper & Lybrand, Inc.
Grubb & Ellis.
Coldwell Banker Commercial Real Estate.

Financial Institutions

Banks.
Savings & Loans.
Insurance companies.

Universities

Departments of Economic and Business Research
Centers for Economic and Real Estate Development

Professional Associations

American Association of Museums.
Association of Independent Schools.
American Hospital Association.
American Corrections Association.

Market Forecasters and Economic Development Consultants

Kenneth Laventhol, CPA—San Francisco.
Economic Research Council—Bethesda.
Pannel Kerr Forster, CPA—San Francisco.
Hammer Siler George Associates—Denver.

11 RESEARCHING FUTURE MARKETS

> "My center is giving way, my right is pushed back,
> situation excellent, I am attacking."
> —*B.H. Liddell Hart, at the 2nd battle of the Maine (1918)*

Forecasting is an essential element of good business. To forecast, you must learn how to identify trends, because trends generate new business opportunities. Your goal is to identify trends that will push and pull certain areas of the economy, and, in turn, to anticipate how your potential clients will respond to these trends.

To begin market research there are several starting points—trends generators—where trends develop. It helps to understand these.

Changes in Attitudes Toward the Quality of Life. For example, the national concern for good health has had an enormous impact on the food industry, particularly the poultry industry, as it has grown to meet the demand of a public seeking to reduce fat and cholesterol in its diet. Other examples are the high value placed on leisure time, and the spreading trend toward environmentalism.

Political Changes. Examples of these trend generators are unfolding now as the Department of Defense plans to close a number of military bases, as we pass through the rise and fall of the nuclear weapons age, and as opportunities open through the fall of Eastern Bloc Communism, as well as in other foreign markets.

Shortages, or Gluts, of Materials. The shortage of whale oil in the late 1800s paved the way for the petroleum industry. The glut of by-products from gasoline production in the 1940s and 1950s sparked the development of the petrochemical industry.

New Technologies. The invention of the telephone, the computer, and any number of other items has meant billions of dollars of business to the firms that serve these industries.

Half Technologies. These are technologies that don't do a job with complete efficiency. Electric generating stations that discard heat via cooling towers are a good example, because heat is wasted. Harnessing waste of all types for productive purposes is an industry that's beginning to take off.

Each one of these trend generators creates opportunities for business today and tomorrow.

These six steps, contributed by Mary Sherry, President of the Economic Research Council, will help you identify areas where there might be business for your firm:

1. Read widely and identify trends. Awareness is the first step, and with practice, you'll find yourself spotting trends in early stages. Read *American Demographics,* the *New York Times,* the *Washington Post, Engineering News Record.* Watch for demographic changes and new legislature that could present new opportunities for your firm.

2. Break each trend into smaller components. For example under "quality of life" issues, the poultry industry is a subgroup of the food industry. While working with food companies may not be your specialty, the same trend may drive another industry, such as the health care industry. Specialty services such as psychiatric care and chemical dependency facilities are smaller, but growing, segments of the market.

3. Examine each likely component carefully. Read trade publications for the field you select and learn about its needs and concerns.

4. Look for exceptions to conventional wisdom. Many of you are familiar with "Silicon Valley" and "Route 128," but how many know there are robust electronic businesses in South Dakota and Utah? And how many pro-

fessional services ever call on them? Seek out market niches nationwide, and cater to their needs.

5. Involve as many people as you can in this process. Brainstorm on a planned topic regularly at marketing planning meetings. Contact industry professionals and interview them. Perhaps you may want able businesses to assemble an informal board of advisors comprised of market participators—hospital presidents if you build hospitals, psychiatrists if you design psychiatric hospitals, and so on. Brainstorming is a wide avenue for forecasting because it encourages off-the-wall ideas that can evolve into profit. It is hard to elicit creative forecasting ideas through other techniques.

6. Identify downward trends and be hardnosed about areas you don't want to spend time targeting. The negative side of trends identification by brainstorming is often overlooked, but it, too, can have time- and money-saving benefits.

This information was kindly provided by Mary Sherry, President of the Economic Research Council, a research publishing and consulting firm focusing on capital investment by industry (Phone: (301) 951-1072).

DON'T FALL PREY TO "FADS"

Many firms' marketing departments are misled by fads. They may fall prey to a "hot" new marketing technique rather than looking at what they are already doing, determining what is working, and applying that technique to the current market conditions.

Understanding market trends and their implications on your firm is probably one of the most overlooked aspects of the marketing of design and construction firms. With some foresight and planning you can train yourself to routinely analyze market trends.

Understanding market trends means you are a *proactive marketer*. When you understand the marketplace, you can: 1) easily target clients with changing operations, 2) identify potential projects, 3) position your firm to offer unique services that meet the market/client demand more easily, 4) sell your firm to that client, 5) virtually eliminate the competition, and 6) identify potential projects before your competitors. In short, you can learn to isolate a niche market before anyone else.

IDENTIFY NEW PROJECT OPPORTUNITIES

One objective in market research is identifying new project opportunities. You've already learned that magazines, newspapers, and industry leaders are the sources for market research. Next you need to know what to look for. For each major news publication or magazine within your targeted geographic area, look for articles that provide your firm with a new project lead. Ask for and seek out new ideas, new trends. The key word in identifying new opportunities is *change*—any sort of change in a particular industry means there's probably a potential project. Growth signals the need for more facilities. Consolidation means something must be done with existing or vacated facilities. Mergers and acquisitions could mean expansion, consolidation, or renovation. Abandonment means reuse of an existing facility or conversion to a new use.

Review newspaper and magazine publications on a daily basis. This is an excellent market research task to assign to an administrative staff person.

NINE BEST INDUSTRIES IN THE 1990S

To help launch your marketing effort, here is some help. According to design and construction industry players the nine major industries that will provide the best project opportunities for design and construction firms for the remainder of the 1990s are:

1. *Community and Cultural Facilities.* Museums (maritime, music, industry, and sport), aquariums, performing arts centers/theaters, sports arenas/convention centers.
2. *Services and Facilities for the Elderly.* Affordable housing/life care, outdoor recreation, health care.
3. *High Tech and Communications.* Telecommunications/

computers/defense, research and development, phar-maceutical/biotechnology.

4. *Health Care.* HMO's/out-patient services, home health care, specialty care hospitals, psychiatric/dependency rehabilitation.

5. *Correction.* Prisons/jails, detention centers/police stations, justice/courts facilities.

6. *Education.* Renovation, expansions, and long-range plans for elementary, secondary, and higher education facilities, day care/child care.

7. *Air Transportation.* New/replacement airport facilities, terminals/airside, support/parking, runways/aprons, food service/retail.

8. *Recreation and Entertainment.* Sports, especially golf, heritage tourism (parks and historic structures), gaming and gambling (casinos and riverboat gaming), hotels, food service, retail, parking.

9. *Environmental.* Recycling/manufacturing, waste disposal/remediation.

LOCATE LEADS THROUGH THE WANT ADS

Stratenomics, a strategic planning firm based in Chicago, identified new potential clients by going through the Sunday Chicago Tribune want ads looking for companies with new positions to fill.

They viewed those classified ads as new business opportunities. If there was a company looking to hire a lot of senior level people, that indicated they were in a growth mode. They called the company, obtained the names of the decision-makers, and suggested it would be more efficient to use Stratenomics to implement new programs rather than hire new employees. By looking for the corporate needs the firm could fill, the firm has added new clients including Coopers & Lybrand, Wick Homes, and RCF Information Systems.

This same technique can be applied to the design and construction industry. Scan the help wanted ads weekly. If a company is planning to hire a large number of employees, change is taking place within their organization. This probably indicates the need for a change in their facilities, whether that be a reconfiguration of internal spaces, addition to an existing building or campus, or maybe just a modification to accommodate new equipment. Contact the company and find out who the key decision-makers are, then call and introduce yourself. They may not be building anything today, but keep your name coming at them and they'll call you first when they are. Get to know them on a first name basis. If you golf, find out where they golf. Make lasting contacts with key individuals at growing companies. You'll be top on their list when it comes to hiring a design professional for their next design project.

UNDERSTANDING YOUR CLIENT'S BUSINESS

Market research has revealed that clients and owners are consistently frustrated by the feeling that design teams do not really understand their client's business. They state that the tendency is for the design team to focus on technical issues rather than on understanding the client's operation. This is a weakness, especially in light of the group trend toward total quality management.

Delivering quality services and products on time and within budget is a client's *minimum expectation*—basically a given. From the owner's perspective, the design team should protect the owner's interest, make him or her look good, and provide an "insurance policy." Clients often use words like: honest, attentive, responsive, friendly, trustworthy, respectful, communicative, square-dealing, and diligent. When interviewing with a client, listen for the kinds of words he or she uses. Pay attention to what kinds of words excite that particular client.

Every time you talk with a client, conduct some mini "market research." Focus your discussion on assessing this type of information. Ask questions that encourage the client to speak of his or her needs and opinions. Confirm your answers and perception of the client's company/operation during your presentation. Test out the "buzz words" and concepts. Ask the client for feedback. "Am I right in assuming that _____ is important to you?"

CLIENT INFORMATION FILE

Maintain a client information file on your computer system. Purchase a card file or rolodex-type software and record information on each client, including interests and the last time you spoke—a little personalization goes a long way!

Successful firms have the following commonalities in their marketing programs:

1. The firm has knowledge of the project before it hits the street.
2. Someone in the firm knows, or gets to know, the people in the project organization.
3. There is a "champion" in the firm with "passion" to have the project.
4. The firm has references who can make direct contact with the prospect.
5. There is time for the firm to do its homework.
6. The team is fit for the job.
7. The marketing effort is followed up in every detail.
8. The firm "nearly always" offers a "sizzle" that makes it truly different from its competition.

What is the common feature needed for a firm to have all of these attributes? Market research and networking are their number one priorities. (Networking will be discussed in Chapter 25.)

MAKING THAT COLD CALL WARMER

Don't ever attempt to visit a potential client without carefully planning your effort. The potential client is undoubtedly a busy person who will probably be irritated by an interruption from "another design firm trying to hype itself." You can orchestrate a strong first impression by deciding how to turn a *cold call* into a *warm meeting.* Here are some steps to help you:

1. Research the company or agency before you make the phone call.
2. Drill anyone you know who has information about the firm.
3. Call the receptionist and ask for the client's annual financial report.
4. Call the firm's marketing people, and, under the guise of

curiosity, ask relevant questions about what is going on, how business is, and so on.

5. Find out about the firm's culture. Are the people who work there relaxed? Are they progressive? Are they hyper and overworked? Firsthand knowledge of a potential client will create a positive impression, and make it easier to arrange a meeting, your major objective.

After you have gone to the library and reviewed every resource to gain information about the agency or firm, then you need to formulate a reason for making an appointment with the right person. The objective in your research should be to identify a special need or an efficiency application or some niche that will differentiate your firm to the client. Use that specialty as the reason for the meeting. Tell the client that you are simply introducing yourself to explain this new service.

Show the potential client that you understand his or her business and offer ways you can improve that business. If you can succeed at this task, you've got your "foot in the door" to be considered for the next design job.

TOOLS ARE NOT JUST FOR FIXING!

Vertical Systems Analysis is a consulting firm that works with property owners and managers to improve and evaluate their elevator service. Several years ago, the firm targeted the high-rise commercial and residential building market. In order to establish a presence in this market and promote their expertise, they adapted charts and forms used in their work to create a 14-page booklet—"Owner's Guide to Better Elevator Service." The firm sent a press release announcing the free handbook to every real estate trade publication in their target market. The firm's owner also used the handbook as a "brochure piece" at his trade show booths, distributed them at speeches and presentations, and mailed them to anyone who called in response to the publicity.

The handbook market technique brought the company new clients such as IBM, New York University, and Westinghouse Elevator. Review your firm's tools used on jobs and develop a similar idea that you can apply to your clients. Create a new tool that will be helpful in your client's operations.

This is known as usefulness selling. Many firms have accomplished the same objective with a client newsletter or even periodic notes sent out to clients with articles attached, relevant to them. There is nothing more powerful than the continual positive presence of your name on the client's desk.

SETTING UP YOUR OWN IN-HOUSE RESEARCH EFFORT

Health care, education, and export-related industries offer some of the best opportunities in the design and construction industry. Also, certain industrial companies are continuing to grow. Growth appears to be centered in industries, and within selected companies within those industries, that are *marketing driven.*

The major commonality among today's successful design firms is that they are servicing their existing clients better than ever before. It is unclear at this time if the higher degree of service is based on better systems the firms may have developed, or on the fact that they have less work and consequently more time to dedicate to their existing clients. However, statistics show that the dissatisfaction level among clients has gone down from 17–21% to 8–11%.

The key for design and construction firms that are not growing at the present time is to devote resources to gathering information. Market research is the only way firms can develop strategies and tactics that will redefine and redirect their practices as well as find the right target.

Interview existing and potential decision-makers and perform such things as a Client Service Analysis. A Client Service Analysis does not consist of asking your client, "How did we do on your job?" Instead it means asking the client, "How can we do our job better to meet your needs?"

Market analysis research starts with the following questions:

1. What are the major influences in the marketplace that affect your business, positively or negatively?
2. What are you predicting to happen in your market, and others, in the two to three years?
3. What could happen to "throw your operation off"? (Laws, regulations, funding, etc.)

You must be analytical and intuitive to conduct this type of research. If you do not have an appropriate person, then hire an outside consultant. A consultant knows the right type of questions to ask, the right type of information to gather, and how to synthesize that information into a strategy for the firm.

How many clients or potential clients do you have to contact to have an accurate reading on a market? You must work backwards. First determine the number of jobs you need to secure for your firm in a given one year period. Then multiply that number by four. That is the total number of already warm and screened potential leads you must make to meet your desired job goal. To understand a particular market, multiply your desired job goal number by twenty. Once you have interviewed and gathered information from that number of clients, you will have a solid understanding of the market.

Here's some general advice for firms attempting to perform in-house market research:

1. Remember, in order to diminish the risk of a misguided strategy, your overall market research objective is to extract information to develop a well-founded strategy and direction for your firm. Consequently, market research must be the number one priority in your firm's marketing program.

2. Set goals. You must have a goal for your market research program and for every market research interview with a client. Ask yourself, "What is my expected outcome from this meeting, activity, or whatever?" Answering that question prior to starting the market research task will provide your direction.

3. Start now! Many firms are too late. This is not the time to be cutting your marketing budget or departments. This is the time to bite the bullet and save your firm!

(This information was kindly provided by Roger Pickar, marketing consultant.)

BUILDING YOUR MARKETING PLAN

Once you've researched the markets and have hard, factual data on the numbers of potential clients in a particular "universe," you can begin to structure your marketing plan. A good number of the smaller firms interviewed for this book did not have as elaborate, or as formal, a plan as we are discussing here. That decision is up to you. The most organized, succinct, and targeted marketing plan you can assemble will obviously ensure the highest return on your investment in the firm. But failure to develop such a plan happens for many reasons, including lack of time, lack of effort, and lack of initiative, all the way down to the fear that if you actually researched the numbers of clients in your targeted universe, you might be proven wrong, to a high influx of work at the present, or to a feeling that there is no need for a plan. Again, you will get better results with a formalized marketing plan.

Every marketing plan should contain the following elements:

1. Executive summary.
2. Goals of the firm.
3. Analysis of strengths and weaknesses.
4. Analysis of the competition.
5. Market trend analysis.
6. Objectives and strategies.
7. Action plan.

Each element is explained in the following sections, and illustrated in the marketing plan of Ronald Gregory Associates, in Figure 11.1.

MARKETING PLAN

XYZ Associates

1994

Table of Contents

EXECUTIVE SUMMARY

The purpose of this plan is to provide a statement of the goals and objectives of XYZ Associates.

The strategy within the plan is to skillfully expedite change by building upon successful activities already in place. This plan also builds on the strengths of XYZ and staff, and in turn, blends and integrates those strengths with market projections and resources available.

This plan is a guide and direction for developing marketing program. One of the major objectives is to assist XYZ in becoming more proactive in its marketing endeavors rather than reactive. Flexibility and exposure are key.

The first two sections of this plan are meant to clearly communicate the goals, strengths, and limitations of XYZ to all staff members.

The next two sections are meant to provide an *overview* of XYZ's competitors and to show how each of them positions themselves in the marketplace, as well as to provide an *overview* of the hospitality/recreation markets, both nationally and internationally, as well as the southern California and southern Nevada marketplace/economy. You will note that as part of the implementation plan, it is suggested that each of these sections be further developed to continually position XYZ competitively.

The following two sections, "Objectives and Strategies," and "Action Plan," are the key to XYZ's marketing program. These sections provide a clear, "how to" outline to implement the targeted marketing program for XYZ.

Figure 11.1

I would like to bring two key points to your attention.

1. In researching your competitors it appears that a major issue XYZ must address is differentiating itself from the competition. In other words, answering the question, "Why should the ABC client hire XYZ over the other firms?"
2. In order to move XYZ ahead, lead generation is going to be essential. This is supported by comparing your fee goals by market segment and to the current fee generation mid-way into the first quarter of 1991. In addition, one of XYZ's objectives is to increase projects in the hospitality/recreation markets. This will only be accomplished by exposure and a dedicated lead generation program.

Exactly how to tackle both of these issues is addressed in detail in the Action Plan.

The success of any marketing plan lies in implementation. The Principal(s) in charge of marketing is the leader and orchestrator. Marketing must become part of every staff member's job in order to reach maximum effectiveness.

Based on this plan, long- and short-term, *prioritized* activities must be implemented. One of the first steps is to develop a detailed marketing budget, specific staff responsibilities, and a schedule to support each activity in the implementation plan (which I would be happy to review with you). I have also provided a milestone schedule for all activities at the end of the Action Plan.

However, it is essential to be *realistic* about which activities can be implemented at any one time. In other words, it is better to do three things right than ten things poorly. Think about a phased approach to implementing the action plan and delegating activities.

Finally, as indicated at the end of the plan, your marketing program should be reviewed and analyzed for effectiveness quarterly. Adjustments should be made as appropriate. The plan should then be revised on an annual basis.

The appendix includes a series of articles collected from A/E Marketing Journal, which will assist XYZ specifically in implementing your marketing program. These are meant as additional reference resources.

XYZ is in an excellent position to capitalize on targeted market segments and has resources within the firm, and staff potential, in order to easily implement a very effective marketing program.

GOAL SUMMARY

The goals of XYZ are focused on expediting change to promote growth—both in terms of clients and fees. Diversifying services offered and targeting market segments are the most important elements in reaching your stated goals.

Figure 11.1 (Continued.)

I. Goals of the Practice

A. Image Statement

1. XYZ offers high end designs coupled with proven design solutions.
2. XYZ provides quality service, on time and within budget.
3. XYZ provides a particular expertise for resort, country club, and golf courses on a national and international basis.

B. Growth and Change

1. **Types of Projects Desired**
   a. Hospitality/recreational
      - Country clubs
      - Golf courses
      - Resorts/hotels
   b. Residential
      - Large, custom homes
      - Single-family tract developments
   c. Large-scale commercial
      - Shopping centers
      - Hospitals
      - Industrial parks
      - Office complexes
   d. Miscellaneous
      - Government
      - Municipal

2. **Types of Clients Desired**
   a. Owner—developers
      - National/international
   b. Corporations
   c. Development partnerships
      - Insurance companies
      - Pension funds
   d. Architects/golf course architects
   e. Governmental agencies/municipalities

3. **Types of Services Offered**
   a. Landscape architecture
      - Planting layout
      - Irrigation design
      - Hardscape design
      - Installation observation

Figure 11.1 (Continued.)

- Bidding coordination
- Site/master planning (limited)

4. **Desired Reputation of the Practice**
   a. High quality design
   b. Service oriented firm that is cognizant of cost and time
   c. Reliable, competent, and professional

5. **Desired Size of the Practice**
   a. Staff size of 20 employees, maximum
   b. Annual gross fees of $2.5 million

6. **Geographic Distribution of the Practice**
   a. Current distribution of projects is Southern California and Nevada.
   b. Expand geographic distribution nationally and internationally for hospitality/recreational projects.
   c. Commercial, residential, and miscellaneous projects will be focused primarily in the Southern California and Nevada areas.

7. **Market to Be Shed**
   a. Small-scale residential
   b. Small-scale commercial

8. **Changes in Technical Capabilities Required**
   a. Add CADD capabilities.
   b. Staffing additions to include: in-house accountant and a project manager for golf course projects.
   c. Strengthen design staff.

C. **Fee Goals**

1. **Hospitality/Recreational**
   a. 40% of gross fees = $1 million
   ($250,000 per quarter)

2. **Large Commercial**
   a. 30% of gross fees = $750,000
   ($187,500 per quarter)

3. **Single-Family Residential**
   a. 20% of gross fees = $500,000
   ($125,000 per quarter)

4. **Miscellaneous**
   a. 10% of gross fees = $250,000
   ($62,500 per quarter)

Figure 11.1 (Continued.)

STRENGTHS AND LIMITATIONS SUMMARY

The strengths of XYZ are clear. There is Principal involvement and attention to all clients. The firm offers strong retention of clients, the capability to effectively evaluate client organizations, and the ability to expedite change. Marketing has been active but requires more focus and priority. XYZ's limitations are not insurmountable.

II. **Analysis of Strengths and Limitations**

   A. **Our Firm**

   1. **Summary/Analysis of Current Position**

   a. Current jobs (February)
      - Hospitality/recreational—fees: $147,950
         - Desert Golf Center
         - Indian Wells Country Club Clubhouse
         - Indian Wells Hotel
         - Mission Hills Hotel
         - RPS Resorts
         - Lake Mirage entry
         - Sun City rec building
      - Large commercial—fees: $71,985
         - Acacia office building
         - Brothers office complex
         - EMC Orthopedic redesign
         - Mitsui Industrial Park
         - San Marcos Shopping Center
         - Shafer industrial building
         - Alessandro/Portola
         - Vista Chino Square
         - Waring Plaza
         - Washington Square
      - Single-family residential—fees: $359,370
         - Cactus Walls
         - Landes Rancho Mirage
         - Marquessa on Lake La Quinta
         - Rancho Palmeras HOA
         - Baker residence
         - Brennan residence
         - Floodberg/Mission Hills
         - Flynn residence

Figure 11.1   (Continued.)

- Holzer residence
- Moss residence
- Pardee residence
- Schlesinger residence
- Strother lot #3*
- Strauch residence
- Thon residence
- Desert Falls Courtyards
- Kaufman project
- Orchard/Strother
- Palm Desert Greens
- Rams Gate
- Rancho Mirage 46
- Sun City
- Villa Europa
- Vistas at Fashion Heights*
- Mission Hills N.
- Miscellaneous—fees: $36,550
  - Cal Poly renovation
  - Second Street Park
  - Indian Wells landscape
  - Manitou gate
  - Presidio Place

*—Fee undetermined.

b. Backlog of jobs
  - None
c. Prospects
  - Resorts/golf courses—fees: undetermined
    - Laughlin Temple Resort
  - Large commerical—fees: $20,350
    - La Puente Shopping Center
    - First Interstate Bank
  - Single-family residential—Fees: $111,350
    - Desert Island building number 4
    - Fritz Burns Park
    - 171-unit single-family residential project

2. Strengths
  a. Design talent

Figure 11.1 (Continued.)

- Lots of potential
- No "prima donnas"
- Flexible staff
- Not interested in becoming "star designers"
- Provides proven designs
- Experience primarily in desert/southwest landscape

b. Technical ability
- Irrigation design/hardscape detailing
- Licensed architect on staff
- Well trained production staff
- Desert, water efficient plants, and water conservation design
- Not interested in being on leading edge

c. Management
- Project
  - Strong project management systems
  - Good tracking of job profitability
  - Good communications with client
- Firm
  - Good financial tracking of all aspects of the firm
  - Good rapport between Principals and employees
  - Attitude of making a profit while promoting a friendly atmosphere
  - Strong Principals with clear division of responsibilities

d. Marketing
- Knowing what does not work for XYZ
- Knowing/promoting strengths of XYZ through personal contacts
- Knowing markets' growth potential

e. Fee structure
- Charge fixed fee whenever possible
- Require retainers for most projects with new clients
- Good billing and collection system

f. Profit margin
- Higher than most landscape architecture firms
- Past seven years, profit has ranged from 15 to 30% of gross fees

g. Growth history
- Steady growth rate of approximately 16% over last seven years

3. **Limitations**
a. Design talent
- Lack of "heavy weights"

Figure 11.1 (Continued.)

- Experience primarily in desert/southwest landscape
- Lack of experience in golf course projects (three to date)

b. Technical ability
  - Lack of familiarity with non-southwest plant material
  - Limited experience with complex hardscape/structure designs
  - Lack of well-trained lower echelon technical people

c. Management
  - Project
    - Project Managers require more experience
    - Follow-through improvement needed
    - Project Managers have difficulty prioritizing and anticipating problems
  - Firm
    - Lack of time for Principals to apply hands-on approach to all projects
    - Lack of time for staff continuing education
    - A reticence toward being "tough" with clients when they exhibit problems

d. Marketing
  - Lack of a marketing plan
  - Lack of an organized marketing strategy
  - Lack of an original slide and/or photo library of past projects

e. Fee structure
  - Need to negotiate for higher fees by "selling" XYZ better up front

f. Profit margin
  - Profit margin not as large as goal
  - Some projects contracted at initial, low profit margin
  - Tracking time budget by Project Managers' should improve

g. Growth history
  - Leaving a considerable amount of money "on the table" with clients due to problems with the clients and own management

COMPETITION

III. Competition—XYZ Associates

XYZ's competition is plentiful, especially within XYZ's target markets. However, it appears that most of its competitors have a broader range of project types that they pursue. In some cases, this is because of the size differences of the firms and the fact

Figure 11.1   (Continued.)

that the firms may offer additional services (for example, environmental analyses as an in-house service).

It is also interesting that XYZ has a smaller staff than any of its competitors. This can be turned into an advantage for XYZ and presents major opportunities to capture a larger percentage of targeted markets.

The question becomes, "Why should the client hire XYZ?" The key is to:

- Understand the client's issues and concerns.
- Build on XYZ's successes.
- Distinguish yourself from the competition.

One idea is to use your firm's staff size to your advantage. Don't promote that XYZ works/functions like larger firms. Distinguish yourself by *promoting* and *demonstrating* through marketing a higher degree of service and key staff (Principal) involvement for every client. Large firms say they offer this, but in reality, it depends how large the project is and what else is happening within the firm.

Another advantage that XYZ offers the client over the competitors is a narrower focus on specific project types. XYZ does not try to be all things to all people. Therefore, XYZ can promote a higher degree of expertise in each project type.

In addition, because of the firm's past project locations, XYZ can offer particular expertise in water management, conservation and related maintenance issues in developing design solutions. Since water is becoming a more precious commodity, this could be a "selling" point even if the potential project you may be pursuing is not located in a "drought" area.

The more you know about the potential client, the easier it will be to sell XYZ over your competitors. How to do this is discussed in greater detail in the Action Plan.

The following is a basic overview of each of XYZ's competitors. Please take special note of the question answered by each firm, "What differentiates _____ from other firms?" This will give you an idea of what each firm promotes to a potential client.

- **Meridian**
  1700 Park Drive
  Irvine, CA 92700
  717-227-2350

  Key staff involved in marketing:

  Bill Millis, Principal
  Susan Millis, VP of Business Development
  Al Grady, Marketing Coordinator

Figure 11.1 (Continued.)

Offices in Irvine, Walnut Creek, San Diego, CA; Orlando, FL; Guadalajara, Mexico. Firm established in 1959.

Staff size: 105 (36 registered landscape architects)
Services: Landscape Architecture, Planning, Environmental

Representative projects/clients include:

- Resorts, hotels, commercial, industrial, parks, residential, institutional, government, municipal, theme parks, equestrian complexes, golf courses
- Most work lies in resorts/hotels, parks and recreation, and residential:
    Ritz Carlton Hotels, Laguna Niguel, CA; La Jolla, CA; Marina Del Rey, CA; Mauna Lani, HI; Amelia Island, FL

    The Four Seasons Kaupulehu, Kona, HI

    The Palm Springs Convention Center and Wyndham Hotel, CA

    La Paloma, Tuscon, AZ

    St. Fields Golf Club, Ibaraki Prefecture, Japan

    Asaka Green Hills Golf Course, Japan

    Forum Golf Hotel, Republic of the Ivory Coast, Africa

    The Citadel Commerce, CA (Trammell Crow Co.)

    Xerox Center, Santa Ana, CA

    Bank of A. Levy Corporate HQ, Ventura, CA

    Irvine Regional Park

    Woodbridge Village Park System, Irvine, CA (including 19 parks, swim and tennis clubs)

    Leisure Village, Oceanside, CA

    Temeku Country Club, Temecula, CA

    Piazza Del Sol Shopping Center, Palm Springs, CA

What differentiates Meridian from other firms:

We are dedicated to creative and technical excellence and high quality service while providing cost-effective, practical designs on time and on budget. We put together a team for each project which is headed by a Principal who is active on the project. We have such a depth and breadth of projects, probably greater than most other firms. We are also on the cutting edge of technology with both CADD and Video Imaging.

—Susan Millis.

- **Harrington, Smith & Miller**
  10 Branwell Drive
  Costa Mesa, CA 92132
  714-775-1255

Figure 11.1   (Continued.)

Key staff involved in marketing:

Alice Smith, Director of Communications
Samuel Harrington, Principal in Charge of Marketing

Offices in Costa Mesa, Riverside, Pleasanton, San Juan Capistrano, CA.

Firm established in 1971.

Staff size: 14, Costa Mesa/50, firmwide
Services: Landscape Architecture, Planning

Representative projects/clients include:

- Commercial, parks and recreation, municipal, transportation corridors, equestrian complexes, sports facilities, bike trails, private golf courses
- For most of the firm's history, they pursued and completed primarily residential projects; now they only do residential on a very limited basis
- Over 300 residential projects, both single- and multifamily housing projects throughout the state of CA
- Parks for municipalities—mini-parks to 1600 acre complex
- Palm Desert Championship Golf Course
- Marriott Time Share, Palm Desert, CA

What differentiates Harrington, Smith & Miller from other firms:

Service is the most important issue in our firm, above anything else—from the beginning of the project through construction. This means that every project is a top priority. We provide excellent response time to all of our clients' inquiries. We offer high design quality. In addition, something that makes us a little bit different than other firms is that we coordinate the bidding phase on almost all of our jobs. This is something we include as part of our original contract.

—Alice Smith

General Information:

Work splits out for firm to be 70% prime vs. 30% sub-consultant. Annual fees equal $5 million. They do not provide services for Environmental Impact Reports but they do collaborate with other firms to offer a complete package to some clients.

- **Sea Village Developers**
  700 College Drive
  Sea Village, CA 92113
  714-272-5500

Figure 11.1 (Continued.)

Key staff involved in marketing:

Jim Baker, CEO/Director of Design
Tammy Taylor, Director of Finance & Business Development

Office in Sea Village only.

Firm established in 1962.

Staff size: 27 (17 landscape architects, 2 designers, 4 administrative)
Services: Landscape Architecture

Representative projects/clients include:

- Public agencies 2% (firm started with government clients but
                         have dropped over the years)
  Private   98%
- Complete projects of all sizes but no private, single-family residential
- The Mirage—3000 room hotel and 100 acre golf course
- 900 unit, 350 acre residential development, Palm Desert
- William Lyme Park Place
- The Golden Nugget, Las Vegas, NV
- 1100 apartment and health club complex, San Francisco, CA

What differentiates Sea Village from other firms:

Our Principal started the whole idea of waterscape design many years ago. From there the firm was built on creating merchandisable projects with a signature design. We concentrate on the environment and softscape elements. We are excellent at negotiating with the nursery industry for mature plants, shrubs, etc. In fact we saved $1 million on a plant material budget for one project. In addition, there is always a Senior Principal at the job site during construction/installation to assure compliance with the design.

—Tammy Taylor

General information:

They provide field observation services on a not to exceed fee structure.

MARKET TREND ANALYSIS

IV. Market Trend Analysis

Figure 11.1   (Continued.)

HOSPITALITY/RECREATIONAL—NATIONAL

Major changes have occurred in the U.S. hospitality lodging business in the past several years. In a summary of the market for the U.S. lodging industry, Laventhol & Horwath reported that many of the problems noted included: an imbalance of supply and demand, an aging supply of middle-market franchise hotels, franchisers segmentation programs that have resulted in cutthroat competition within franchise families, proliferation of independent management companies, pressures on publicly held corporate management to maintain growth, escalating human resource problems, the savings and loan crisis—which has eliminated local sources of funding—and major reductions in hotel development.

An overabundance of hotel rooms was built in the 1980s as tax-sheltered investments without much regard for profitability from regular hotel operations. These were, by and large, mid-range properties, a slice above the low end motel/hotel range. Their quality was far below the executive/luxury/suite hotels and resorts.

Now, with the current economy, many of these properties are simply unable to compete in today's hospitality marketplace. Most of the properties have changed hands on one or more occasion.

Thus, many savings and loan institutions and many banks were burned by repossessions as tax-sheltered hotel deals fell apart with tax law changes, regional economic slumps, and lack of hotel management skills at many properties. This then translated into the lending institutions reselling the properties at far below real or market value. As a result, many banks and savings and loan institutions refused to finance any new construction or to rehabilitate the U.S. hotel/motel industry.

However, opportunities always follow these types of market conditions. A whole new industry niche has been created by firms offering hotel management services as "turn-around experts" for these depressed properties. That service has now evolved into "workout specialists" for new properties to be built.

Purchasers of these properties and other depressed/failing hotel properties are now potential client targets, such as American General Hospitality Inc. (AGH), Dallas. AGH represents a number of investors who are interested in buying some of these troubled properties. AGH and Westbrooke Hospitality Corp., Dallas are currently handling about 40 properties.

In addition, there are firms such as Global Hospitality Resources, San Diego, that emphasize consolidation among hotel chains. One of their recent projects was overseeing the $100 million renovation of the 482 room, golf course property, La Costa Hotel & Spa near San Diego.

This trend is predicted to continue in the United States for the next several years and presents excellent project opportunities.

Hawaii is a major growth area for Hyatt, as Mexico is for Marriott in the resort market. In addition, Hyatt is more active in the continental United States, with recent

Figure 11.1 (Continued.)

projects in Beaver Creek (near Vail, CO), Lake Tahoe (near Incline Village, NV), desert facilities in Palm Springs, CA and Scottsdale, AZ, and urban developments in San Antonio, TX.

Marriott has taken off in several directions, such as timeshare hotel/mini-resorts in Mexico, Colorado, Florida, and South Carolina; several planned resort hotels in Mexico, and Pelican Hill, a 1200 room complex on a huge beach site in Orange County, CA. They also have a new thrust in golf resorts, which prompted the establishment last year of a new division, headed up by Roger Maxwell, Vice President of Golf Operations and Development. This new division is devoted entirely to golf management services worldwide and offers its skills at golf-oriented resorts, based on its 20 years of experience in the United States.

Golf is a $20 billion industry in the United States with a growth rate that is phenomenal. The National Golf Foundation estimates that 22 million people currently play golf, up 25% in two years. The market is expected to hit $40 billion within ten years, and the demand for new golf courses has skyrocketed.

Inter-Continental Hotels' approach has been to take over first-quality properties as operator or to acquire property for other investors in locations around the world. Over the next five years they intend to spend $300 million on rehabilitation and refurbishment for resort properties.

Orlando, FL has 12 all-suite properties already built and 8 more properties are in the works according to Houston-based Pannell Kerr Forster. Orlando and Anaheim are ranked in the top ten U.S. cities that are described as the "hottest" by the hotel consultant, Laventhol & Horwath.

"The Un-Hotel," described as having 100-plus properties, is reporting remarkable growth in residence-inn, extended-stay facilities. Many apartment owners are trying to convert their properties to residence-inn facilities in order to take advantage of this new market.

The real casualty is the middle sector of the U.S. market—the full-service, mid-priced hotel, which is having the most economic difficulty. The high and low end properties perform well.

The luxury hotel market is more recession-proof than the middle market. In Dallas and Houston the luxury hotels have enjoyed significant occupancy increases over last year. Following this trend Sheraton will debut five to nine all-suite hotels in 1992.

Consolidation of the hotel/motel/resorts industry will probably be one of the biggest buzzwords in the industry for the next five years. With 800 or so hotel companies and 400 to 600 management companies, consolidation must happen.

Japanese investment in the U.S.'s hotel/resort/golf industry is enormous. In resort hotels alone, the Japanese investments for 1989 was $3.6 billion, 1990 was $4.2 billion. The attraction to these properties is most likely because resorts are the best per-

Figure 11.1   (Continued.)

forming and most profitable of all types of full-service lodging properties. According to an independent study, resort occupancies average 75%, the average daily rates top $100. The resort properties studied show gross operating profits ranging from $14,000 to $27,000 per available room. Few commercial hotels can match this performance.

HOSPITALITY/RECREATION — INTERNATIONAL

The hotel industry is globalizing. Overseas hotel building opportunities are the target for many American hotel/lodging chains. In 1990, of the over $1 billion in hotel development, $650 million was outside of the United States. Hotel/lodging industry experts agree that many major European cities' hotel/lodging accommodations are completely undersupplied.

However, there are two major problems in setting up European hotel operations. The first is a lack of well-trained employees who are able to offer services commensurate with the high room rates. The second problem, especially in Eastern Europe, is zoning. Due to the scarcity of rooms, existing hotels are able to charge very high rates.

However, with Eastern Europe joining the free economy and Western Europe ready to lower trade barriers, that side of the world offers many temptations to the large hotel companies. Eastern Europe provides particularly intriguing opportunities if economic stability follows political stability.

The whole Pacific Rim is a target for companies such as Hyatt International and Hilton International. This year Hyatt International expects to open hotels in Algiers, Algeria; Sydney, Australia; Beijing; Bali, Indonesia; and Mauritius, off the African coast, and will continue to develop new properties well into the 1990s.

Australia will continue to provide excellent project opportunities.

San Juan, Puerto Rico's Costa Isabela, a $1 billion resort community, is in the first of five phases, to build on a 2,500-acre site on the north coast. The project site plan includes five hotels totaling 2,000 rooms, more than 1,400 houses, and 5 golf courses, as well as sports and leisure facilities. The projects developers are I.D.G. Development Corp., Irvine, CA and TSA International, Honolulu, HI. First phase includes a 650 room Conrad International Hotel, a 350 room Four Seasons Hotel, and 2 golf courses. Dedication of the first two hotels is planned for Oct. 12, 1994. Amenities at Costa Isabela will include the Cabana Beach Club, a health club, a Spanish Colonial shopping village, and a tennis complex with 36 tennis courts and a tennis school. CYP Inc., an architectural and planning firm based in Irvine and Fort Lauderdale, FL, is designing the project.

Sheraton Corp. has a global outlook and views its real opportunities in the overseas market. It has targeted the Asia and Pacific area for its major thrust. In the United States, however, it operates the Walt Disney World Dolphin Hotel in Orlando, FL. The developers of the Dolphin Hotel were Tishman Realty and Construction Corp., Aoki

Figure 11.1 (Continued.)

Corp., and Metropolitan Life. In July 1993 they signed a contract to build a resort and casino operation in St. Martin, Virgin Islands, scheduled to be completed in 1996.

One strategy to obtain international project opportunities is to follow the reverse investment philosophy. Target international clients, such as the Japanese, who are investing and developing properties in the United States. Complete their work locally and then let your client take you into the international market.

Another approach is, of course, to do the reverse. Focus on U.S. investors, developers, and hotel/resort chains who are targeting the international market. The project on San Juan, Puerto Rico's Costa Isabela is an excellent example—the operators, developers, architectural designer/planners are all U.S. firms.

COMMERCIAL/RESIDENTIAL—SOUTHERN CALIFORNIA/SOUTHERN NEVADA

It appears that southern California and southern Nevada have not been hit by the recession as in other parts of the country and provide some excellent commercial, residential, and limited hospitality design opportunities. It is clear that San Bernardino, Riverside, and San Diego counties as well as southern Nevada are where most project opportunities are available. These areas are predicted to continue to grow while Los Angeles, Ventura, and Orange counties are slowing to allow supply to catch up with demand.

Los Angeles County. There are differing opinions as to whether the Los Angeles commercial market has been hit by the recession as in other areas of the country. Overall demand slowed due to fears of economic recession and an apparent halt of businesses moving into the downtown area. Vacancy levels and downward pressure on rental rates have increased.

Despite a bleak picture painted by some real estate observers about downtown, vacancies in southern California are among the lowest in the nation and many service sector and institutional type companies are in search of expansion space.

However, development activity is not limited to the downtown core. Santa Monica is a healthy submarket for commercial based mixed-use developments.

Active developers in this area include:

Snyder Co. and Davis Gray Co.—The Water Place

Thomas & Jones Partners—Colorado Place and Santa Monica Hotel

Peel Enterprises—Arborteum

Beta Corp.—Northpoint in the Davies Center

Urban Development—1999 Avenue of the Stars Building

The South Bay area is a buyer's market. The Tri-city areas, comprised of Glendale, Burbank, and Pasadena, were once considered residential suburbs to the downtown

Figure 11.1 (Continued.)

market. However, in recent years each city has developed its own viable commercial base. The San Fernando Valley remains flat.

Throughout the county, most industrial projects have been build-to-suit rather than purely speculative endeavors. The retail market has felt the effect of a recessionary economy in some areas, but other areas are booming. The San Fernando Valley has a large amount of retail space. However, for the most part, developers are expanding or are involved with rehabilitation projects. Mixed-use is becoming a popular alternative.

The residential market is uncertain. With single-family developments built out, new construction and unemployment are two major factors impacting the multifamily housing market in Los Angeles, particularly in the San Fernando and Hollywood areas.

Ventura County. During the past decade, Ventura County has experienced strong growth in terms of population and employment. While growth has been strong, almost all local governments within the county have severely restricted residential development. There are many companies that would like to locate in Ventura County, but their employees can't afford housing.

Active developers include:

> TOLD Corp.—Oxnard Towne Center
>
> The Sammis Co.—Sammis Business Center, McInnes Ranch, and Del Norte Industrial Park, Oxnard
>
> U.S. Postal Service—purchased 20 acres in McInnes Ranch for a Regional Mail Facility
>
> Carlton-Browne & Co.—Westlake North, business park, hotel, community center, residential townhomes
>
> City of Simi Valley is considering a 76,000 square foot office structure in the civic center

Retail continues to be strong throughout the county with low vacancy rates and moderate construction levels. The majority of new retail construction is in Oxnard and is predicted to continue. The industrial user market continues to be sluggish.

The Inland Empire: Riverside and San Bernardino Counties

Riverside County. The area around the Ontario International Airport has mushroomed. Growth has spread toward Riverside County and is expected to continue because of lower land costs, lower home prices and business costs, and the area's transportation network system.

Corona has become a star player in Riverside County's growth and development. Most projects have been commercial/industrial, mixed-use, and residential developments.

Figure 11.1 (Continued.)

There are many local and national players involved in Riverside County's growth including:

Centrelake, a joint venture project of Centremark, San Diego, The Sickels Group, San Diego, and Mission Land Co.

Tri-City Corporate Centre by Rancon Financial Corp. of Temecula, CA.

CenterPointe by Ferguson Partners of Irvine, the master developer.

Riverside Marketplace, a Birtcher urban redevelopment in Riverside.

Rancho Cucamonga Distribution Center II by O'Donnell, Armstrong & Partners, Irvin, CA

The huge increase in residential growth throughout the Inland Empire has been followed by retail growth. The Riverside/San Bernardino market has eight regional shopping centers with Rancho Cucamonga's Victoria Gardens, and a 1.2 million square foot regional shopping mall by The Hahn Co. coming to the market soon.

San Bernardino County. Maturation is the best word in describing the west end of San Bernardino County. Affordable housing is now becoming an issue. High-rise office instead of low-rise, garden variety is predicted. Retail is focusing more on the upscale discount outlets.

Major players who have projects throughout the county include:

Chevron Land & Development	Lincoln Property
Kline Development	Birtcher Campbell
The Koll Co.	Ferguson Partners
Santa Fe Pacific Real Estate	Arcial Properties

Even with a maturing market, businesses are continuing to locate in San Bernardino County. Growth is expected to continue.

Orange County. Construction and leasing have slowed in Orange County but are still active. The office building market is expected to slide significantly in the next five years. However, there are still many active developers such as:

Robert A. Alleborn Associates—Century Centre

Birtcher—Lakeshore Towers

Brinderson Real Estate Group—Brinderson Towers

The French & McKenna Co.—Main & Von Karman

Hillman Properties—Irvine Plaza

As in Los Angeles County, industrial developers are focusing on build-to-suit rather than spec space.

Figure 11.1 (Continued.)

The residential market will continue to tighten and therefore offer more project opportunities. Affordable housing will become more of an issue in the future.

San Diego County. The City of San Diego has been on a roll and if the end is in sight, no one is expecting it soon. Even in the face of growth controls championed by individuals and groups concerned about shortfalls in vital infrastructure development, growth will continue.

San Diego is the sixth strongest economic region in the country and economists predict it will be the third strongest within three years. Growth will continue to expand into the outerlying areas of the county, providing project opportunities in most market segments.

Contributing to this growth is the fact that Japanese funds are estimated to be involved in 70% of the city's major real estate deals. Coldwell Banker's Nobuo Okumura notes a recent Japanese survey identified San Diego as the fifth most popular U.S. city for Japanese investments.

Office markets downtown and to the north in the Golden Triangle are overbuilt. The retail market is solid and is expected to continue to be the same this year. Industrial occupancy is strong, R&D construction is giving way to more light industrial and warehousing projects. Several downtown residential projects are planned as part of mixed-use complexes, hotel and retail will also be included.

Hospitality market appears promising but suffers from overbuilding near the new convention center. The resort sector is the only hotel component not overbuilt. New projects include:

400 room Sheraton Grande Torrey Pines

400 room Hyatt Aventine

490 room Four Seasons Resort Aviara with a conference center and golf course

210 room Ritz-Carlton joint venture in La Jolla, CA

430 room, $89 million Stouffer resort/conference center on Harbor Island, by developer R. B. McComic

Southern Nevada. Strong hotel and industrial markets make the Las Vegas area a national contender in the real estate market. Last year, four projects representative of commercial development in southern Nevada were announced:

Excalibur, a Circus Circus Enterprises hotel-casino opened in June

Sunset Galleria, Henderson, NV, broke ground. This 1.4 million square foot indoor mall will be the focal point of a new urban commercial/residential area

T. J. Maxx stores started construction on a 400,000 square foot warehouse

Construction was started on the 35 story Minami Tower with completion due in 1992.

Figure 11.1 (Continued.)

Within five years, the Sunset Corridor area in the southeast valley has become Nevada's leading area for commercial development. There is still room to the east and south of this newly identified urban area, particularly as the resort/residential communities of Silver Mesa (Cosmo World-Caesars World-Spanish Trail), Lake Las Vegas (Transcontinental Properties), and McDonald Ranch come on line in the 1990s.

The same thing is happening in the west valley, which is predicted to become the second "true suburb" in the valley.

Another major area north of Las Vegas will house major Las Vegas and out-of-state relocations. Three major industrial/warehouse centers that are continuing activity are Park 2000 (Ribiero), Hughes Industrial Park near the airport, and Lewis Properties' Spectrum in the northeast valley.

Other trends to watch are:

- Neighborhood casinos combined with a form of entertainment/sport
- Resort destinations—the largest of these is Transcontinental Properties' Lake Las Vegas with eight resort sties, some with gambling and golf course/tennis/spa amenities as seen at Summerlin

Land prices worry developers and investors in Las Vegas as dramatic increases in prices in some areas of the valley are not controlled by planned-community interests.

Related Information

Based on our research, the following is a "laundry list" of developers, operators financiers and chains and other contacts active in the hotel/resort marketplaces.

Carl Marks & Co. Inc.
New York, NY

TSA International
Honolulu, HI
Takeshi Shekiguchi, Principal

I.D.G. Development Corp. (resort development company)
Irvine, CA

Stouffer Hotels & Resorts
Cleveland, OH

Loews Hotels
Jonathan M. Tisch, President and CEO

American Hotel & Motel Association
Kenneth F. Hine, Executive Vice President and CEO

Morgan Stanley Realty
Peter Krause, Principal

Figure 11.1   (Continued.)

Park Inns
Robert "Bob" L. Brock, President and CEO

Global Hospitality Resources,
San Diego, CA
Howard "Bud" James, Chairman
Donald E. Stephenson, President
Robert Harp, Vice President of Real Estate

Omni Hotels

JMB Realty Corp. (Four Seasons-Chicago, Hans Willimann)

Windsor Hotel Group
Los Angeles, CA
Carlos C. Lopes, a Principal

Lodging Unlimited
Westchester, PA
Morris Lasky, President

Hawthorn Suites Associates
Boston, MA
Joseph McInerney, President

Equitable Real Estate Investment Management
Atlanta, GA
Richard Dolson, Executive Vice President

Diamond Hospitality Group Inc.
Nashville, TN
Drew Diamond, CEO

Doubletree
Phoenix, AZ
William Sinclair, Vice President

Hyatt Hotels Corp. (Classic Residences)
Hyatt International
Hyatt Development Corp.
Chicago, IL
Doug Geoga, Executive Vice President
John Burlingame, Vice President of Development

MHM Inc. (an AIRCOA Company)
Dallas, TX
Joe Leising, Vice President of Marketing

Berins & Co. (division of Arthur Anderson Real Estate Service Group)
David Berns, Principal

Mariner Hotel Corp.
Dallas, TX
Archie Bennett, Jr.

Landauer Associates

Figure 11.1 (Continued.)

New York, NY
Sean Hennessey

Omni Hotels
Hampton, NH
Roger Cline, Senior Vice President

Guest Quarters Suite Hotels
Richard M. Kelleher, President

Lexington Hotel Suites

Tollman Hundley

VMS Realty Inc.
Chicago, IL

Ramada International Hotels and Resorts (Renaissance hotels)
Phoenix, AZ
Werner Braum, Senior Vice President

Pannell Kerr Forster (accounting firm)
Peter Quek

Marriott Corp. (Fairfield Inns, Courtyard, Residence Inns [extended-stay])
Washington, DC
Dan Cohrs, Vice President of Project Finance

Stephen W. Brener Associates Inc.
New York, NY
Stephen Brener

Inter-Continental Hotels
Emmett Gosen, Executive Vice President of Corporate Development

Sheraton Corp.
Boston, MA
Bill Wilson, Vice President and Director, Strategic Marketing

Jones Lang Wootton USA
New York, NY
Neil Teplica, Director of the International Hotels Group

American General Hospitality Inc.
Dallas, TX
Bruce Wiles, Executive Vice President

Urban Land Institute
Washington, DC

McCarthy Co.
St. Louis, MO
Jerry Murphy, President
Laughlin, NV (new hot casino area in southwest)

JBS & Associates (real estate auction house)
Chicago, IL

Wyndham Hotels and Resorts

Figure 11.1 (Continued.)

Wyndham Garden Division
Mack Koonce, Senior Vice President, Marketing

Manor Care Inc. (parent company The Choice Hotels International)
Robert N. Weller, Group President

Interstate Hotels Corp.
Pittsburgh, PA
Bob McKinley, Vice President, Sales and Marketing

Brookshire Hotels
Columbia, MD
Stephen Taylor, Executive Vice President

Holiday Inns
Kirk Kinsell, Vice President, Development

Hampton (Holiday Inns)
Dave Sullivan, Vice President, Development

The Promus Cos. (parent company of Embassy Suites, Hampton Inns, Homewood Suites, and Harrah's)

Aztar (operates gaming business; TropWorld Casino, Entertainment Resort—Atlantic City, NJ; Tropicana Resort and Casino—Las Vegas, NV; Ramada Express Hotel and Casino—Laughlin, NV)

Blackstone Capital Partners (parent company Howard Johnson, Ramada, Hospitality Franchise Systems) New York, NY

Accor S.A. (French conglomerate, parent company Motel 6)

Trusthouse Forte (United Kingdom; parent company Travelodge, Crest [new owner Holiday Inns])

R&B Realty Group (parent company Oakwod Corporate Apartments—extended stay residence) Van Nuys, CA

OBJECTIVES AND STRATEGIES

The objectives clearly and simply state what XYZ is trying to accomplish. The strategies state the methods that will be implemented to reach each objective. Both direct and indirect marketing activities are proposed.

V. Objectives and Strategies

A. Maintain and enhance image of the firm.

1. Make XYZ known in the clients' realm.

2. Make XYZ more visible in targeted communities.

3. Distinguish XYZ from competitors.

B. Develop contacts/leads with the objective of obtaining larger, fewer jobs to meet fee goals.

Figure 11.1 (Continued.)

1. Enhance network in client oriented groups.
2. Develop a targeted lead generation program.
3. Enhance current XYZ client relationships to receive referrals and expanded/additional assignments.
4. Renew relationships with past XYZ clients.

C. **Be more focused and targeted in XYZ marketing efforts.**
   1. Clearly communicate marketing objectives to *all* XYZ staff.
   2. Involve *all* XYZ staff in marketing.
   3. Target XYZ Principals' marketing efforts.

D. **Develop/revise marketing information, tools, and support systems.**
   1. Develop/revise promotional materials to support marketing effort.
   2. Develop/update information systems in order to quickly and consistently respond to clients' needs.
   3. Develop/revise strong, effective follow-up systems.

ACTION PLAN

The action plan is composed of three parts—promotion plan, sales plan, and plan for monitoring the program. The key is diversification and flexibility coupled with a very targeted and prioritized effort in both the promotion and sales plans.

The Action Plan is the step-by-step guide to implementing your marketing program. It clearly outlines what needs to be done, suggests who should be responsible for each activity, and provides a specific time frame during which each activity should be completed for maximum effectiveness.

Before embarking on each marketing activity, always answer these questions:

- What needs to be done? What is our expected outcome? How will we follow up?
- Who will be the "project manager" for this activity? Who will be involved in supporting this activity?
- When will this activity be completed? What are the milestone dates I need to establish to meet the final deadline?

In addition, you must make sure that each marketing activity fits within your marketing budget.

Included in this section is a schedule that indicates an appropriate time frame for each activity. This naturally develops some priorities in the implementation of your marketing program. There is also a note at the end of each outlined task item to indicate who should be responsible for that task.

For XYZ, there are several basic guidelines for responsibility:

Figure 11.1   (Continued.)

1. Principals should spend the majority of their marketing time in Direct Client Contact—being in front of the potential client.

2. Any public relations activity should be handled by your PR Consultant and/or should be a shared responsibility with a designated person on your staff—a PR Coordinator. The PR Coordinator could be a part-time position and should be the only *marketing* focus for the designated person.

3. XYZ will need direct, in-house support in marketing—a Marketing Coordinator. This could be handled by moving an administrative person already on staff into this position or by hiring a new staff member. This person's responsibilities will be to manage all of the in-house marketing activities and directly support the implementation of the marketing program. The Marketing Coordinator may start as a part-time position, but should become a full-time position.

Monitoring of the program rounds out an effective action plan by providing the opportunity for evaluation, analysis, and modification, to meet the demands of the marketplace and the goals for XYZ.

VI. Action Plan

A. Promotion Plan

1. **Mark XYZ known in the clients' realm.**

    a. For each of the project types listed in the Goal Summary, I. B.1, research to identify *client oriented* publications, conferences, and other events. Make a list.

    b. Develop an annual calendar listing each opportunity for participation and determine how your firm can gain the most exposure. For example, write an article, become a featured speaker at a conference, have an exhibit/display or put on your own in-house seminar. Focus on a particular subject of interest to your potential clients. Use your past projects to illustrate your points. In other words, position yourself/firm as an "expert" on the subject.

    c. Before you engage in each activity, develop a specific marketing plan including your objectives and how you will follow up. For example, when you are a speaker at a conference you should:

    • Obtain a list of all attendees prior to the conference. Target specific people you would like to meet at the conference and/or you would like to invite to your session. Arrange meetings prior to the conference. Send personal invitations to your session.

    • Arrange to include appropriate material in the registration packet for each attendee.

    • Make sure you have a sign up sheet of all who attended your session.

    • Create your follow-up packets for all appropriate attendees prior to the conference. You may have cover letters including: Enjoyed

Figure 11.1 (Continued.)

meeting you . . . Glad you attended my session . . . Sorry you were unable to attend my session . . . And so on.

- Send out follow-up packets upon your return from the conference. Call to arrange a meeting to discuss their upcoming plans and further introduce your firm.

  d. Primary staff responsibility:
- In-house Marketing Coordinator
- Supported by PR consultants and XYZ technical/administrative staff and Principals

2. Make XYZ more visible in the community.

  a. Develop a PR program for all projects. At the beginning of each project, meet with the client to join in their PR efforts or create a joint program. Tie the PR program into getting press on projects in client oriented publications.

  b. Contact targeted and local publications for an editorial calendar. Aim at special issues on design or building types, best firms, top ten lists, and so on.

  c. Sponsor visible, community events.

  d. Create an opening event, in conjunction with the client, for appropriate projects. Develop a special PR campaign around the event. Include prospective clients on the guest list.

  e. Investigate the opportunities for exhibition of XYZ's work through universities, ALSA, museums, libraries, design schools, traveling exhibits, corporate and public agency gallery spaces.

  f. Primary staff responsibility:
- PR Consultant/PR Coordinator
- Supported by XYZ technical/administrative staff and Principals

3. Distinguish XYZ from competitors.

  a. Review the general overview of each of XYZ's competitors provided in the section on Competition of this marketing plan.

  b. Develop a competitive analysis of each firm, either by an in-house staff member or an outside consultant. Present finding of each competitive analysis to key XYZ staff.

  c. Conduct a survey to determine how XYZ is perceived in the marketplace and by clients, and what clients are looking for from their consultants.

  d. Conduct a brainstorming session to determine XYZ's "niche" in order to differentiate itself from the competition.
- Promote XYZ's "niche" through direct client contact, PR, and all promotional literature.

  e. Primary staff responsibility:

Figure 11.1 (Continued.)

- Outside marketing consultant
- Supported by Marketing Coordinator, Principals, and key staff

4. **Clearly communicate marketing objectives to *all* XYZ staff.**

   a. Share the marketing plan with all staff members.

   b. Hold weekly marketing meetings with a prepared agenda.

   c. Determine and share each individual person's role in marketing with all staff.

   d. Institute simple marketing reporting methods:

      - For example, when you are awarded a new project, let everyone know how much closer this project brings the firm to the year-end fee goal.
      - Issue a quarterly summary of marketing activities, including new project fees versus year-end goals.
      - (Refer to Section C, "Monitoring The Program," at the end of this section.)

   e. Institute a yearly marketing retreat.

   f. Primary staff responsibility:

      - Principals
      - Supported by Marketing Coordinator, technical/administrative staff

5. **Involve *all* XYZ staff in marketing.**

   a. Make a list of all of the marketing activities that XYZ will engage in—be as specific as possible.

   b. Make a list of all staff members, including each person's marketing strengths.

   c. Match each marketing activity with each staff person:

      - Confirm your assessment with each individual person.
      - Develop specific goals and rewards with each individual.

   d. Provide appropriate marketing training for all staff members.

   e. Primary staff responsibility:

      - Principals/Marketing Coordinator
      - Supported by technical/administrative staff

6. **Target XYZ Principals' marketing efforts.**

   a. Clearly define, in writing, roles of XYZ Principals for marketing.

      - Of your available marketing time, how will marketing activities be split between Ron and Bill? Consider client contact, proposals, potential client contact, and so on.
      - For example, Ron should aim for:

        20% overseeing marketing program and all efforts, including

Figure 11.1   (Continued.)

> training/coaching staff members, and so on.
>
> 80% direct client contact.

b. Delegate other existing marketing responsibilities by involving all staff members in marketing.

c. Primary staff responsibility:
  - Principals
  - Supported by Marketing Coordinator

B. Sales Plan

1. Enhance network in client oriented groups.

a. Research and make a list of all client oriented groups that support project and client types listed in the Goal Summary, I.B.1 and I.B.2.

b. Make an annual calendar of events/activities.

c. Require all appropriate staff to participate in at least one event per month.
  - Tie contacts into lead generation program.

d. Primary staff responsibility:
  - Marketing Coordinator (organization)
  - Principals/Technical staff (participation)

2. Develop a lead generation program.

a. Require each member of the firm to generate qualified leads.
  - Provide suggested lead sources to all staff including newspaper articles, past/current clients, networking contacts, capital improvement plan budgets, consultants, and so on.
  - Develop a list of questions/information required to qualify a lead.
  - Train each staff person in order to create a maximum comfort and effectiveness level.
  - Develop individual goals for all staff, in terms of number of leads per week, and rewards.

b. Institute an intelligence gathering program.
  - Compile a prioritized list of new, potential clients, based on market segments identified in the Goal Summary, I.B.1, including name of contact person, phone number, and address.
  - Develop a list of questions/information to be determined from each potential client.
  - Identify appropriate people on staff to participate in program.
  - Train each staff person in order to create a maximum comfort and effectiveness level.
  - Develop individual goals for each participant, in terms of number of contacts/leads per week, and rewards.

Figure 11.1 (Continued.)

   c. Create a market overview every six months to outline the direction of targeted markets and client/project opportunities.

   d. Primary staff responsibility:
- Marketing Coordinator (organization)
- Supported by Principals and all staff

3. **Enhance current client relationships to receive referrals and expanded/additional assignments.**

   a. Create a client service review program.
- Meet with the client to determine client satisfaction on each project. Target specific milestones such as 50% completed, 100% completed, and post occupancy.

   b. Develop an entertainment program for your clients.
- Identify events on a monthly basis, which will match your budget, to which you could invite a client. For example, sporting events, cultural events, take a client to lunch at a new restaurant, or invite him or her to a luncheon with a featured speaker of interest to the client, and so on.
- Make a list of all clients you would like to include in this program and identify who in your firm would accompany the client (Project Manager, Principal, etc.?).

   c. Ask what other projects the client has coming up.

   d. Ask who the client would suggest you contact for additional assignments.

   e. Primary staff responsibility:
- Principals/technical staff (participation)
- Marketing Coordinator (organization)

4. **Renew relationships with past clients.**

   a. Make a list of all past clients.

   b. Arrange a meeting to discuss the condition of the job after completion.

   c. Invite the past client to a special event.

   d. Ask what other projects the client has coming up.

   e. Ask who the client would suggest you contact for additional assignments.

   f. Primary staff responsibility:
- Principals/technical staff (participation)
- Marketing Coordinator (organization)

5. **Develop promotional materials to support marketing effort.**

   a. Review all existing marketing materials to determine what is useable, what needs to be eliminated, what needs to be updated/revised, and so on.

Figure 11.1 (Continued.)

- Specifically evaluate consistency of information and image and in accordance with section VI.A.3 of this Action Plan.
  b. Develop/update a "kit of parts" marketing materials support system:
    - All elements in XYZ's kit of parts must provide consistent information and image.
    - All elements in kit of parts must distinguish XYZ from the competition and reflect findings in section VI.A.3 of this Action Plan.
    - Create a plan to obtain/create an original slide/photo library of past projects.
  c. Primary staff responsibility:
    - Marketing Coordinator
    - Supported by all staff/Principals

6. **Develop information systems in order to quickly and consistently respond to clients' needs.**
   a. Create consistent, computerized marketing information systems including:
      - Project descriptions
      - Resume materials
      - Boilerplate material
      - References
   b. Primary staff responsibility:
      - Marketing Coordinator
      - Supported by administrative staff

7. **Develop strong, effective follow-up systems.**
   a. Establish follow-up procedures for all contacts including:
      - Standard, consistent brochure packets for individual client/project types
      - A computerized lead tracking system in a database program that will enable you to produce a monthly "tickler file" of contacts
   b. Primary staff responsibility:
      - Marketing Coordinator
      - Supported by administrative staff

C. **Monitoring the Program**
   1. Establish a weekly marketing meeting with a prepared agenda with key staff. Each meeting should review what has been accomplished, the success rate, and plans/assignments for coming week. This meeting should be a forum for communication and should keep the marketing program focused and targeted.
   2. Quarterly, the marketing program should be evaluated against the established goals. A report to all XYZ staff should be issued indicating

Figure 11.1 (Continued.)

accomplishments, direction, new project fee goals versus year-end goals, targets for the next quarter, assignments, areas of change, and so on.

3. Annually, the entire marketing plan should be reviewed. Appropriate modifications and revisions should be made at that time.

Please refer to the following schedule of activities for a more detailed list of action items.

Promotion Plan (Refer to section VI.A of the Action Plan)	Time Frame
1. Make XYZ known in the client's realm.	
Identify client oriented publications, conferences, and other events. Develop annual calendar and strategy for exposure.	June/ongoing
2. Make XYZ more visible in the community.	
Develop a PR program for every project.	June/ongoing
Contact local/targeted publications for editorial calendar. Develop strategy for exposure.	June/ongoing
Sponsor at least one major community event per year. Exhibit XYZ's work in a public exhibition space at least once each year.	September 1994
Create an opening event for at least two major projects per year.	June/ongoing
3. Distinguish XYZ from competitors.	
Review general overview of competitors.	June–July 1994
Develop competitive analysis.	June–August 1994
Conduct XYZ image survey.	June–September 1994
Determine market/service niche.	September–October 1994
4. Communicate marketing objectives to all staff.	
Share marketing plan with all staff.	June–July 1994
Institute weekly marketing meetings.	June/ongoing
Determine each staff member's marketing role. Institute reporting methods. Yearly marketing retreat.	June–July 1994
5. Involve all XYZ staff in marketing.	
List all marketing activities. List all staffs' marketing strengths. Match marketing activities with staff.	June–July 1994
Provide training for all staff.	June/ongoing
6. Target XYZ Principals' marketing efforts.	
Define roles. Delegate responsibilities.	June–July 1994

Figure 11.1 (Continued.)

Sales Plan (Refer to Section VI.B of the Action Plan)	Time Frame
1. Enhance network in client oriented groups.	
Prepare list of client oriented groups. Make annual calendar of events.	July 1994
2. Develop lead generation program.	
Require each member of firm to generate leads. Institute intelligence gathering program.	June/ongoing
Create a market overview.	October 1994 and April 1995
3. Enhance current client relationships to receive referrals and expanded/additional assignments.	
Create a client service review program.	July 1994
Develop an entertainment program for your clients. Ask the client what other projects are upcoming. Ask the client who you might contact for additional assignments.	June/ongoing
4. Renew relationships with past clients.	
Make a list of all past clients.	July 1994
Arrange a meeting to discuss the condition of the job after completion. Invite the past client to a special event. Ask the client what other projects are upcoming. Ask the client who you might contact for additional assignments.	June/ongoing
5. Develop promotional materials to support marketing effort.	
Review all existing marketing materials to determine what is usable, what needs to be eliminated, what needs to be updated/revised, and so on.	July 1994
Develop a "kit of parts" marketing materials support system	June/ongoing
6. Develop information systems in order to quickly and consistently respond to clients' needs.	
Create consistent, computerized marketing information systems.	June/ongoing
7. Develop strong, effective follow-up systems.	
Establish follow-up procedures for all contacts.	June/ongoing

Figure 11.1 (Continued.)

In addition to the schedule, the following are specific, minimum monitoring milestones for XYZ's marketing program.

Promotion Plan

1. Publish one article per month in a client oriented publication. Reprints of these articles should then be utilized as promotional pieces for potential and current clients. Include them in brochure packets. Plan and execute a mass mailing including each article upon publication.

2. Become a featured speaker at one major client oriented conference for *each* of XYZ's project types per year. By devising and carrying out a follow-up plan (as outlined previously in this section) with a session attendance of 100 people, this activity should result in a minimum of five to ten solid project leads per conference. (This number will increase as conference attendance increases.)

3. Have an exhibit or display of XYZ's work at one client oriented conference/ event for *each* of XYZ's project types per year. By devising and carrying out a follow-up plan (as outlined previously in this section) with a session attendance of 100 people, this activity should result in a minimum of five to ten solid project leads per conference. (This number will increase as conference attendance increases.)

4. At a minimum, get three pieces of press per project—announcement of project award, project in progress, and completed project. Reprints of these articles should then be utilized as promotional pieces for potential and current clients. Include them in brochure packets. Plan and execute a mass mailing including each article upon publication.

5. Be included on at least one major listing or feature article in a targeted area's local publication per year. Associated PR activities should be tied into this activity to assure community visibility.

6. Sponsor at least one major community event per year in targeted areas. Associated PR activities should be tied into this activity to assure community visibility.

7. Create an opening event for at least two major projects per year. This should result in community visibility and direct project leads with current and potential clients.

8. Exhibit XYZ's work in a public exhibition space at least once annually. Associated PR activities should be tied in to this activity to assure community visibility.

Sales Plan

1. Require each appropriate staff member to participate in one client-oriented event per month. Through this activity, each staff member should be able to generate at least one lead per month, at a minimum.

Figure 11.1   (Continued.)

2. Each technical staff member should provide at least two qualified leads per month.

3. XYZ should be making at least 20 qualified intelligence-gathering calls per week. This should result in at least two qualified leads per week.

4. Create a market overview every six months.

Note: Remember to create a *follow-up* program for each marketing activity, prior to commencing any marketing activity.

Figure 11.1 (Continued.)

THE MARKETING PLAN AND ITS COMPONENTS

Executive Summary

This section introduces the need for the marketing plan, and explains the sections in the plan and their purposes. It also calls out any "Key Points" that should be noticed by yourself, key officers, bankers, and so on. The Summary then briefly explains how the Action Plan section of the plan will complete the goals of the firm.

Goal Summary

This section introduces the focused goals of the marketing effort. Transfer the goals you developed in the previous sections, and state them clearly, without any verbiage on how to achieve them. It may be helpful to include several types of goals—a set of goals on your image and on your growth plans, client types, services offered, desired reputation, desired size, planned geographic distribution, markets to target and those to shed, and fee goals. Each firm will have its particular set of goals.

Strengths and Limitations Summary

In this section you should honestly assess what you do best, and where to set your limits. It is easy to have boundless enthusiasm for endless possibilities. It's much harder, and a lot less scattered, to concentrate your approach into particular strengths, and seek to minimize your weaknesses. This is another section that is not always entirely spelled out in a firm's plan, mainly due to fear—to the fear that you may not have any strengths at all, or that your beliefs about your firm's strengths are not justified. Again, we cannot stress enough the importance of setting out these particulars on paper. The whole effort is a process of honing your focus and placing your assets where they will best prosper.

Competition

This is another tough, albeit necessary section. In this section it is most helpful to specifically research the competitive firms serving the same geographic area. List their strengths and weaknesses, and keep in mind that you are trying to build reasons why clients should choose your firm for design projects, rather than theirs. If you list the competition, you will have honed your purpose to produce very clear, specific reasons why the client should hire your firm.

Market Trend Analysis

In this section, you utilize your demographic trend research and your market research to forecast trends in the market. This section should be extremely specific, and you may want to have this section written by a marketing consultant, depending on the size of the market you wish to tackle. Remember, in preparing this section, that any banker or financier will be particularly interested in looking your reasoning behind opening your firm. Your credibility is naturally greatly elevated if you can back up your assumptions with concrete evidence of trends and therefore of future work. The most successful design firms in history have been those with the ability to anticipate a trend, and then to get into that market before anyone else realizes it's a trend. If something is going around as a new "trend," beware of how many other firms are out there performing the same service you are planning to offer.

In this case potential clients are excellent sources of trend forecasts, and the closer you can get to the client, the better. A specific listing of potential clients is essential in this case.

Objectives and Strategies

Your objectives and strategies are clearly defined here, for both direct and indirect strategies. In this section you should keep each objective/strategy to one sentence, and keep the section to a one-page maximum.

Action Plan

The Action Plan is the "meat and potatoes" of your marketing plan, because it describes in specific details the tactics you will use, step by step, to meet your firm's marketing goals. In the sample marketing plan shown here, the first page of the Action Plan summarizes how the action plan works and how to implement the plan given budgetary considerations. Basically this section is the who will do what, when will they do it, why, and how! Review the Action Plan shown here and use it as a framework against which to structure your own plan. This particular plan is well researched and thought out. It includes specific time frames for each element of the plan.

As may be evident thus far, each element of the strategic plan builds on the preceding activity. Your vision comes first, then your mission, and then the marketing plan grows out of those broad guidelines, turning the subjective vision into an objective reality, and outlining the steps to build a design firm with enough forward motion to propel itself into success, and enough stability to withstand the inevitable economic downturns.

12 DESIGN AS A BUSINESS

"In the 90s, the externally-focused firms will be the only design firms to prosper."—*David Rinderer, Mngt. Consultant*

Before setting up your financial controls system, you need to consider your financial objectives—what are you selling? Are you selling time? Expenses? Computers? Intangibles? What percentage of your work is not billable? What percentage is billable? How much should you ask for up front? What is your loss potential? What about accounts receivables and collections? What kind of profitability are you expecting? What is your expected return on investment?

Before you overwhelm yourself trying to answer all the questions posed above, consider the explanations of the various aspects of financial reporting in the upcoming pages. Use this section to familiarize yourself with the various aspects of controlling your finances, so that when you approach your accountant or bookkeeper to begin to set up your financial system (which you should do even if you plan to keep the books yourself at first), you will be familiar with the purpose of each item and the jargon you'll encounter.

The following are important concepts to understand. Be sure that you comprehend each one:

1. The difference between gross revenues and net revenues.
2. How to look at revenue by project type and client type.
3. How to set up a pension/profit sharing system for your firm.
4. Why staff turnover is important.
5. Average operational size of your projects.

6. Measurement of project backlog and its ramifications for hiring.
7. What a balance sheet is and why it is important.
8. Income and expense statements.
9. The difference between accrual and cash accounting.
10. Fiscal year-end statements.
11. Profit planning.
12. Billable ratios.
13. Labor analysis reports.
14. Firm overhead.
15. Income and retained earnings.
16. Firm valuation.

Another important tool to understand is the nature of financial reporting. Financial statements are useful in the process of assessing your business posture. Be advised, however, that although they have the appearance of completeness, exactness, and finality, they nevertheless have definite limitations. First, financial statements are interim reports. That means they cannot be "final" because the actual gain or loss of a business can only be determined when it is sold or liquidated. However, it is necessary to get this "snapshot" of the business in the form of a monthly balance sheet. An annual profit/loss statement every 12 months, and (once you have it) a three to five year comparison of your profit/loss statements.

GROSS VERSUS NET REVENUES

For a service business, there is, like any other business, a gross revenue and a net revenue, and likewise, a gross profit and net profit.

It is important to produce two separate analyses in order to understand how well your firm is performing as a whole, and how well particular areas are doing. Hence the difference between gross and net revenue becomes important.

Gross revenue is the total amount of dollars that come into a firm. This figure includes any "pass-through" dollar—for instance photocopies, airline tickets, and other reimbursables. Generally these expenses are charged off to the client at cost plus a 5–10% markup. Gross revenue also includes overhead and profit, and any income generated and paid out to subcontractors or consultants.

On the other hand, net revenue is the revenue generated by your professional staff only, not including "pass-through" dollars, not including income generated through outside consultants. It is simply the money your staff alone has generated.

Net revenue shows the actual performance of your staff—the people directly employed by you. Gross revenue reflects the performance of your staff plus all reimbursable expenses, outside consultants, and overhead costs. Both measurements are helpful in understanding what's going on with your firm's financial status.

When starting up your own firm, you basically need to know the difference so that you can request reports based on gross revenue, net revenue, and also gross profits and net profits. If you neglect to measure financial data on the basis of net revenue, you will be misled about your actual profits: are they coming from your staff or through consultants? Are you losing too much through consultants? Through pass-through dollars? Be sure that your accountant clearly defines the two amounts, so that you understand where you are making money and where you are losing money. The result can be surprising.

REVENUE BY PROJECT VERSUS CLIENT TYPE

Another critical area to define is your revenue generated by client type. Each client type represents a separate "market" and a revenue report by client type will help you determine where you are making a profit and where you are taking a loss, in terms of marketplaces you serve.

How are you doing, for example, with institutional clients? What about your commercial shopping center clients? Each client type represents a different mix of variables in overhead, workload, productivity, and so on, and your results by market can vary significantly. What you want to be able to determine is whether or not you are making any money on one market versus another. You may find that you're making no money on developer projects and tons of money on educational projects, and a report of revenue based on client type may help you decide that you should get out of one particular market.

The fact of the matter is that, if you are not making money in a particular area after a given period of time (two to three years generally is allowed), then you have to stop fantasizing about all the money that could be made in this market. It is simply not going to be there for you. Yes, the market may have great potential, but if you are not doing these projects efficiently, and you can't turn them around in a six month period, then delete the service!

The same process should be measured each month based on project type—in other words for all office buildings versus multifamily housing. This is simply another cross-check to determine which areas of business are profitable and which are not.

As simple as this all sounds, believe it or not there are too many firms out there producing ten page reports each week that never get read—and that simply do not highlight the key ratios. Remember what you can handle, and use only specific measures to take a snapshot of your firm. And keep your reporting system short, sweet, and frequent.

This is an important area for very intangible reasons. The kinds of decisions you make based on client-type reporting and project-type reporting will make or break your business—and oftentimes these are hard decisions. Your ego can be tied to projects and markets that are not necessarily productive. Know when to balance that ego with a real facts report on the profitability of markets. Get out while you still have a choice!

The other critical point to recognize in performing the client and project type analyses is whether or not your organization in internally or externally focused. Is your internal operation geared toward the client or project type? Or geared inward, toward inward control? How well are you really serving the client? Does your service truly meet the client's needs or are you superimposing your own needs on the clients? You have to be willing to look honestly at these points and answer yes or no to some difficult questions.

Remember, today's successful firms are small, they move swiftly, and they focus on specific markets. The more specific your market niche, the more money you can charge and the more work you will get, because, hopefully, you'll be alone in your market! You should aim for that narrow a focus, all the while providing the utmost in service to the client.

SETTING UP A PROFIT-SHARING AND PENSION PLAN

These days, the setting up of employee benefits plans is getting easier and easier, as companies such as IDS American Express and many others seek to serve the small and large business alike in 401K and other investment plans. Everyone's getting smaller, and as that happens the possibilities for providing added benefit to the employees grows.

STAFF TURNOVER

I've said this in many speaking engagements and in many of my books and publications, and I often meet with objections—but I stick to my philosophy that you should actually plan for and strive to meet a 5–10% staff turnover ratio each year. This is an unusual goal, but honestly, there are always dregs, in every company. The successful company has the guts to get rid of the dregs.

Each year, divide your staff into thirds. The top third are the top performers, the second third are the average to good performers, and the bottom third are the ones who are not pulling their weight. Of those bottom third, fire the last 10%. Do it swiftly, and definitively. If a person has been dragging along for a year, get rid of him or her. Here are the reasons why. Many times an employee needs a change in order to realize his or her productivity level needs to be adjusted. It's a simple, well proven fact of management. The employee may have outlived his or her usefulness, or have outgrown the job, but is simply staying there because the place is familiar, the paycheck is regular, and the employee doesn't know what else to do.

Of course, you have to be fair, and give sufficient warning. But be decisive. If you see no progress, then let that employee go. You're not doing nonproductive employees any favors by retaining them when they are not performing.

AVERAGE OPERATIONAL SIZE OF PROJECTS

When setting up your financial controls system, you should take a look at your first three projects, and determine an average size for your projects. Doing so in advance can help you determine, with the help of your accountant, just exactly which financial control system is best for you. This will also be critical in choosing a software program for financial reporting. Take a look at the kinds of projects you plan to service, and simply come up with an average—you'll save significant amounts of time and money that would otherwise be spent on your accountant and your computer system.

BACKLOG

Project backlog is the easiest measurement to determine whether or not you need additional staff (or additional upcoming projects). This should be looked at periodically, at least once every other month, to determine your needs, staff-wise, and project-wise. Look at the available hours you have for each project. Divide those hours by the number of hours you have available, and you will come up with the length of time it will take to complete the work. For example, if your project requires 10,000 hours to produce, and you have 1000 man-hours available per month, then you know that it will take you 10 months to complete the project. You then need to analyze all of your projects in this manner, and compare the length of time needed to complete with the client's schedule. If they need the project done in 5 months, then you need to add another 1000 hours per month to your staff, usually by way of a temporary staff person.

When does your backlog trail off? Your company should normally have a trail off of three to six months, at which time if you didn't have additional work, you'd go out of business.

If your backlog is 18 months worth of work, then you could confidently hire another employee. On the other hand, if your backlog is down to one month, then you may have to consider firing someone. It's as simple as that.

All firms should maintain at least a 12-month projection of their current backlog of signed contracts to help in manpower and business development planning. One of the most common management shortcomings among professional firms is a failure to foresee and take corrective measures for impending peaks and valleys in the workload.

THE BALANCE SHEET

A balance sheet is basically a "snapshot", a "Polaroid photograph" of the finances of the firm at a given moment. You want to know, each month, whether or not you are getting a good return on your investment into the firm. The balance sheet gives you a snapshot of your own net worth.

Most design firms do not look at their firm from a return or investment (ROI) perspective. They do not consider its net worth, and whether is increasing or decreasing. However, this is important, and you should look at your balance sheet each month.

Smith Architects, Inc.
Pro-Forma Income Statements and Balance Sheets 1994–1995

	1994 ($)	1995 ($)
Income Statements		
Project revenue	$500,000	$550,000
Other income		
Total Revenue	$500,000	$550,000
Operating expenses		
Project expenses	$200,000	$225,000
General overhead	248,000	270,000
Total Expenses	$448,000	$495,000
Net Profit Before Taxes	$ 52,000	$ 55,000
Balance Sheets		
Assets		
Cash	$ 48,000	$ 33,000
Accounts receivable	120,300	135,300
Work in progress	78,200	98,200
Other current assets	25,600	25,600
Fixed assets	85,000	85,000
Total assets	$357,100	$377,100
Liabilities and equity		
Liabilities		
Accounts payable	$ 75,000	$ 57,000
Notes payable	25,000	20,000
Other liabilities	42,000	30,000
Total Liabilities	$142,000	$107,000
Equity	$215,100	$270,100
Total Liability and Equity	$357,100	$377,100

Figure 12.1

Figure 12.1 is an example of a balance sheet.

MOST RECENT INCOME AND EXPENSE STATEMENTS

The income and expense statements are important in measuring your profit and ROI. You start to compare your profits to your balance sheet. Is your ROI, as measured by profit divided by your equity in the company, going up or down? You

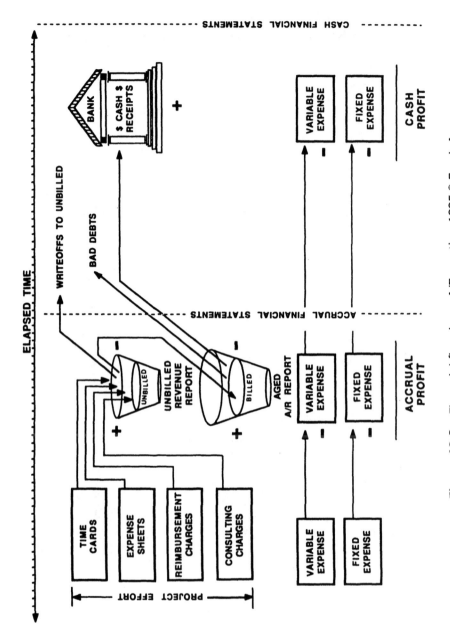

Figure 12.2 Financial flow in an A/E practice. 1985 © Frank A. Stasiowski, AIA, Practice Management Associates, Ltd.

need the income statement to figure out whether or not you are profitable.

Look at ratios between the balance sheet and the income statement. Where are you making money, where are you losing money? Are you controlling overhead or not controlling overhead? Is your net worth going up or down each month?

CASH VERSUS ACCRUAL ACCOUNTING

A monthly, accrual basis, profit and loss statement is important because it provides the most accurate picture of your position. Most firms do not get such a statement, or if they do, it is a cash-based statement. Cash-based accounting is adequate for very small firms, taxes, and cash flow purposes, but it is a dangerously misleading basis for management reporting. For example, on a cash basis the firm usually loses money while it is growing, makes abnormally high profits when it first levels off or whenever a big check comes in, and appears profitable during the first months of decline—all because cash income is our of phase with cash expenses. Therefore, if your firm maintains cash-basis books for tax purposes, you should make the appropriate accrual adjustments when developing your monthly statements.

Figure 12.2 is an illustration of the difference between cash- and accrual-based accounting.

FISCAL YEAR-END STATEMENTS

To properly manage your firm, you need to look at monthly statements and year-end statements. Basically, year-end statements are important to "keep score" each year, and also to look at five year periods, and to make projections based on trends. It is important to understand both uses for the year-end statement.

PROFIT PLANNING

Many weak or marginally successful design firms do not focus enough on planning out their financial results as a whole. Most service firms recognize the need to plan the operations of individual projects, to develop a time schedule, a program of work to be accomplished, a staffing plan that assigns personnel to tasks, and a budget that sets forth the desired financial results for the project. Developing and monitoring a comprehensive financial and operating plan for the whole firm is just as important as performing that task on a project by project basis, yet in many firms "firmwide" financial management is often focused on cash management and maintaining good borrowing relationships. The need to focus on cash and on borrowing relationships, rather than on firm-wide financial management, is a by-product of mediocre financial results. Mediocre results, in turn, are the by-products of poor or nonexistent planning.

Successful planning and monitoring of a firm's financial condition can be described as a three-step process that includes: 1) creating a financial "model" of how the firm should ideally operate in the long run. 2) establishing a profit plan and a budget that test the model against what management feels are the "realities" of the business over the next six months or year, and 3) monitoring the short-range results, which includes projecting the results of near-term operations before they occur and then reporting those results after they occur, so that the actual and the projected results can be compared.

Key Steps

While there are certainly no "correct" goals in setting a profit level that is desirable, you should try to allocate at least 20% of your accrued fees as pretax profit over and above your base salary. Now, in starting out, this may be impossible, especially in difficult economic times. However, according to past statistics, 20% is high, but not unachievable. Before the 1991–1992 recession, the *Professional Services Management Journal* measured average profits for architectural and engineering firms to be about 8 or 9%. But there is no reason why you can't plan for and eventually achieve higher numbers. However, don't spend it in advance, if you don't know whether or not you'll make it. This seems to be common sense, but you'd be surprised how many firms will believe in nearly impossible projections, and spend accordingly. Don't fall into this trap.

Clearly define the firm's and your financial goals. Be sure to translate that into a budget for every area of operation. Then have a good understanding of the cost-volume-profit interrelationship.

The profit percentage you choose will first depend on your targets and the salary targets of your employees. For a start-up firm, the typical design firm owner earns $80,000–$100,000 a year (and that has actually been going down in recent times), but you may have to forego such high earnings until you develop a client base and good reputation. However, you may realistically need to earn $50,000 to maintain your current personal assets. In any case, know that prevailing small office targets are often too low, as are the salaries small firms offer their employees.

Encourage employees to help make projects more profitable by:

1. *Achieving Utilization Goals.* Let all team members know their target utilization goals (which should be upwards of 85%, including that of the principal). Produce regular reports informing employees of their progress, as compared with their goals. Every individual target should be both ambitious and realistic.

2. *Working Within Budgets.* Each work item requested from an employee should be accompanied by a targeted number of hours for task completion and a due date. Each individual is responsible for completing the task within budget.

3. *Selling Additional Work.* Every employee should help expand work on existing projects and solicit additional projects from existing clients. Educate all staff members on the firm's strengths, and be sure they know how to communicate this directly to the client.

4. *Securing New Clients.* Getting new clients shouldn't be the sole responsibility of the firm's principals. Every employee can and should look for new work. Offer a bonus system or comp time for the employee who brings in the most work each month. Everyone can do it.

The first two contributions listed will result in work profits. The second two will increase work volume. If each employee is aware of and participates in each of these four activities, profits will increase.

BILLABLE RATIOS

Hundreds of design practices across the country can conjure up a hundred different ways to monitor project progress. In this book you'll be presented with various ways to monitor project progress, company financial status, and budget control. Perhaps the most important task you face as manager of yourself and of others is in maintaining the highest productivity levels possible. Use the following guidelines to monitor project and overall company productivity levels:

1. Technical staff should be working at 90% utility ratios, meaning that 90% of their time is billable.
2. Professional staff with minimum marketing responsibilities should be 85% billable.
3. Project managers with administrative and marketing responsibilities should be 75% billable.
4. Senior project managers and principals (like you!) with project overview responsibility should be 60% billable.

In addition to these individual staff members' targets, consider that the entire team should have an aggregate 80–85% billable ratio. (The average firm has an average billable ratio of 65%. Why be average?)

LABOR ANALYSIS REPORTING

Simply put, a labor analysis report provides a weekly "snapshot" of who charged time to all active projects during the preceding week, how much of the fee budget remains, and the "financial percent complete" status of the project. Jayne Subwick of Ft. Lauderdale-based James M. Montgomery Engineers (JMM) says the firm's use of weekly labor analysis reports has helped the company's project managers catch and correct virtually all miscoding and unapproved time coding since implementing the system.

This report also provides project managers the opportunity to review job cost reports and make corrections "on their own." Each week a project manager can look at financial versus job progress percent complete. They have the freedom and responsibility to take care of any variances without interference from management.

OVERHEAD CONTROL

Probably no other financial measure in design firms receives more attention than overhead rates. The most basic computation, overhead is the relationship of all nonproject costs to direct project labor.

A general way to compute your firm's overhead is to add up all firm expenses, then deduct all your direct project costs (direct labor, subconsultants, travel, printing, etc.), and divide this total by direct labor.

The problem with overhead rates has long been the debate over what constitutes a cost. Firms can either "expense" costs as project costs or consider them as overhead. The confusion comes because different overhead rates result with the two methods, even when dollar expenses are identical. This is one reason why it's difficult, if not impossible, to compare your firm's overhead rate with that of another. According to the *Professional Services Management Journal's Financial Statistics Survey,* the average overhead rate for design firms is 149% (or 1.49) of direct labor. Here are two examples:

To calculate firm overhead and determine if you are making a profit, you can prepare a simple profit and loss statement (P&L), using only net multipliers and overhead rates.

If your firm's net multiplier is 2.74 (meaning that your overhead rate is 1.49), a simple P&L can be shown as:

Net multiplier	2.74
Direct labor	(1.00)
Overhead	(1.49)
Operating profit	.25

Immediately you can tell whether your firm is profitable.

Measuring overhead is one of the key financial analyses needed to determine, on a periodic basis, whether or not your firm is profitable.

INCOME AND RETAINED EARNINGS REPORT

Retained earnings arise from the profitable sale of goods and services in the normal course of business, from gain on the sale of fixed or other assets such as investments, and from irregular revenue transactions such as retirement of liabilities for less than their face amount. Retained earnings may be appropriated or unappropriated, depending on your wishes. Typically, retained earnings are appropriated for the following reasons:

1. To cover a loss occurring in the future—appropriation for possible future decline in inventory, for flood loss, and for unfavorable decision of a lawsuit.
2. To expand, retire preferred stock, or pay off a long-term debt.
3. To replace assets at a higher cost—appropriation for asset replacement at a higher price level.
4. For self-insurance purposes.
5. To maintain a larger amount of current assets necessitated by a substantial increase in sales volume, to be used for working capital if need be.

Figure 12.3 is an example of a statement of income and retained earnings.

FIRM VALUATION

It is important to understand why there is a need to have your firm valued each year. Basically, there are several reasons, and many design firm owners ignore all of them. First, you want to see how you are faring in your worth each year. Second, valuations may be necessary in order to secure bank loans for equipment and other costs. Third, you will eventually want to think about ownership transition, the inclusion of partners, and so on, and an annual valuation is a necessary ingredient to this process.

Figure 12.4 is a sample design firm valuation.

| | Year ended January 31 | |
	1993	**1992**
Income		
Professional fees	$3,448,069	$2,804,201
Interest earned	10,281	13,971
	3,458,350	2,818,172
Expenses		
Architectural consultants	— —	2,500
Bad debt recovery	— —	(18,130)
CADD terminal charges	269,038	100,322
Capital tax	980	0
Courses and conventions	1,835	10,274
Donations	— —	7,300
Dues and fees	2,285	3,511
Employee benefits	782	— —
Engineering and mechanical consultants	1,038,724	841,238
Insurance	61,309	55,476
Interest and bank charges	9,840	3,766
Management services	1,411,963	1,149,757
Professional fees	2,700	3,396
Promotion	75	3,284
Vehicle expenses	650	8,770
	2,800,181	2,171,464
Income before bonus and income taxes	658,169	646,708
Bonus	556,000	547,000
Income before income taxes	102,169	99,708
Income taxes	23,500	23,500
Net Income	78,669	76,208
Retained earnings at beginning of year	205,047	128,839
Retained Earnings at End of Year	$ 283,716	$ 205,047

Figure 12.3   Statement of income and retained earnings (unaudited).

FIRM OVERVIEW

ABC Design was founded in 1986 as an independent Interior Design firm. Operations have been continuous since its founding.

The firm operates as a sole proprietorship under the laws of the state of Iowa. There is currently one owner and two employees. The firm makes regular use of contract labor.

The firm offers interior design services but does not offer purchasing services to its clients.

The firm operates from offices in Houston, Texas. Its geographic market, while inclusive of all of Texas, is largely focused on the Houston area.

The firm's clients are largely private in nature and focus on corporate and residential clients. The financial statistics of the firm strongly suggest that these clients are those which permit the firm to be chosen as a result of its qualifications rather than on a price/bid basis.

CONCEPT OF VALUE

For a professional service organization, value is composed of two elements. The first is the accounting-based "book" value of the organization as expressed on an accrual-basis method of accounting. A determination of this value results from an examination of the balance sheet of the company and the making of appropriate adjustments for "realizable" value.

The second, and usually greatest, value is "good will." The assumption is that there is a realizable value associated with a firm's continuing existence, client base, reputation, history of revenue production, recognizable name, profitability potential, and so on.

The following section of this report addresses the issue of the book value of ABC Design. Successive sections primarily address the evaluation and valuing of "good-will."

BALANCE SHEET

A professional service firm's balance sheet provides the base upon which a total firm value is developed. It is also a way of determining the value of the organization under a "close the doors" assumption—what the value of the firm would be in the event that it decided to cease operations. The following comments were reached as a result of an examination of ABC Design's balance sheet dated 1/1/93 and conversation with the firm's owner.

Figure 12.4 Financial Analysis of ABC Associates

As presented by the firm's internal statements, the firm's debt/equity ratio is 0.10–1. The industry average is 1.12–1. The organization obviously has a very strong financial base. Given the firm's assets and the industry average, the organization may be considered to have an excess capitalization above industry average of $513,178.

The firm's current ratio is 8.2–1. The industry average is 2.19–1.

The balance sheet as presented by the firm does not include a provision for "Deferred Taxes Payable." This defines the theoretical tax liability on the difference between cumulative cash-basis and accrual-basis incomes. Since there is an assumption that the firm will continue to operate on a cash-basis method of accounting for tax purposes, it is unlikely that this amount would ever need to be paid. Therefore, no adjustment is made to the presented balance sheet.

In the event, however, of an outside sale of the entity, it is possible that a conversion to accrual basis would be required for tax purposes and a true liability created. Some discount in value might be considered by the accrual-based purchaser.

It was indicated in conversations that the accounts receivable balance is accurate as stated. It was also stated that the firm bills substantially all its projects at the end of each month and therefore does not carry on its balance sheet any recognition of value for "unbilled earnings."

Since the firm's fixed assets do not indicate any asset that would be likely to appreciate or represents a significant portion of total fixed asset value, the value of assets is accepted as presented. No appraisal on actual value would be recommended. It is likely that any prospective buyer would accept the value indicated.

It was stated that the firm does not have any pending professional liability or other legal actions that could require a provision for potential loss.

The financial statements presented by the outside accounting firm indicate a firm investment in an outside organization. It was stated verbally that this investment does not have a substantial value so as to impact significantly total firm value.

On the basis of the above, the firm's balance sheet value is accepted as presented on 1/1/93 as $1,063,265.

INCOME STATEMENT

The income statement presented by the firm allows for an analysis that is standard within the design professions. The following comments were as a result of calculating certain key indicators from statistics presented on the income/expense statement for the six month period of operations 6/30/93–1/1/94.

Figure 12.4   (Continued.)

Total revenue	$2,015,392
Direct and reimbursable expenses	386,736
Effective fee revenue	$1,628,593
Direct labor	516,464
Net revenue	$1,112,129
Overhead:	
Labor $469,953	
Other 482,886	952,839
Operation profits	$ 159,289
Effective labor multiplier	3.15
Overhead multiplier	1.84
Labor utilization ($)	52%
Profit margin (gross revenue)	8%
Profit margin (net revenue)	10%

These statistics are consistent with previous years' performance with the exception of the labor utilization rate. Despite the current economic recession the firm has been able to maintain profitable operations. It has, however experienced a significant reduction in its profitability and increase in its overhead as a result of not reducing work force commensurate with the reduction in work load.

The firm's effective labor multiplier is consistent with its largely private clientele and a non price competitive market. The firm's overhead costs are in line with its market's typical cost structure and even somewhat low in non labor costs. There is some indication that the firm should consider increasing its marketing expense to reinforce its price position and increase work load.

Any outside purchaser might evaluate favorably the potential of increasing profits through marketing investment and reduction in non direct labor costs.

CASH FLOW

The primary financial purpose of the closely held professional service firm is to generate cash. While some portion of the cash is used to finance growth and expansion, the major use of cash generated is to fund ownership distributions, employment bonuses, incentive compensation programs, and tax deferred retirement plans. Cash is also required to allow any funding of internal ownership transition programs.

For an outside buyer valuation estimates may be based upon calculations of cash flow and availability to complete purchase payments within a given number of years.

Figure 12.4   (Continued.)

The valuation of any design organization requires not only an examination of the historic ability of the firm to generate cash but also the potential of the firm to produce additional cash. This additional cash can be produced by employing one time steps to increase cash balances or increased annual cash flows through profits.

Cash is produced for an organization by:

1. Increasing revenue.
2. Decreasing expenses.
3. Decreasing assets.
4. Increasing liabilities.

Items 1 and 2 result in increases in profits. Items 3 and 4 represent a change in the firm's financial structure.

The examination of the firm's asset base does not suggest the organization could generate significant cash through reduction of assets. "Assets per total staff member" for the firm is $21,200. The industry average of assets per total staff member is $31,150. The firm's accounts receivable represent 58 days of earnings while the industry average is 67 days.

The firm is, however, virtually debt free as has been noted above in the discussion of the balance sheet. Significant lending ability is certainly available to the corporation. Any buyer could consider this ability to secure debt financing as a vehicle for cash generation. The firm's "equity per total staff" is $19,300, the industry average is $12,900. The organization has the potential of securing perhaps $750,000 through debt financing.

Operationally the firm is achieving an effective direct labor multiplier of 3.15. While some increase in effective pricing may be possible, it is not immediately felt significant enhancement of profits would be available through these means. Increasing of revenue would probably come through increased volumes of revenue. The firm's statements regarding percent of repeat clients, limitation of the geographic market, and limited marketing expenditures all suggest the potential of volume growth even considering the present economic conditions.

The firm's financial statements strongly indicate that management maintains a close cost control over expenditures. The total overhead of the firm is 1.84% of direct labor in 1993 and was 156% in 1992. The latter is significantly low for a firm achieving its current prices. The growth of this number in 1993 is attributed by this writer to the low labor utilization rate being achieved.

Management attention to labor costs should allow a return to previous years' very significant profit achievements.

The total analysis is that the firm represents a very positive prospect for significant cash generation through increased debt, increased volume of work, and return to labor cost controls.

Figure 12.4 (Continued.)

COMPARISON WITH INDUSTRY STATISTICS

One approach to the valuation of a professional service firm is to compare the firm with the value determined for "similar firms rendering similar services."

This has led some individuals to attempt to compare the value of the closely held relatively small firm with that of the publicly held firm providing the same services. This is done because it is often possible to gather operating information about larger public companies. Private firms are not required to reveal meaningful data about their operations or their stock price.

This is an erroneous approach since the public company and the privately held firm are driven by separate objectives. The management of the public firm is primarily concerned with the stock price of its company. The small closely held professional service firm is concerned with the generation of cash and other nonfinancial motives. Therefore, financial decisions will differ.

For evaluation purposes, however, there is a value in undertaking a comparison of an individual firm with statistical information gathered in a confidential survey of firms.

It is our opinion that the current profit achievement of the "average" professional service design firm is not commendable. It does provide, however, a bench mark against which to measure an individual firm in a valuation process.

The chart below compares ABC Design with industry medians for some significant financial indicators.

The ABC Design statistics are drawn from the 1/1/94 balance sheet and income statement. The industry medians are drawn from the PSMJ Financial Statistics Survey. It is noted that the industry medians would have been drawn from individual firm fiscal years ending in 1992 and 1993. It is anticipated that 1992 statistics will show a decrease both in profitability and in equity position for the industry as a whole.

	ABC Design	Industry
Net profit margin before profit distribution	8%	7.3%
Overhead as a percent of direct labor	184%	152%
Net multiplier achieved	3.15	2.8
Net revenue per total staff	$59,222	$62,790
Labor utilization	52%	63%
Return on equity	36%	24%
Assets per staff member	$21,200	$31,150
Equity per staff member	$19,300	$12,900
Debt/equity ratio	0.10–1	1.12–1
Current ratio	8.2–1	2.2–1
Days in accounts receivable	58	67

Figure 12.4   (Continued.)

PROFIT ANALYSIS

The most difficult part of any valuation is arriving at a value for good will. For our analytical purposes, the value of good will is best demonstrated by the firm's historic profitability and an analysis of the firm's chances of having future profitable operations.

At this point it is appropriate to examine the past profit history of ABC Design.

Up to this point the analysis of the firm has been on the basis of the financial statements as presented. When one looks at the profit of the firm for valuation purposes, one must look beyond the revenue and expenses as presented.

Most professional service firms use the cash-basis method of accounting for tax purposes. For this reason, at the end of the fiscal year, each firm undertakes a considerable number of cash transactions to reduce the firm's cash-basis profit to a minimum amount.

Some of these transactions are, in effect, distributions of profits. Any profit analysis requires that "book" profit be adjusted by amounts that can be considered profit distributions.

The following chart is a presentation of ABC Design profit achievements:

	1992*	1991	1990	1989
Gross income	$4,030,658	$5,542,357	$7,782,937	$3,899,211
Fee revenue	3,257,186	3,627,050	4,621,955	2,721,384
Net profit	318,578	36,580	293,304	218,356
Distributions	0	480,869	1,334,512	391,662
Profit/operations	318,578	517,449	1,627,816	610,018
Beginning capital	$ 903,975	$ 876,690	$ 638,091	$ 437,474
Employees	55	59	56	46
Net revenue per employee	$ 59,222	$ 61,916	$ 82,905	$ 58,841

* Annualized.

In valuations, in order that one specific year's profit does not inappropriately influence evaluation of firm's profitability, it is common to use a weighted average of profits to arrive at a "calculation" of good will under certain transition scenarios.

Calculation of weighted average of profit:

$$
\begin{array}{llll}
4 \times \$ \ 318,578 & = & \$1,274,312 & \text{(1992 annualized profit)} \\
3 \times \$ \ 517,449 & = & 1,552,347 & \text{(1991 profit/operations)} \\
2 \times \$1,627,816 & = & 3,255,632 & \text{(1990 profit/operations)} \\
1 \times \$ \ 610,018 & = & \underline{\ \ \ 610,018} & \text{(1989 profit/operations)} \\
& & \$6,692,309 / 10 & \\
& = & \$ \ 669,231 & = \text{weighted average of profits}
\end{array}
$$

Figure 12.4 (Continued.)

According to subjective evaluation of the firm, its operations, future profit potential, and various transition scenarios, different multiples of the weighted average of profits are used to set the firm's value.

EXTERNAL VALUATION

The current market for the sale of an architectural/engineering firm is not strong. These are currently more firms available for sale than there are buyers for such organizations. Despite this fact there does remain a market for strong organizations that have certain desirable characteristics.

The following factors would make ABC Design a favorable acquisition candidate and add to a subjective evaluation of its value in the event of an external sale.

1. Long presence and established name within a defined market.
2. Demonstrable history of profitable operations.
3. Potential for enhanced profitability through control of administrative and other overhead labor costs.
4. Strong presence in defined market, especially the health care market.
5. Well defined geographic market.
6. Potential for growth through geographic expansion.
7. Ability to generate work and produce profits in slow economic periods.

On the basis of the above factors and the examination of the firm's financial statistics, we would place an external sale value on the firm of $3,350,000–3,900,000.

This was calculated as:

1. Five (5) times the weighted average of profit from operations ($3,346,155). Our work with firms both being acquired and acquiring, and our survey of large firms who have undertaken numerous acquisitions suggest that these organizations expect to be able to "pay back" their purchase price over a five year period.
2. Five (5) times the weighted average of profits plus the excess capitalization of the firm according to industry norms ($3,859,333). No additional monies should be required by a buyer to fund operations above purchase costs. Some monies could be immediately drawn from the balance sheet value of the firm.
3. Capitalization (book value) plus three (3) times the weighted average of profits ($3,070,959).

Outside buyers usually base their top acquisition price on the cash flow and profit potential of the organization rather than on the book value.

Figure 12.4   (Continued.)

Any amount in excess of $4,000,000 would be considered to be a very attractive offer for the firm.

If the firm were to offer itself for sale on the open market, a number of the following conditions would probably be attached to any purchase agreement.

1. Acceptance of employment agreement and/or noncompete agreements by the current owners and other defined key employees.
2. Some portion of the purchase price would be contingent upon continued profitability. (Additional bonus payments could be included as part of an agreement for current owners who assisted in the generation of profits in excess of expectations or stated goals.)
3. Some portion of the purchase price would be guaranteed but payable over a specified period of time. (Initial payments may sometimes be equal to the book value with good will paid out over a longer period.)
4. Agreement regarding potential liability on past projects.
5. Reconciliation of current employee fringe benefit plan with standard plan of acquirer.
6. Availability of 100% ownership of the firm.
7. Acceptance of terms that allow an acquirer to expense good will value through employment compensation or noncompete agreements.

INTERNAL VALUATION

The most common ownership transition procedure within the design professions today is the transference/purchase of equity interests from current owners by younger successive generation employees. Among younger professionals, it is expected that eventual ownership opportunity will be made available to them.

The major problem that arises in internal transition is financial in nature. Most younger employees do not have the financial resources available to them to allow them to purchase equity interests within firms without the money actually or eventually coming from the firm itself. Under most internal transition scenarios "firms buy themselves."

It is also a financial truth that internal transition valuation procedures result in selling at a value that is lower than could be achieved through an external sale. Firms cannot generate sufficient earnings to pay off former owners, compensate current owners, maintain financial health, and fund potential growth without there being a significant reduction in value.

In the event that the firm were to be valued as of 1/1/93 for internal transition proposes we would set a maximum value on the firm of $2,400,000. This is approximately book value plus two (2) times the weighted average of earnings. The lowest price that should be considered is the book value of $1,063,000.

Figure 12.4 (Continued.)

The achievement of the higher internal value would require significant financial and tax planning in order to meet all cash flow requirements. It would also probably require a reduction of the equity value of the firm through debt financing and the distribution of these proceeds to current owners.

An alternative internal transition option is available through the use of an Employee Stock Ownership Plan (ESOP). While this option does allow for a higher internal valuation, it is only under certain specific circumstances that we would recommend this option to firms with as few employees as ABC Design. If you wish further information regarding this option, please contact us.

Figure 12.4 (Continued.)

SUMMARY

It's important that you comprehend the items explained above before visiting your accountant. Otherwise, your accountant will be spending his metered time explaining them to you. If your effort is well planned, then hopefully you will succeed. If you add the ingredients together, you should be able to produce a viable financial controls system. There is one area that will only be touched upon lightly later in this chapter, and it bears mentioning, because of its importance, and that is cash flow. Cash flow management is an art form at best, and it is such a large topic that we cannot give it anywhere near its full due here. However as the owner of a design firm, you should seriously consider reading a book on cash flow. *Cash Management for the Design Firm* (Wiley, 1993) is a good start.

The rest of this chapter presents you with some tips to consider in putting together your financial controls system.

PROJECT COST CONTROLS

SIMPLIFY, SIMPLIFY, SIMPLIFY

People often say, "If only I knew that then, I wouldn't have. . . ." The best advice I can give you in preparing your firm's finances is to consider the simplest way to get to the goal — managing the finances of your firm. Here are 10 tips provided by Lowell Getz, accountant, on keeping financial reporting simple. This applies whether you're preparing financial reporting for yourself, a board of advisors, or a bank officer.

1. Gear the level of detail to the needs of the audience. Provide only as much information as the reader can absorb.

2. Use graphic illustrations for strong visual impact, to create interest, to hold the reader's attention, and to spark discussion.

3. Keep graphic illustrations simple to avoid confusing the reader with extraneous information.

4. Report by exception to focus on problem areas and evaluate specific performance.

5. Use comparative data to illustrate variances that should be analyzed.

6. Bracket or otherwise give emphasis to unfavorable changes.

7. Use ratio analysis to study key indicators of performance; compare with projections, historical data, and industry averages.

8. Limit reports to those on which management can take corrective action.

9. Continually review the usefulness of all reports; eliminate those that no longer serve any purpose.

10. Recognize that reports must be timely to be useful.

GET THE GRAPHIC EDGE

Believe it or not, half of the battle in financial reporting is the presentation. Direct the reader's eye to the right figures, by preparing reports in a graphic, user friendly format. Follow the suggestions below for preparing financial reports.

1. Use an interesting and descriptive title to clearly identify the report.

2. Use plenty of white space for eye appeal.

3. Keep the report neat and easy to read.

4. Be consistent in style so the report can be interpreted quickly, minimizing the need for reader reorientation.

5. Emphasize figures by using color, lines, and spaces or halftone overlays.

6. Box insignificant figures or use different typefaces for added impact.

7. Be sure the information displayed is relevant to the purpose of the report and in enough detail to be useful.

8. Take care to present information correctly, accurately, and objectively.

BUDGET PROBLEMS?

Inevitably in running any design practice there comes a time when a project runs over budget. When you realize you're about to exceed budget, take immediate action. Implement one or more of the following action steps:

1. Stop evaluating alternatives. Take the best design solution you have and go with it.

2. Cut dead wood. Review the performance of all team members. Reassign those who are not making progress.

3. Reduce staff, keep schedule the same. Tell those who remain that they will just have to get by with one less person.

4. Work overtime, without compensation. Or, at a minimum combine overtime as a ratio of compensated and noncompensated time. Check the prevailing laws for guideline on overtime for exempt and nonexempt employees.

5. Shorten the schedule. Take some time out of the schedule. It is human nature that the work will get done even though there are fewer days in which to do it.

6. Review your contract with the owner as well as your contract with consultants. Can any of these fees be adjusted to give more money to you?

7. Take a "nuts and bolts" approach to production. Simplify detailing and make document production quicker.

8. Ask for more money. If all else fails, meet with your client, candidly apprise him or her of the situation. Request additional funds.

The key to solving budget problems is to take charge early, and implement actions quickly.

CASH PLANNING

Ultimately, the goal of all planning, control, tax analyses, and related efforts is to ensure ample cash for firm operations and for adequate cash reserve. To achieve the desired level of solvency requires considerable planning and control. The basic elements of cash planning are as follows:

1. *The Cash Flow Projection.* This particular projection is most important when there is any question about the adequacy of the firm's cash resources over the next 6–12 month period. It also is a good basis for making application for a back-up line of credit, long-term loan, or a short-term investment plan for excess cash. (This last point is important, for many firms have short-term cash peaks, but do not realize that their banks can arrange for a no-risk 30-day investment so that the money does not sit idle in the checking account.)

2. *Accounts Receivable and Accounts Payable: Aging Schedules.* Each month, you should gather a list of accounts receivable and accounts payable, and arrange them by age to plan for collections calls and cash projections.

13 HOW TO DEAL WITH A BANKER

"The world is his, who has money to go over it."
—*Ralph Waldo Emerson,* The Conduct of Life *(1860)*

Design firms frequently borrow money to finance capital equipment, such as computers, office furniture, photocopiers, or CADD equipment. For most new design firm owners, borrowing to finance capital equipment is a new experience. In fact, for many this will be the first time you've ever had to borrow money for items other than short-term capital needs.

Loans for capital equipment are considered "term loans." In lender's language this means that they are of medium term length, generally from three to ten years. With this type of loan, lenders advance a percentage of the equipment cost, the highest percentage of which goes to general purpose equipment that can easily be transferred or sold to another company in case of default. Conversely, lenders loan a smaller percentage of the asset cost for special purpose or custom-made equipment.

When considering taking out a loan, consider all sources available. Banks are not the only source of funds. There are other entities in the business of lending money for the purchase of capital equipment:

1. *Leasing Companies.* These companies are active in this market and their rates are competitive. They can offer rates similar to or better than banks because of their large portfolios of loans and their experience in obtaining funds. The seller of the equipment may have a "tie-in" with a leasing company and can put together a package deal at the time of the sale. In addition, if a leasing company is familiar with your firm because you've dealt with them in the past, a more favorable arrangement can sometimes be made. If you are considering a leasing company, shop around. The leasing business is highly competitive.

2. *U.S. Government Small Business Administration.* This is another source of funds. Generally the SBA works indirectly with clients through banks and guarantees up to 90% of the funds lent by the bank up to a maximum of $500,000. In some cases it might be advantageous to inquire as to the availability and rate for an SBA loan. One major drawback, however, is the considerable amount of paperwork involved in preparing the SBA loan application and the time it often takes for approval. Of course, you must first qualify as a "small business."

3. *Small Business Investment Companies.* Such companies can be a source of funds and are often affiliated with banks. These companies take greater risks in lending by concentrating on smaller companies and, as a result, generally expect an equity participation. Historically, "venture capital" firms (as they are commonly called) have not been a significant source of funds for design firms, but they could be in the future.

APPLYING FOR A LOAN

Once you've decided to go for a bank loan, the best advice for getting the loan approved is this: sell your proposal to the banker as you would sell architectural or engineering design to a potential client. Be as comprehensive in presenting yourself to the banker as you would be in trying to convince someone to hire you for a project. Prepare a complete loan package that includes the following:

1. A description and brief history of the firm (include a copy of your brochure and other descriptive material).
2. Résumés of the principals of the firm.
3. Full description of the capital equipment with photos, descriptive brochures, and names of other firms that are hiring you.
4. Most recent year-end audited financial statements (income statement, balance sheet, and statement of changes in financial condition). Note: Even if you do

not have business financials, you'll need personal financial statements to show a bank.

5. Interim financial statements through the most current period.

6. Projected financial statements that include the borrowing. Use footnotes for assumptions.

7. Projected cash flow statement showing how the loan will be repaid.

8. Selected financial ratios compared with industry averages.

9. Cover letter indicating how much you wish to borrow, over what period of time, and at what interest rate. When you propose the terms of the loan, it shows that you have thought through your request and serves as a basis for negotiation.

In your initial visit, review the loan request proposal with the banker and be prepared to answer any and every possible question. Remember, a banker is interested in three things: 1) purpose of the loan, 2) collateral, and 3) repayment schedule. Put yourself in his or her position and make certain that by the end of the first meeting you've presented a clear picture of these three points.

Design professionals are at a disadvantage when negotiating a bank loan because banks deal primarily with wholesalers, retailers, and manufacturers. A banker relates to these people because there are so many of them. Most bankers see so few architects and engineers that you must take the time to explain your work and how you are paid for your services. In obtaining a bank loan, this is the single most important task.

When requesting a loan for capital equipment, you must make the banker understand how the equipment will be used and its economic justification. In the case of "state of the art" equipment, the banker must understand how the equipment will be used and why it is necessary. Use experts when necessary to support your proposal. For example, you may bring your accountant to the meeting and state that he or she has reviewed your numbers for reasonableness. The accountant can answer questions on the financial statements even though he or she is not ethically permitted to state an opinion on your projections.

One of the banker's main concerns is the amount of capital

the owners have committed to the firm and the rate of withdrawal of that capital in the form of salaries and bonuses. A request that the principals of the firm personally guarantee (with collateral) the loan may be in order, particularly if the firm is small or has not been in business long. Be prepared to deal with this question because often it will make the difference on getting your loan.

OTHER CONSIDERATIONS

Generally a bank officer has loan approval authority up to a certain dollar limit. When these limitations are lower than the amount you require for capital equipment, the loan officer's function is to present information for review by a loan committee composed of senior officials of the bank. The loan officer presents your case and acts as your proxy by answering questions raised by members of the loan committee. He or she must be thoroughly briefed on your proposal.

The loan committee looks at the total relationship with your firm when deciding whether to grant a loan. This total relationship includes the other services provided for the principals, such as checking accounts, other loans, cash management services, investments, trust services, and so on. In addition, your loan is one of many under discussion by the committee, and obviously the bank has a limit on its capacity for granting loans.

Since term loans for capital equipment are for a relatively long duration, the bank may impose certain conditions on the borrower.

For example, working capital may have to be maintained at a certain level; audited financial statements and interim reports may have to be provided: and the firm may have to abide by certain covenants. The covenants may prohibit paying dividends, redeeming capital stock, entering into a merger or acquisition, or creating any further debt obligations. While term money lenders usually require the pledge of the capital equipment as security for the loan out of current earnings, these covenants are of primary importance to them.

If your application is rejected, meet with the loan officer to discuss the reasons. Often it may be no fault on your part, but rather that the bank feels it has enough of a particular loan of this type. In that case, the loan application may be taken as is to another bank for perhaps better results. If there is a weakness in the firm or in the structure of the loan, it must be corrected and a new loan package prepared that could produce more favorable results at another bank. It is often difficult to establish a relationship with a new bank by coming in with a loan application by itself. Be prepared to improve your chances by offering to move your personal and business accounts to the new bank.

DON'T LEAVE BANKING UP TO CHANCE

Many years ago I read an article in *Inc.* magazine written by then Associate Editor John Halbrooks, and it so impressed me that I've kept it in my files and passed it along to design professionals beginning their own practice. This story is a lesson in self preparation and presentation. The article is reprinted here with permission from *Inc.* magazine.

> On a hot summer day in 1975, Warne Boyce stood quite still outside Mellon Bank in Pittsburgh. He'd just been refused a loan and he felt humiliated. Humiliation turned to anger as he realized that being turned down was all his own fault.
>
> Boyce had built his company on the strength of his relationship with his bank. In the years since, Boyce had expanded through acquisitions financed through bank loans. His firm managed an acquisition a year for about six years, when the bank turned down Boyce's application that summer.
>
> And Boyce had known almost as soon as he sat down in the bank office that he was going to be turned down. He knew because he was breaking all the rules he'd followed for six years in his dealings with the bank—rules he had only intuitively understood until he broke them.
>
> Boyce's cardinal rule was this: Let your banker know what you're up to, even before you're up to it. All the other "Rules according to Boyce" are variations on that theme.
>
> Boyce broke his rules in a couple of ways on that visit to Mellon Bank. First, the loan officer had heard nothing of Boyce's plans until the morning he called for a loan interview. Second, Boyce compounded the error by walking in with only some doodling on a legal pad to back up his application.
>
> "I was so caught up in day-to-day operations that I failed to see how much we had grown," recalls Boyce, "I needed a

much more sophisticated balance sheet. We'd been so successful in the past, I became a little too casual."

Boyce was scheduled to leave for Montreal on business immediately after stopping at the bank. He'd been looking forward to relaxing on the trip, but instead spent the entire two nights transferring figures onto cash flow projections.

Back in Pittsburgh, Boyce returned to the bank immediately and this time, he got the loan. His effort to repair the damage he'd done himself reflects the importance he places on credibility. Rejections tarnish credibility. And credibility with banks is like honor in battle—you lose it just once.

After going after 17 loans, Boyce has only been turned down twice, so that 15–2 record makes him somewhat of an expert at getting bank loans. Boyce knows how important it is to get on the right side of a bank—and to stay there. "Your banker has to be an ally. If you're a success, your banker is also. You're a hero to your banker."

Mellon Bank was the first place that Warne and his wife, Doreen, had turned to when all they had was a dream. They chose Mellon because they'd been doing their personal and business banking there.

When they went in to propose their business scheme, "We didn't pretend to be thinking of anything on a tremendous scale," says Doreen Boyce, "we recognized our limitations. On the other hand, we recognized our strengths."

Both were considerable. Their experience was great, but their assets were meager. They couldn't have raised even $15,000, if they'd both cleaned out their bank accounts, and neither had lived anywhere for more than six years.

But the Boyces had a knack for turning negatives into positives. The couple stressed their commitment to Pittsburgh. Doreen was already serving on a local school board. And they were willing to throw all their assets behind them.

And they cultivated an image.

It helped that they were a handsome couple with British accents, not typical of small business owners in the locale. They appeared to be among the elite who could deal successfully with banks in a city dominated by big business. Before they even approached the bank, the couple practiced their presentation. Doreen played devil's advocate to Warne, as they ran down all the "what if" scenarios.

Coached by Doreen, schooled inch by inch on the intricacies

of the installment loan by his attorney, and armed with projections of income and cash flow over five years, Warne Boyce set off for the bank.

"The last thing you want your banker to think is that you're naive," says Boyce of a loan interview. "Even if you don't have the answers, he should at least realize you know the questions."

Boyce knew the questions and he had the numbers. As he walked through the door, he straightened his tie. When he came out, he carried a check for $26,000. Microbac Labs was born.

Boyce drew the following intuitive laws of banking.

1. Stop by to see your loan officer at least once every nine months.
2. Discuss any potential acquisition with the loan officer in advance. The loan officers tend to know a lot about the community.
3. Be realistic about the possibility of sickness or disability. Have a plan in the case of disability or death.
4. Provide more information than you have to. Send the bank a cash flow statement every six months. Send an income statement once a quarter.
5. Keep the banker informed of everything you do. This is "preventive banking." This ensures that the banker understands the inner workings of your company and you.
6. Be ready for a crisis three or four years into the business. At this point, you're expected to stand on your own two feet, but you're still strapped financially, cash flow is tight, and you're paying high interest on your debts. The natural reaction, according to Boyce, is to conceal your problems. That's the wrong reaction. The banker needs as much ammunition as possible when he or she goes before the loan committee.
7. Provide annual forecasts of sales for the year, broken down by month and service category.
8. Expect the next crisis seven to eight years into the business. At this point, the bank might think, "These people have grown pretty well, but their long term indebtedness is still pretty stretched. Maybe they ought to cool down a bit and establish themselves as a reputable little business (before getting more in debt)." Be sensitive to the bank's position, but don't be intimidated by them. Believe in your convictions, even if one bank turns you down.
9. Don't give up if the bank turns you down. Continue to

send your statements and keep in touch. They'll grant you your next loan once they know more about you.

10. Diligent care and feeding of the bank pays off. You'll be invited to bank functions, and introduced to the right people once you get to know your bank personally and you let them get to know you.

Warne Boyce's final words of advice: Expecting your bank to be an ogre becomes a self-fulfilling prophecy. Don't be intimated.

See Figure 13.1 for a 14 point loan checklist.

Here's a 14 point single page loan checklist conceived by Bruce Posner that forces you to think out the answers before you meet with lenders:

1. *Date.* Gives your application a frame of reference and sets things in motion. When do you need the money?

2. *Borrower.* Who gets the money?

3. *Type of Loan.* Speak their language: "Line of credit." Show them you know the terminology of their business.

4. *Amount.* Credibility is key. Don't be unreasonable, but make sure you ask for enough the first time so that you don't have to go back for more.

5. *Use of Proceeds.* Be specific: "Working capital for funding growth." This one comes right off of your business plan.

6. *Term.* Longer is better.

7. *Closing Date.* Give yourself 60 days.

8. *Takedown at Closing.* Reveal your plans, or "as needed," if you can't be specific.

9. *Collateral.* Explain what's of value. As a service organization, that's probably your receivables.

10. *Rate.* You name it. Prime plus 1% is norm in the A/E industry.

11. *Repayment Schedule.* Manage lender expectations. Balance by a certain date; interest only monthly.

12. *Guarantee.* Hold that guarantee: "None."

13. *Source of Funds for Repayment.* How you will pay the money back?

14. *Alternative Sources of Funds for Repayment.* Your backup plan.

Figure 13.1 Fourteen point loan checklist.

14 CREATING THE COMMUNITY

"We must be the change we wish to see in the world."
—*Mahatma Ghandi*

Next comes the task of defining your organizational structure. Give this some thought, even if you are setting up a one person firm. Planning your intent now will make a difference down the line when you do decide to hire others. You'll already know where they fit in, and what kind of people to hire.

Your design firm's organization is dictated by your vision and your mission—as it is the outgrowth of your definition of what is most important in your firm. The kind of organizational structure you assemble for your firm will affect how clients perceive your firm, how you market yourself, and how employees operate and feel within the environment.

Firm organization has been a source of hot debate in design firms, mainly because there are two opposing issues at work: quality control versus client service.

The ongoing debate centers around whether you want to focus on providing high quality or outstanding service. The issues can be oppositional, even in a one person firm.

First you need to define which element is most important to you and to the marketing of your firm. The small firm of two to ten persons will likely focus on client service— meeting the schedule and budget requirements, as well as the other myriad requests that keep the client focused, in touch with the firm, and satisfied. A 25 to 50 person firm doing government work for hazardous waste cleanup is more apt to require strict quality controls because of liability considerations, even at the expense of some level of client satisfaction (budget, schedule, design). The exceptional firm combines both to meet the client's needs.

Whether you choose to focus your firm on providing excellent service or providing unequivocal quality will dictate the type of organizational structure you choose. In traditional organizations, principals are at the top, project managers next, and technicians and draftspersons below. However the options for innovative firm organization are boundless.

One thing to keep in mind while defining an organizational structure is that you should define your organizations to be human and functional. According to Warren Bemis in *On Becoming a Leader,* this means that you must build a flexible organizational structure—a structure that is fluid—one that, like the world, is dynamic, not static, and must be renewed, adapted, and continually adjusted. And when it becomes unfocused, it must be abandoned and replaced. Figure 14.1 is an example of Schmidt Associates Architects client-focused team approach.

Studies have shown that there are certain characteristics of a firm's organization that produce long-term success. Tom Peters, in *Thriving on Chaos,* says that organizations that succeed over time generally share the following organizational characteristics:

- A flatter, less hierarchal structure.
- More autonomous units.
- An orientation toward high-value-added goods and services.
- Quality controls.
- Service controls.
- Responsiveness.
- Innovative speed.
- Flexibility.
- Highly trained and skilled workers who use their minds as well as their hands.
- Leaders at all levels, rather than managers.

This suggests a flexible environment in which people are not only valued, but encouraged to develop their full potential, and treated as equals rather than subordinates. The organization must take on a shape that focuses on creativity, auton-

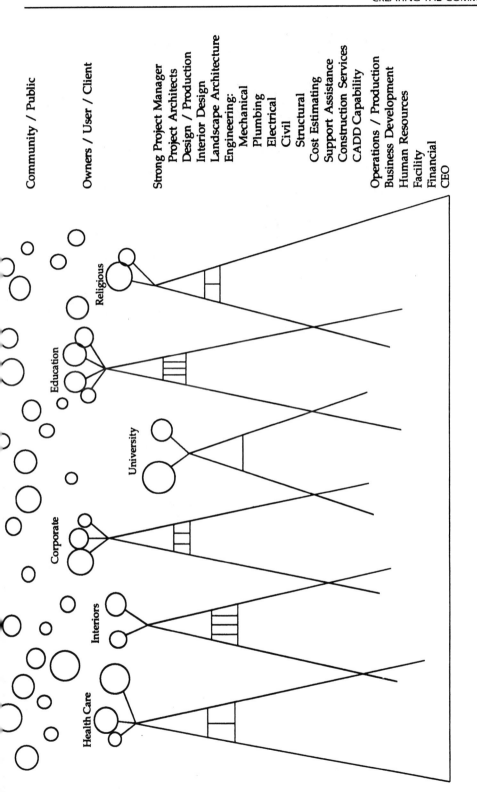

SCHMIDT ASSOCIATES ARCHITECTS
BUSINESS ORGANIZATIONAL CHART

Figure 14.1

omy, and continuous learning, rather than obedience, conformity, and rote; one that encourages long-term growth and relationships.

My consulting firm is a god example of a flat hierarchy. I've been known to offer outrageous opportunities and high levels of authority to individuals who are new to the firm. Company managers often take issue with my belief that when employees are given the opportunity, they will rise to the occasion. And given enough freedom, they will define their best role and the function they will serve me best. The result is well paid and well appreciated employees who are functioning in the roles they want to be in, rather than accommodating themselves to roles that they were assigned.

Remember that the organization is the means, not the end, and that it functions best when it functions as a community, not as a hierarchy, when it is truly a team offering autonomy to its members, as well as testing its opportunities and its rewards. As aviator Brooke Knapp once said, "Life isn't about limitation, it's about options." A healthy organizational culture encourages options.

Don't be afraid to go out on a limb. You can always come back in again. Realize that there is an element of risk taking involved in creating that ideal organizational structure. As aviator Brooke Knapp also said, "There are two kinds of people: those who are paralyzed by fear, and those who are afraid but go ahead anyway." Forge ahead with your new idea, your new belief on how to set up your firm. There can be no true growth without risks and no progress without mistakes. If you don't make mistakes, you are probably not reaching high enough.

"Life is either a daring adventure or nothing at all."
—Helen Keller

15 OWNERSHIP TRANSITION

"Everything exists, nothing has value." —*Edward Forster, 1924*

Some design firm owners wait until they are in their 60s to think about transition; others begin in their 30s and then pick the wrong leaders. Still others begin in their 40s and 50s, handling transition only when forced to by catastrophic events. Too many people face these events, such as divorce, with inadequate planning. They find their values can be skewed either up or down, or find that agreements based solely on tax planning are ineffective. All of this is needless—it would take very little effort for most principals to plan effective ownership transition and thus put their minds at ease.

LEADERSHIP

First off, consider your approach. Typically, firm owners invest and ponder heavily for six months to two years thinking about how to structure an ownership transition, and then give the designated employee or employees two weeks to sign the agreement. Keeping transition a secret can lead to disaster. The best solution is to involve everyone in the firm in the process of learning about leadership transition.

Good transition is a matter of balancing four issues: the buy/sell agreement, leadership, valuation, and financing. The purpose of this chapter is to show you how to transition evenly; by not tipping the scales you'll maintain your focus and the right perspective.

Leadership is the cornerstone upon which all other aspects of ownership transition rest. Hence the next task is to define leadership in terms of your particular firm. I've seen too many firms transfer ownership to the wrong person because the current owner did not consider the issue of true leadership. Identify the qualities of leadership you want in a new leader.

One common mistake is that the owner looks to his or her second tier of management for a new leader. Many strategically led firms with bold entrepreneurial leaders transfer ownership to a group of second-tier followers, only to find that the firm wallows in indecisiveness. Don't make loyalty your only criteria for leadership. Chances are that your loyal followers are not the future leaders of your firm.

Leaders must have the freedom to fail. Many followers are fearful of failure—they will preserve the group "status quo" instead of taking the risk of failing. By contrast, leaders are bold—they make things happen. They have a vision of the future, a clear picture of where they want to be. They give lots of credit to the team and little credit to themselves. On the other hand, they will take the blame for things that go wrong. They anticipate well. Leaders will anticipate your every move and take action before being told to do so. You do not want someone as leader who waits for direction. Leaders are people who anticipate and take action!

One element that helps you to promote and choose appropriate leaders is *career tracking*. Design professionals have traditionally become owners through the "management route." Today, the trend is moving toward career tracking, with promotion in firms available through several channels: 1) the management track, which may lead to becoming CEO, 2) the technical track, the track within which most design professionals started, 3) the administrative track—people like marketing and finance directors who are vital parts of today's design firm and who must be recognized as they move up through the ranks. Does your firm recognize each track equally and allow equal opportunity for ownership within each track?

Leadership Criteria

Several firms have created "leadership criteria" within a written document that they publish and distribute to everyone in their firm. Anyone considering the issue of ownership transition should develop an ownership criteria listing. These criteria include:

- Minimum of 7 years with the firm, or demonstrable

equivalent experience with another firm in an ownership position.

- Minimum age (not less than 35 years old)—this may be contested within the area of equal opportunity, so check on this
- Registration license or other professional equivalent.
- Acceptable personal characteristics such as a stable personality, a stable community reputation, and acceptable personal habits.
- The ability to participate in firmwide planning and management.
- The ability and willingness to participate in marketing efforts.
- Acceptance of the principle that the position is not limited to a 40-hour week—in many cases, firms do not write this down.
- Ability and willingness to make a personal financial contribution to the firm.
- Willingness to express a long-term commitment to the firm (and to sign an agreement committing his or her career to the firm).
- Acceptance of the firm's philosophy regarding quality control.

Here are some additional criteria you may want to add:

- Any new owner must have the unanimous vote of all pre-existing owners.
- He or she must have an absolute commitment in terms of ability to sell work; all owners must be willing and able to get their own clients.
- It must be a person already registered or licensed (I disagree slightly with this one because topflight people might be eliminated this way).

Leadership selection is the foundation of ownership transition. If you don't pick the right leaders, everything else is meaningless.

FIRM VALUATION

The next issue is the value of your firm. Most of what I'm saying relates to corporations. However, value has little to do with how you're organized from a legal point of view. Value has to do with somewhat subjective criteria.

Here are ten reasons for wanting to know the value of your stock:

1. It lets you keep "score."
2. Value allows you to give gifts of stock for tax-saving reasons.
3. It put proper valuations on your buy/sell agreements.
4. It creates a determination for the amount of your inheritance tax.
5. It can be used for applying for loans.
6. It can let you know your true financial position in order to avoid misjudgments in personal business situations relative to bringing in people to the partnership or letting them out.
7. It helps you deal with untimely deaths, establishing the valuation from the point of view of heirs.
8. It helps you if you are given an offer to purchase—you should know the value so you can decide whether or not to sell.
9. It allows you to know whether you have enough assets to expand via a merger or acquisition, giving you enough time to value your company and pledge those assets.
10. It allows you to tell your employees that you are a growing company.

There are hundreds of valuation methods, each twisted and turned for a particular reason. As an overall philosophy, keep your valuation formula simple. My recommended valuation formula is accrual book value plus a weighted average of the past three to five years' profits. Pure accrual book value takes into consideration all of the rules and regulations that apply to depreciation and marketable assets. Accrual is superior to cash—never set your value based on cash. Cash literally captures the flow of funds in and out of your firm. Accrual, however, takes into consideration all swings and takes a more accurate "snapshot" of your firm at a particular point in time. Important issues to consider are: 1) work in process— value work in process at billable value to get a true value of the firm, 2) use of depreciation within the firm, 3) real estate—do you really want real estate showing on your books? I recommend not including it because it has an inflationary value.

Multiple of Profitability Based on a Weighted Average

My biased opinion is that you should never put good will into a buy/sell agreement—it is too subjective. It is always arguable. Capture any value you hope to achieve within the multiple of averaged profits. Multiply the book value and a weighted average by 2 or 2.5. If you take a multiple earnings approach to valuing your firm, a firm is generally valued at four to six times its net earnings. Potential buyers will buy your firm at a multiple of four to six times net earnings because they are looking for a payback in four to six years.

Net earnings are those earnings prior to any discretionary disbursements to avoid taxes and prior to any taxation, so capitalization of earnings is another way to value your firm. Other methods average book value over five years. Any method you use must fit for your owners and your particular circumstances. *Do not change your valuation formula each year.* Keep the same formula for as long as possible; otherwise, you will demotivate current owners and provide an unstable market for future owners.

Consider the present value of cash flows. It may sound cumbersome, but you don't want to do it the day after somebody dies.

SEVENTEEN TERMS TO INCLUDE IN THE BUY/SELL AGREEMENT

The following 17 issues should always be addressed in any buy/sell agreement. Make sure they're included in yours.

1. Purchase obligation under death.
2. An option upon voluntary transfer—you need the right of first refusal in order to control stock.
3. An option to purchase under involuntary transfer—if you fire someone, you must have first right of refusal on the stock.

4. Purchase obligations under termination of employment.

5. Option upon permanent disability—most of us are living with disability insurance terms that are predetermined by insurance companies designed for working class people. They don't define disability in a professional sense. Does your policy determination and your definition of disability in your buy/sell say what you want it to? Are you disabled if you physically can't make it into the office, even if you could work from your bed? Most firms don't choose to do this and are later forced to buy stock from a partner based on this definition of disability. Perhaps you need a better definition of the word disability.

6. Valuation of your stock—remember to keep it simple—accrual book value plus a multiple of the past five years' profits.

7. Stockholders rights to obtain a different valuation—don't allow them to tell you that your valuation formula is invalid.

8. Payment terms—how long do you want it to take for payment to be made in all of the above circumstances?

9. Security for payment obligations—if you are a departing partner and I sell 100% of my stock, should you get any security?

10. Term for closing stock certificates—do you need spousal consent? Sometimes the wife's signature looks mysteriously like the husband's signature, or vice versa.

11. Know what certificates mean—should they be kept within the firm or not?

12. Termination of the agreement.

13. Insurance funding—do your policies penalize junior partners? Do they penalize you? A good solution is for the estate of a partner who dies to receive 50% of the life value, while the firm receives the other 50%. The valuation used is that of the day before the date of death.

14. Use of escrow accounts.

15. Nonsolicitation and noncompetition covenants. Be as specific as possible in these agreements—you don't

want them to be broad and generic. Don't allow anyone to take your known clients away.

16. Use of severance pay to increase your tax deductions.
17. Waiver of all spousal rights in case of divorce or bank-
ruptcy.

FINANCIAL MEASURES TO FINANCE TRANSITION

Most design firms raise partner's compensation so they can
buy stock—technically a "giveaway." Understand all the ramifications before you decide how to structure your buyout. In
addition, every employee should be forced to buy 5,000
shares to make an initial purchase out of their own funds.
Otherwise they won't take buying into the design firm seriously. If you do any internal borrowing among partners, keep
the interest rate to junior partners at least at half of the normal bank rate so they perceive the deal as tremendously beneficial. Another method of financing is through an ESOP. Like
raising compensation, the ESOP provides some a path to finance the transition.

Make sure you understand that the buy/sell agreement is
not written in stone, but should be periodically reviewed.
This is especially true if the transition takes place over a pro-
longed time period. Finally, when you choose a new partner,
remember it is a glorious moment. Have a party—publicly!
Announce the new partners in front of clients and family
members and have a positive impact on transition.

16 MAKING STRATEGIC PLANNING WORK

> "Strategic planning is simply the process of figuring out how you're going to use your resources. Your people, your money and your time. It's also the trigger that unleashes an awful lot of latent energy within a firm. It causes people to work together to make things happen."
> —By West, AIA, Principal, West Carroll Bates & Bergmann Assoc.

Byron West, AIA, Principal of West Carroll Bates & Bergmann Associates, shares his views on strategic planning, and the CEO's role in the strategic planning process. Figure 16.1 is a profile of the firm that West recently started with partners Kevin Carroll, David Bates, and Donald Bergmann in 1992. According to West:

Strategic planning is simply the process of figuring out how you're going to use your resources. Your people, your money and your time. It's also the trigger that unleashes an awful lot of latent energy within a firm. It causes people to work together to make things happen.

Since strategic planning is a process that never stops, all you need to do is formalize it to coincide with your forthcoming fiscal year. That means starting six months in advance of implementation. It also means structuring your mission and overall goals before you begin.

The formal process itself only takes about four months. That means that for four months out of every twelve, you have some type of formal activity going on about you that gives you a basis for building your budget.

It's like a tennis game between top management, the CEO if you will, and the staff. Obviously the CEO can't do the plan

Firm name:	West Carroll Bates & Bergmann Associates
Size:	8
Principals:	Byron West, Kevin Carroll, David Bates, Donald Bergmann
Focus:	Architectural design, health care, infrastructure
Address:	6629 W. Central Ave.
	Toledo, OH 43617

West Carroll Bates & Bergmann Associates was established in October of 1992 for several reasons: client demand, a desire for greater control, a desire to create a nationally recognized firm, and the desire to launch a gifted, talented young architect, according to Byron West. The firm's objective from the beginning was to make a strong mark on the industry. "Our goal is to become the most significant consulting firm in health care and infrastructure in the Michigan Region, to be one of the 25 most profitable design firms in the nation, and to grow to the size of 50 staff over the next five years with an average income of $100,000 per person."

Can it be done? According to West, the firm is "only six months old, and already we are ahead of schedule."

The advice that West offers to anyone starting their own venture is to "write out your own, clearly stated goals and objectives, make quality your hallmark, participate in community activities, hone your interpersonal skills, and network with local business leaders."

West says that starting his own firm has been worthwhile. "Beyond a doubt!" West says he puts in about 50 to 60 hours a week, and loves it. "Each of us has an obligation to live up to his or her capabilities. If the basic skills are there, then it is necessary to take action to fulfill oneself and to better serve those around us."

West sees design professionals in the future taking greater command of a larger segment of the construction market.

Figure 16.1

alone, nor can the staff. Therefore, it becomes a series of vollies back and forth, with a plan emerging by the end of the game.

The CEO asks the staff for their assessment of where the organization currently stands, what needs to be changed, and what are its aspirations. In return, the CEO and top management can see where the areas of concern lie, and can set broad goals based upon what the staff is trying to tell them. That's the "what" ball from the staff. Now the ball goes back to the staff to determine how to implement the goals. Back comes the "how" ball, which is formulated into specific quantifiable goals, and returned for the staff's blessing and buy-in.

Since there has to be a measure of creativity in the process, you often hit the net. There's also the marketing aspect: the task of looking at trends and demographics. All of the basic research pieces must go hand-in-hand with the strategic planning process. You can't do one without the other. You've got to get them working together.

You end the game when you come away with actual numbers that can be implemented and measured. Now it's the CEO's responsibility to publicize the plan and make it known to the whole organization. To make the plan work, everyone in the firm must understand the mission and goals.

In setting up the process, West says, you need to recognize that there's a certain amount of stretching, challenging, and aspiring that has to happen. And while you may not have all of the information available to make flawless decisions, you ultimately have to say:

This is the way we're going to go; we'll reassess it in six months, and if it isn't working out, then we'll adjust our course. Also remember that you're the symphony conductor. Your staff knows how to play their various instruments; it's your job to make them play together in harmony.

Simply having a formalized process in the works has tremendous value. It energizes the organization and makes things happen. When people know there's an opportunity for feedback, and they know where you're going, they begin thinking, even off of the job, about what's going on in the world around them.

FIVE TIPS TO GET THE MOST OUT OF YOUR STRATEGIC PLANNING

Strategic planning shapes morale, motivation, and the work environment in your organization. Remember its value as you translate your plan into day-to-day operations. Here are five "extra value" products of strategic planning.

1. *The Marketing Plan.* How will your firm secure the types of clients and projects, geographic reach, value and profit margins that allow it to make its goals?

2. *The Company Budget.* What to spend in which categories to attain your firm's targeted revenue and profit objectives. The company budget, in other words, is an annual monetary expression of your strategic plan.

3. *The Capital Expenditures Plan.* What long-term assets are needed to reach your firm's goals and how will the firm pay for these assets?

4. *The Personnel Plan.* How many employees do you need, in which categories and with what qualifications, to meet your objectives? Where will you find these employees, and how much will you pay them?

5. *Ownership Transition.* What your firm does must be consistent with possible future changes in ownership.

NO MORE EXCUSES—SIT DOWN AND DO IT NOW!

Design professionals can usually think of a hundred reasons why they can't plan now. Below are nine reasons why you should sit down and do your strategic plan today.

1. Strategic planning introduces a new process of decision forces into the firm. If properly done, it brings together people who often aren't involved in the decision-making process.

2. It asks and answers questions of importance to the firm that previously might not have been asked or even considered.

3. It imparts a sense of participation in setting objectives and policies for both owners and employed management and staff. (People "buy in" more readily when they have the chance to give their input, even if they don't agree with the final outcome.)

4. It creates an initial and annual formal, comprehensive review of all critical impacts, resources, and expectations in the firm.

5. It integrates owner/employee expectations and internal and external perceived structure and administration, finance and accounting, marketing, human resources, and operations.

6. It's essential to discharge management's responsibility to undertake strategic planning.

7. It considers the futurity of today's decisions and their impact on the firm, to make tomorrow's decisions today.

8. It can put the fun back into the design professions.

9. The strategic plan is a compass and chart to the firm's future, and the management control and operational control action plans are the chronometer keeping you on track.

IMPLEMENTING THE PLAN

Files. Folders. Stacks of paper. Research. Market research. More market research. More paper. How do you control your organizational planning so it doesn't take on mammoth proportions? One way is to beware of overplanning and over-reaching. Strategic plans can try to accomplish too much or try to overplan events, and as a result such plans never get implemented. When a planning document is too long and too overwhelming, it tends to sit on your desk or your shelf, never to be opened again.

For this reason, the strategic plan should be short and to the point. Management consultant Ben Rawls suggests keeping your strategic plan under ten pages. When you produce a plan that is longer than ten pages, take a second look at it a few weeks after completing the first draft, and eliminate any unnecessary planning. Work through it several times, paring it down each time until it is brief, concise, and easy to read.

According to Rawls, a short plan is easier to communicate to employees. Employees understand exactly who is responsible for an action, when it should be started, and when it should be finished, thus ensuring better implementation. To successfully communicate and implement the strategic plan, include employees who will implement the plan in the planning process. This will give them ownership in the plan, and therefore the incentive to see that it gets successfully carried out.

If you cannot include everybody, give the written report only to the key people who were involved in preparing it. If you give it to those who were not involved, you may only upset and confuse employees who do not understand what the firm is trying to accomplish.

If you decide to distribute the planning report to everybody, first set up a communication process. Be sure everyone has at least had a chance to express their views, whether on paper or in person. Then, when handing the plan out, be sure to hold a meeting to clarify what you are trying to achieve with the strategic plan.

> "A rut is a grave with the ends blown out—and you can choose to climb out before you get buried."
>
> —Anonymous

PART

IV

THE NEXT STEP, ACTION!

17 GETTING THE BALL ROLLING

> "We are not here to sell a parcel of boilers and vats, but the potentiality of growing rich beyond the dreams of avarice."
> —*Samuel Johnson, April 4, 1781*

A great number of new firms—in every field—have gone out of business immediately after an initial period of success because they did not recognize the need for profits and retained earnings. Any growing firm consumes large amounts of money—to finance accounts receivable, major promotional efforts, and related requirements. Assuming that you can begin to obtain a base of work, you must set out to build a cushion to help ensure survival during the inevitable slow periods.

At times you have to "spend money to make money"—on promotional efforts, on staff, or on other necessary expenses. As a general rule, however, you should try to avoid extra staff, nicer space, and other discretionary overhead expenses. Invest your savings and profits into building the firm's capital or into well planned promotional efforts. New firms that do not control overhead and do not build a cash reserve die fast.

Profit in the early years is that amount over and above what you, as principal, can live on as self-imposed starvation wages. Normally, as the principal, your salary would reflect your level of responsibility and effort, but as the owner of a new firm, be prepared to put out an effort over and above any reasonable level of compensation.

New firms can rarely build an early reputation as the most experienced, but they can—and the successful ones usually do—build a reputation of giving more service for the money. That takes time, thought, planning, and commitment.

HOW MUCH CAPITAL DO I NEED?

Even if your firm has plenty of initial work, you must still ensure that you have the staying power to maintain business, should client payment fall through. At any point in time a firm should have working capital to equal at least three—and preferably four—months of its average volume to finance accounts receivable, purchase supplies, and carry the firm and its principals during slow periods. This could be as little as $20,000 but often is more. In addition to the working capital needed, your firm will require several thousands of dollars just to cover the cost of legal and accounting fees, purchasing an advertisement in the yellow pages, furnishing an office, and other start-up costs. The final amount of capital required to start your business depends on the number of owners and their required salaries, the amount of work the firm expects to generate right away, the likely payment schedule, and the degree of overhead necessary to run the business.

Hopefully, you are starting off with as few partners as possible (you and perhaps one other), and as low an overhead rate as you can (a home or small office space with one secretary). Be conservative about spending, even on yourself.

THE $100,000 BACKLOG QUESTION

Most firms record the amount of work under contract but not yet performed, because the firm needs to know how much work remains to plan staffing, establish marketing goals, predict cash flows, and manage the business.

Backlog is often stated in terms of "number of days of backlog." This number of days can be calculated by dividing the dollars of backlog by the firm's average daily earnings. There is no preformulated "magic number" that a firm should maintain. Each firm differs according to the nature of its work, average project size, average project duration, and the nature of the firm's clientele.

However, a firm can determine its required backlog by tracking its backlog over a period of time and watching the backlog number in relation to other operational statistics.

Most firms are aware that it will take more than 60 days to complete a specific 60 days dollar backlog. Work doesn't continue at a full pace and then just stop when finished. Work tapers off over time. However, utilization rates begin to fall when backlog falls below a specific number. Project budgets will also suffer as "work expands according to the time available for accomplishment."

Track backlog on a monthly basis and determine your own magic number. Watch the backlog trend over time to predict when your firm will reach that "magic number." Advance knowledge of a slow period allows you to plan in advance, and to act accordingly—whether that be to crank up marketing, leave a vacant position open, or plan for layoffs.

You may also wish to track the backlog number that requires staff overtime hours on a regular basis. Watch for the trend toward this number. Once this number reaches a certain point, it is time to hire another technician, draftsperson, or designer. Be particularly wary of promising ambitious project schedules, but if you have gotten your firm into that bind, discourage vacation time and identify ways to streamline the production process.

MAKE SURE THE MONEY'S THERE

One of your worst nightmares is to find out at the end of the preliminary design phase that the client cannot afford to do all that was originally intended, or what is needed to finish the job. When this happens, the client is not only disappointed, but is usually scrambling to devote as much money to construction funding as possible. Therefore, getting paid for redesign and/or value engineering efforts becomes more difficult than ever.

Dave Sholthauher and Terry Parker of AvPlan in Cincinnati offer the following suggestions to avoid the no money trap:

1. Before beginning design, ask to see the client's budget—what is the program of requirements and what costs does the client expect. Be sure the included costs cover more than the actual construction budget.

2. Test the program and budget for compatibility. Do not begin design until you are convinced there are adequate funds to cover all costs such as construction, equipment, fees, moving, administrative, and finance costs.

3. Verify the financial stability of the client via reference

checks, as well as contacts with other consultants who have previous experience with the client.

Schlothauer and Parker, who specialize in planning and financing aviation projects, note that the most important first step for a project manager is to verify the bonding and/or financing capacity of the client. They note that in too many cases, a client may appear to have appropriate budgets authorized and allocated; however, the client may learn later that the financing markets will limit his or her financing capacity.

You may even devise a preprinted company checklist of steps you should go through to check and recheck the client's financial status and ability to pay you. This is a worthwhile exercise, given the resources you will expend over time in fulfilling the client's design. Use the following checklist as a guide.

1. What is the client's anticipated or allocated budget for the project? _____
   (If a client cannot specify a number, then draw up a preliminary budget to give that client an idea of whether or not this is in the right ballpark. If not, you're out.)

2. Ask for three credit references. Approach this in a very friendly manner, as this is a touchy subject. If the client cannot provide the names of three consultants with whom he or she has a good working relationship, then take that as a warning.

3. Where is the money being held? Does the company make adequate profits? Is there an allocated fund for design work? Is the owner still trying to secure financing (in which case, get the design fee up front!)?

4. Devise a Go/No Go Checklist such as that shown in Figure 17.1, in order to measure whether or not you want to take on the project. As I stated in my first book, *Staying Small Successfully,* (New York: John Wiley & Sons, 1990) your success will be measured by the number of projects that you turn down. Be selective. Choose only those who can pay. Or don't run your own business!

TAKE NOTE OF THESE . . .

This listing first appeared in an issue of one of the newsletters that my firm publishes, entitled *Project Management*. The list

THE WORLD'S MOST COMPLETE GO/NO GO CHECKLIST

How can you determine which projects to say "no" to? It's not always wise to have a strict formula for project evaluation. Often the best decisions are made on "gut feel." But every firm should have a documented "Go/No Go" checklist in place.

Use the following checklist as a means to arrive at your own criteria. You may want to add or delete either categories or questions, or divide the list into more or fewer groupings. The important thing is to tailor it to your firm, based on your known competitive strengths and weaknesses. Use it to make decisions, not to make decisions for you.

Adherence to the Marketing Plan

1. Does the project meet our design objectives and goals?
2. Does the project fit our target markets and services as defined in our marketing plan?
3. Is the project within our geographic reach?
4. Is the project consistent with our minimum/maximum project size objectives?
5. Does the project present us with an unusual opportunity to break into a new market that we had not foreseen?
6. Does the project offer repeat client potential?

Profit Potential

7. Can we make a profit on this job?
8. Are there any prevailing reasons to want this job even though we can't make money?

Project Viability

9. Are project funds secured? If not, how likely is it that they will be?
10. Is the client experienced in contracting design services?
11. Is there a discrepancy between the proposed scope and the fee? Is the fee adequate?

Selection Process

12. Is the selection process reasonable?
13. Is the job already wired to another firm?
14. Can we compete effectively under the conditions of the selection process?
15. Can we influence changes in the selection process?

Skills and Experience

16. Do we have the capability to perform the work?
17. Do we have a solid track record and relevant experience in the project type?

Figure 17.1

18. Is the project the right size for us in terms of our objectives, our ability to compete and our ability to produce the work?

19. If these are weak, do we have a strategy or other credentials to offset these disadvantages?

20. Will a joint venture or association be required to compete effectively?

Location and Available Staff

21. Is our location favorable in terms of the client's criteria?

22. Do we have the available staff to produce the work in the client's time frame?

23. Do we have the staff and time available to market in a first-class fashion?

Client Contact

24. Are we known to the client? Is it a past client with whom we have a good reputation?

25. Have we become known by the prospect?

26. Will we have adequate opportunity to research the client's needs before the selling process begins?

27. Do we have an inside track with the primary decision maker?

Competition

28. Who is the likely competition? Do we have a chance against them?

29. Does this project offer us an opportunity to compete at a "higher level" against firms with whom we would like to be identified with in the marketplace?

30. Do we have a strong "message"?

31. What do we have that makes us uniquely qualified to do the job? To compete effectively?

Odds Calculation

32. What are the odds of being shortlisted?

33. What are the odds if and when we do make the shortlist? (If your odds are 50% that you will be shortlisted and 25% that you will be selected, then your overall odds are 50% x 25% or 12.5%)

Cost to Pursue

34. How much marketing time and effort will be required in proportion to our odds of winning?

35. What are the marketing costs relative to the potential profit? (Spending your profit to get the job may be sufficient reason to decide not to pursue it.)

Figure 17.1 (Continued.)

was written by Editor Scott Braley, who is Vice President of Heery International in Atlanta, Georgia. This list is invaluable, and you should hang it up on your bulletin board and use it as a standard business practice.

Best time to call a contractor	7:00 am
Best time to call a client	Tuesday at 8:45 am
Best time to run a meeting	11:00 am
Best day to hold all meetings	Tuesday
Best time to do manpower planning	8:00 am Monday
Best day to mail invoices	23rd (so they pay on 1st)
Best time to open mail	4:30 pm
Best place to eat lunch	At your desk
Best place to eat with clients	At breakfast
Best meeting format	Standup meetings
Best way to control meetings	Take meeting minutes yourself
Best position among six firms competing in a presentation	Last
Best form of contract	Lump sum
Best type of client	One who pays
Best employee	One who initiates action
Best length of workday	Nine hours—no more
Best day to avoid interruptions	Saturday
Best time to get things done	Before hours
Best way to avoid conflict	Straight communication
Best marketing brochure	Never saw one
Best title on a business card	None at all
Best interoffice memo	Handwritten
Best time to fire someone	9:00 am Monday
Best boss	One who teaches you daily

TWENTY-TWO EASY STEPS TO YOUR BUSINESS PLAN

In case you are really having trouble getting started, here's the quick and dirty plan to get it all going, all in one sitting! These are some basic exercises to go through in developing your firm. This is a very basic, all-in-one outline, but it will

Firm name	Gail Sullivan Associates
Size	2
Principal	Gail Sullivan
Focus:	Community and small institutional buildings, educational buildings, and housing
Address:	85 Jamaica Street
	Jamaican Plain, MA 02130

Gail Sullivan started her own firm because "I wanted to extend the scope of work to include more active work with nonprofit clients, especially in the pre-design phase: helping to define the project, extensive architectural programming, as well as design and construction documents."

Sullivan's original objective was to help nonprofit organizations provide the best quality environments possible, which enhance their work, encourage a sense of community, and bring joy to those who participate in their programs. Her start-up money was scarce. "I started with no money and capitalized as I went—but also began with minimal expenses, put in lots of time. But mainly toward meeting clients needs and doing design."

As far as financial goals go, Sullivan's are clear, but could be better quantified. "I would like to make a decent living and establish a stable financial base for the company. I'd like to grow slowly but maintain a small firm which works as an effective team."

Which objectives has she reached? Thus far, Sullivan is still struggling with her original financial goals; however she is hiring her first full-time staff person this year. The effort, she feels, is absolutely worth it. "I'm doing exactly what I want to be doing—only a little too much of it."

Sullivan recommends that, in starting up your own firm, you should: "Know what you want to do, figure out your unique contribution, begin with some passion for the substance of what you're doing rather than only the form."

Over the next five-year period, Sullivan plans to continue to build her client base, and to expand enough to hire a business manager who takes over the direct control of the business issues so that she can focus on clients' needs and design.

Figure 17.2

get you on your way to the important strategic planning necessary to properly launch a design firm. Figures 17.2 and 17.3 are two profiles of design firms, one a small architectural firm and the other an aviation design and planning firm. These profiles are of interest here as examples of firms who have successfully started their practices.

1. Draft a one sentence vision for your firm.
2. Now draft a one page mission statement describing how you will reach your vision.

Firm name	Talmon & Albright Inc.
Size	16
Principals	J. T. Talmon and W. S. Albright
Focus	Avaiation design and planning
Address:	Exchange Place
	3 Front Street
	Lexington, NC

Talmon & Albright Inc. was truly founded to fill a market niche. "We started the firm in 1989 because we saw a growing gap in consultants serving general aviation airports versus air carrier airports, as well as expanding overhead costs for those serving GA airports, thereby enhancing the market niche for a small aviation consulting firm," say John Talmon, partner and CEO of Talmon & Albright Inc.

The firm's objectives from its inception were geared toward beginning to build a practice in the southeast (North Carolina, South Carolina, and Virginia), and then to expand as opportunities are presented. They expected, after bank payoff, to produce profits of 15–20%. They felt that with controlled growth and continual evaluation of the marketplace demand, they could achieve those goals. How has the firm fared in reaching their own expectations? "At four years old we are still working hard toward them, with some project managers doing well and others still struggling," says Talmon.

The firm provides, along with their billing rates, a note that says, "We haven't raised our prices in 18 months, in order to stay competitive." (See price list that follows.)

Talmon's advice to the new design firm owner is to, "Get some business training if you want to make it to the top. Learn about the marketing side of a business as soon as possible. And realize that putting in just 40 hours a week won't get you to the top." And, "The more time and energy we put into it early resulted in less personal resources needed later to keep things up and running."

The firm's vision for the future, says Talmon, is to stay cautious about overoptimism; to concentrate on profitable project managers, projects, and clients; and to reward excellence in every aspect of the business.

Talmon feels that, despite the hard work, operating his own business has been rewarding: "You can control your own destiny—lots of work can result in lots of satisfaction and high levels of compensation."

Figure 17.3

3. Select three design companies you'd like to emulate.

4. Contact and try to obtain the following information about these firms. Gather as many of these items as possible:
   - Marketing brochure
   - Any other marketing materials
   - Marketing newsletter
   - End of year fiscal report
   - Project management policy/manual

- Personnel policy/manual
- Job description of CEO, marketing director, director of operations, director of finance, and project managers
- Copy of their buy/sell agreement

5. Study the materials from these firms, and use them as a basis for setting your policies (see later steps).

6. Develop a list of 12 sources for market research for your firm.

7. Write/contact/subscribe to these 12 sources.

8. Gather demographic information on your chosen markets by using local newspapers and magazines, *American Demographics Magazine* (your local library will have back issues), state and public reports/project bids, Construction Market Data (local offices set up throughout the United States), and other sources.

9. Draft a set of marketing goals, including a list of target markets and a targeted number of projects per year per market. Do your goals match the demographic information you gathered?

10. Assemble a three-ring binder with tabs to begin compiling your business research data.

11. Prepare an initial draft financial plan for your business. Include a pro forma budget and summaries of all potential expenses for the first year.

12. Submit your financial plan to your accountant for review and ask for suggestions for revision.

13. Draft a set of goals for each of the following areas: marketing, finance, delivery of service, human resources, and ownership structure.

14. With these goals in hand, map out a plan for each area on how to reach the goals. This is time consuming, but once it's done, it's done! Without a formal plan, you will flounder!

15. Write a three- to four-page summary of how you plan to organize and deliver your projects; include how you'll organize your project teams, how you'll get projects done, and why your service delivery is better than other firms in your niche.

16. Now pare the service delivery plan to one page (or hire a professional writer to do so), and prepare a formal version of this to include in all of your business planning, banking requests, and client proposals.

17. Write a revised version of your own résumé and draft a cover letter selling yourself to future clients. Make several copies of this and keep it on hand for inclusion into the business plan, the banking applications, and proposals.

18. Assemble your complete business plan in your binder—including vision and mission statement, marketing plan, financial plan, project delivery plan, human resource plan, and ownership structure/plan. *This is your business plan!*

19. Contact three CAD software and hardware vendors and request presentations on their systems. Choose one! Write a one-page summary of costs for a start-up system.

20. Draft a convincing letter to a bank requesting financing for your business. Attach your résumé, financial plan, and annual budget; the one-page CADD summary if that is going to make up the bulk of your financing; and a one-page summary of your basic mission statement. *This is your bank presentation package.*

21. Submit your business plan and your bank presentation package to three to five colleagues for review. Be sure to include one of each of the following professionals: an accountant or financier; an attorney; and another service firm owner.

22. Incorporate changes suggested by your reviewers, and finalize the bank presentation package and the business plan. Remember, the shorter the better! Now hit the pavement!

18 THE CLIENT FOCUS

"We don't know what it is, but we love it when we get it."

—James H. Donnelly, Jr., author of Close to the Customer

ON ACHIEVING EXCELLENCE IN THE EYES OF THE CUSTOMER

Why has it become so important to bring the customer further than the old expectations (however vague) of some combination of quality and price? What is new in this decade is the way in which customers define value: they now judge other factors that have grown to be highly important in this fast-paced, immediacy-of-delivery, excellence-of-service business environment. They look at convenience, post-service satisfaction, dependability, and many other factors. In short, they are harder to please than ever before, and the way to please them is to find out what they want and then do a better job at giving them more than they expected. That is how you will soar above your competition, and in this economic climate, there is no other way.

"Most service businesses sell 'brown paper bags.' Thus, when your services are the same, you will win or lose on the performance of your people," says James Donnelly, author of *Close to the Customer* (Richard D. Irwin, 1992). Donnelly writes about the necessity of becoming intimate with your customers so that you are not just "selling paper bags," but are providing outstanding multifaceted "paper bags." He also emphasizes the value of training your staff to provide peak performance—which really means teaching them to leave a lasting impression on the client. According to Donnelly, you should encourage your staff (and yourself) to commit to peak performance using the following tactics.

1. Tie compensation directly to performance; this enhances both the efficiency and the effectiveness of the organization or unit.
2. Give tangible and public recognition to people who perform beyond the acceptable level.
3. Accept completely the idea that employees should share directly and significantly in overall productivity gains (however you define them).
4. Encourage joint participation (management and employees) in defining recognizable goals and standards against which individual performance can be judged.
5. Provide special attention to, as well as training to deal with, the problems and difficulties that middle managers face in supporting and implementing programs of change in the organization.

HOW-TO-DO-IT TACTICS

Basically the firms who have taken leadership positions in their markets today are those that have narrowed their business focus, and deliver superior valued service in one of three avenues: 1) operational excellence, 2) customer intimacy, or 3) product leadership. The top firms are expert in at least one of these areas, and meet industry standards in the other two.

Becoming an industry leader depends as much on your own and your staff's attitudes toward the client as it does on being proficient at your craft. Quite frankly, being proficient these days is just not enough! According to Fred Wiersma and Michael Treacy (*Harvard Business Review,* January–February 1993), sustaining your position as an industry leader requires that you choose a value discipline that takes into account your customer's strengths and weaknesses. That is, choose to excel in one of the disciplines listed above: in operational excellence, customer intimacy, or product leadership. This goes back to the choice between being inward oriented (toward quality) or outward oriented (toward the client). Is it most important to your client that you know the absolute ins and outs of their business? Is it most important that you provide the leading service product? Or is your client looking for operational excellence (in this case, fastest and cheapest service delivery)? It is up to you to develop a profile of your typical client, and to find out whether or not they are looking for a bargain quick, looking for only exactly what they want, or looking for high technology state-of-the-art computer technology and customer service delivery. Complete the exercise shown in Figure 24 to determine which kind of a client you will be servicing, and which need is most important. Define what value is to your customer, and then deliver!

> "A great many customers will not return bad service with bad behavior. They are always polite and never get loud, cause a scene, or scream for the manager. They just never come back."
> —James H. Donnelly, Jr.

UNDERSTANDING CLIENT EXPECTATIONS

In a recent survey of design firm clients, it was found that clients' biggest concern is in *getting the firm to understand the client's expectations for the purpose of the project.* Design firms cannot deliver a quality project if they do not understand what the client really wants. And the client's true needs can be hidden. For instance, if you are doing a project for a city and its mayor is up for reelection the following year, then you've got to realize that the mayor's hidden agenda is to be reelected. So your task is not only to design the project to meet the needs of the town, but also to complete the project on time, under budget, and make the project a resounding success—all in order to enhance the mayor's reputation.

After all, isn't that the business we're in—managing projects for our clients? Taking care of their needs and expectations? Your task then is to hone the client's expectations. Here are some ways in which you can hone your understanding of their expectations to get to the true heart of the matter.

Initially, assume nothing. Whenever you go into a marketing meeting, strategy meeting, or client presentation, count how many times the word "assume" creeps into your discussions. Design professionals typically assume too much. It is part of the process, and often assumptions are made in order to get the project going. It's easy. But dangerous. You start to assume what that client will do and where he or she will go and the kinds of issues the client has. You assume the phases needed and the functions within each phase. In doing so, you are assuming the project will proceed the traditional way you've always handled projects in the past, and thereby you are canceling out client input on the true nature of the client's needs. In making all of these assumptions, you are not listening to your client.

So how do you really listen to the client? Before making any assumptions, listen carefully to determine *what the client wants delivered* in the real project. It may be helpful to pre-print a checklist of items to include in your discovery process.

If the client seems unclear about what he or she needs, communicate your experiences with similar ventures to trigger discussion. Clients are not always experts at honing exactly what they want. They may not have a lot of experience with design projects. It is your job to present them with options that will lead to an ultimate fulfillment of goals.

What Does the Client Want Delivered, and When?

In most cases, the client wants a project delivered on time and within the budget. The quality of the project from a design or specifications point of view is always subject to discussion. Understand the client's expectation for quality, not your own firm's expectation for quality. (This is one of the main points being made across the board in total quality project management these days—strive for the quality that the *client* defines, and document the agreed quality standards.)

In addition to underlying assumptions, the issues of schedule and budget should be defined. Clearly explain to the client the tasks that comprise your schedule. Give a specific number of man-hours and then try to fit that into the client's needs. The client must understand the impact of certain schedule demands on the budget. For instance, if a condensed schedule is required, the client must understand the cost of overtime needed to meet that schedule, or the cost of hiring additional temporary workers.

Extension of a design for any reason to accommodate client needs will add money to the budget. For example, in Massachusetts there is an ongoing Harbor Tunnel Project, which will extend the state's main artery going north and south by building it underground, and installing a third tunnel that will provide direct access to the airport. The project was delayed for over five years and the resultant cost has nearly doubled.

Your client must understand the impact of any schedule change on the budget. Explain all budgetary, schedule, and even interest rate changes. Define expectations clearly prior to assembling a project plan.

Communicate Your Assumptions

After fact-finding and interviewing the client on his or her needs, make a list of 12 to 18 assumptions about the project:

"We assume the client wants this level of quality."

"We assume the client has _____ level of tolerance for schedule flexibility."

"We assume that the client's budget can go plus or minus 5%."

"We assume that the client will not switch project representatives midway through the project."

List each and every possible assumption. With list in hand, review the assumptions with the client carefully. Agree on correct assumptions, and add and delete as necessary. For self-protection add a caveat to each assumption. "If this assumption is not held true, our action as a professional firm will be the following." For example for the last assumption above include the following:

"If the project representative is changed by the client, our action will be to halt the project for one week to orient the new project representative. This adds one week to the schedule and *XX* dollars to the budget."

If you work out a list of assumptions with the client, you'll perform your best work without complications or misunderstandings. The client will know the penalty or price for each and every change initiated, of the changes you can anticipate.

Without a clarified list of assumptions, the wrong assumptions may stay in your mind while the client has another set of assumptions, a situation that can only lead to misunderstanding, disappointment, and lost projects.

WHY SHOULD THE CLIENT SELECT YOU?

Outside of the proper qualifications, it is how well you respond to the above question that guides clients in the selection process. Why *should* the client select you, anyway? The better your firm conveys why you are more qualified, how you provide better service, the more likely it is that your firm will be selected.

The answer to this question could make the difference in your firm's being awarded this agency's next contract, according to Sylvia F. Hartley, Consultant Services Engineer with the Utah Department of Transportation. Hartley offers the following advice for self-promotion:

1. Understand all criteria that the client will use to compare firms and answer each criterion completely and concisely.

2. Materials you submit to a client represent your firm on paper. Hire technical writers if you don't have a good writer in-house. Many firms lose because of poor, unclear writing. That lack of clarity will signal to the client how difficult (or easy) it would be to communicate and work with your firm.

3. Promote previous experience on similar projects. Experience is *number one* with most clients. If you don't have the necessary experience, team up with another firm that does have it.

4. Attend conferences that client market groups sponsor to meet client staff members. Develop a working relationship before you go for a contract by learning more of their needs and policies in advance. This is also your opportunity to present your firm's image in a nonpressure situation. Remember, you represent your firm, and what you say about yourself will be reflected back on your firm.

5. After you're awarded a project with a client, consider yourself an extension of their agency. As with any clients, represent them in a positive way. Take pride in making the effort to sustain and, if needed, improve their image. This will reflect positively on your firm and help position you for the next job.

EIGHT CLIENTS, ONE MESSAGE

A port authority land development manager, two office building developer/managers, a state department of transportation official, a county purchasing agent, a transit district representative, and two higher education construction directors all had the same message about what's important to them: *They want firms who can become part of their team.*

All of these clients say they are looking for the firm that has creative ideas and solutions. They want a firm that brings something extra to the table—like a project for them. They want quality services that are timely and within their budget. And they distinguish between consultants by looking at past experience, knowledge, rapport, approach, and listening skills.

Here's what these clients told Jackie Bonney, Marketing Director for Moffet, Nichols & Bonney Consulting Engineers, about what they look for when interviewing design consultants:

1. *Prove Yourself.* The ability to produce a good reference list is crucial. Show that you have performed well for other clients. This is a strong indicator that you'll do well again. If you're starting up your own new business, don't attempt to break into projects that are completely unfamiliar to you. Include a list of references along with descriptions of similar projects. (Always get permission before listing someone as a reference.) For start-up firms with little prior experience on projects under that firm name, obtain personal references on your own work from past clients.

2. *Communicate your Knowledge.* Understand the client's business. Outshine your competition by learning as much as possible about the prospective client's industry and specific concerns. Firms that demonstrate an understanding of the client's business needs will be the consistent winners.

3. *Make an Effort to Communicate your Image from the Start.* You have just seconds to make a good first impression. Good or bad, first impressions are lasting.

4. *Be Creative!* Your approach to their project gives the client insight into your management style. Tailor the approach for each project, noting all of the issues that may come into play and how to deal with them.

5. *Develop Outstanding Listening Skills.* Clients are looking for people willing to listen to what they want. If you do all the talking, you won't learn what the client thinks.

From an abundant supply of professional service firms, clients have to choose a firm that will solve their problems. Most firms have the capability. Those who are successful are the problem solvers, and those who provide a higher level of awareness of client needs and who can best communicate their work.

COMMUNICATE STRENGTH AND MINIMIZE WEAKNESS

Clients consider consulting engineering firms best at:

Being able to understand technical problems.
Providing expertise not available in-house.
Designing constructable projects.
Providing objective, unbiased recommendations.
Being able to identify and diagnose problems.
Providing complete and accurate designs.

Clients consider typical consulting design firm weaknesses to include:

Difficulty in meeting time schedules.
Difficulty in staying within budget.
Difficulty in communicating with nontechnical people.
Inadequate project supervision by senior management.
Poor service during a project.
Poor service after project completion.

BUILD TRUST INTO YOUR PRESENTATION

A design team's ability to communicate *trustworthiness* in a presentation is one of the major issues when selecting a firm through the presentation process, according to Wayne Bingham, Assistant Director of Design and Construction for the State of Utah.

As with so many projects these days each of Bingham's projects are funded with scarce resources and have tight budgets. Design teams that exhibit their *trustworthiness* are most successful teams with the State of Utah. For Bingham, trust means:

- *An Ability to Provide a Highly Skilled and Trained Staff.* The staff must have the needed skills for each specific job—the State does not want to incur any training costs.
- *Adequate Room in the Workload.* The design team must be able to prove they will manage and staff the job within the established time and budget.
- *Skills in Problem Solving.* Project issues must be identified, addressed, and resolved as they arise. Teams must be able to use their professional judgement to make the best recommendations for the State and for the end user.

In the presentation, you should:

- *Visit the Site.* Meet the user and project coordinator to ascertain key project issues.
- *Demonstrate your Abilities.* Show past related projects and provide a record of good performance on past jobs.
- *Illustrate Problem Solving Abilities.* Describe unique solutions to specific project challenges.

In marketing there's an old adage that you can't sell a lie twice—in other words you can't really sell yourself if you don't believe you're providing quality services. Your client will not feel trust in you if you do not have trust and confidence in your ability to conceive, design, serve, and deliver. If you work on building self-belief, you'll naturally exude a feeling of confidence and generate a sense of trust.

BRING UP THEIR ISSUES

One of the major objectives in any presentation is demonstrating to your client what it would be like to work with your firm on the job. To accomplish this, focus your presentation around the key issues of the project.

Make a list of the key issues to be addressed and/or solved. That list then becomes the agenda for your presentation. Weave past relevant projects into the presentation as they relate to the specific issues.

Instead of starting your presentation with a standard welcome and introduction, get right into the meat of the problem. Display your "issues board" and ask each selection committee member, in one word, to state their major concern on the project. Write any new items on the "issues board." Then inform the selection committee that the objective of your presentation is to demonstrate how your team will solve each of these issues. This approach demonstrates:

• Your knowledge about the client's project.
• Your ability to resolve project issues and your experience with the relevant past projects.

This method also "breaks the ice" with the selection committee, encourages interaction during the presentation from the beginning, and is generally a terrific way to distinguish yourself from the rest who start with an introduction, then explain the history of their firm, then review all their past relevant projects.

SEEING DOUBLE

Many projects require a funding or fundraising phase after completion of the conceptual design. Some design firms today are offering to prepare fundraising documents for the client, and in some cases prepare complete fundraising packages for their clients. This may include preparation of presentation quality drawings. Rather than funding the cost of these drawings yourself, require that the client do so in order to improve their chances of receiving funding.

Possible presentation drawings to consider include:

Renderings. Best prepared at small, quick scale and photographically increased in size. Ideal when a single drawing may be used for multiple uses ranging from small vignettes to jobsite signs.

Models. Study models can be photographed, perhaps with enhancements, and serve as presentation quality resources. Finished models can be photographed from multiple angles, making them more economical than multiple view renderings.

CADD Documents. These can be enhanced to serve as camera-ready art for presentation materials. MacIntosh is one company that is developing 3-D presentation packaging allowing you to actually "walk through" designs.

Offset Printing and Color Copying. Consider the immediate and long-term quality needs. Color copy technology has made great advances in the last few years. Consider a limited edition offset printing of materials, and multiple "second generation" color copies.

Seek complete participation from the client. And make sure you get the right to publish and/or use the materials in your business development, award submittals, and other promotional uses.

When arranging to prepare presentation quality materials, be sure you and your client agree in writing to the following:

Compensation.

Audience or geographic restrictions.

Type and duration of use.

Credits and acknowledgements.

IMPROVING PRESENTATION SKILLS

"Everything you say has to pass the "so what" test."
— Spring Asher, Chambers & Asher Speechworks

Chambers and Asher Speechworks are speech and media training consultants. Spring Asher specializes in helping design and construction professionals improve their presentation skills. She has this to say:

First, remember that the goal of any presentation is not to impress people—the goal is to "connect" with your audience and make them feel comfortable. Focus on letting them know that you can solve their problem. Second, 50% of your nervousness and discomfort can be eliminated by preparation. Get your act together, prepare, and the presentation will go well.

For technical people making a presentation, remember that the subject may be technical, but it relates to people and the things they care about—such as money, or getting good press. The key to making a good presentation is to show how what you do can solve a problem and enhance a project.

Beware of technical jargon. If you're talking to a "techie" who understands the vocabulary, use it sparingly. Otherwise absolutely avoid all jargon. Jargon intimidates, and you lose the audience. Remember, if they knew—or wanted to know—about the technical aspects of your profession, they wouldn't need you!

In the initial sales call, listen. Take the time to determine the client's needs. Find out intended uses, costs, schedule and expectations. Then give *specific* examples of how you have solved similar problems in the past.

In a formal presentation the keys are: *organize, rehearse, connect,* and have *conviction.* Address the client's needs *specifically.* Present three points that will solve this client's problem, and bring each of those points to life with real life solutions. "Remember, everything you say has to pass the "so what?" test." As Asher explains:

> The rule for presentation length is "shorter is better." Make your three key points in no more than 20 minutes. Interestingly, George Bush's speeches were cut from 20 minutes to less than 15 minutes—people simply do not want to hear you go on and on.

> If one of your colleagues starts to ramble, wait until he takes a breath, then redirect the focus to yourself. For example, say "Bob, that is a very good point, but . . ." or "Bob makes an excellent point, and I'd like to add to it. . . ." You then are in control, and can bridge to another point.

> The best offense is a good defense for those tough to answer questions you get during a presentation. To anticipate questions brainstorm with your colleagues. Identify the ten most common or important questions you are likely to be asked. Then think of the five questions you hope they don't ask. Prepare answers for each, and be sure to have an example to illustrate your point. This is exactly what George Bush did, and he had an 85% hit rate on predicting the tough questions. Or, as Henry Kissinger once said at a press conference, "Does anyone have questions for the answers I have prepared?"

> The bottom line is be prepared, be convincing, be confident. Presentation makes the difference. All things seeming equal to the client—the presentation is going to make the difference. For any kind of presentation, the rules don't change. Listen, prepare, present.

DANGEROUS AREAS

If You Must Bid . . .

Generally it is best not to have to resort to a bidding arena; however in public works projects and even in private sector projects, you may find yourself putting in a bid. Here are a few tips to help you through the bidding process. If you are handling a project that is being bid, or was bid, remember these few pluses of bidding:

1. Bidding will focus your firm to manage the project better to survive.
2. Bidding encourages you to negotiate lump sum contracts, thereby pricing the service based on value, not on cost.
3. Bidding will force design professionals to be accountable for everything they do—including design.
4. Bidding will improve the financial accounting procedures in most design firms.
5. Bidding will drive poorly managed firms out of business, leaving more work for well-managed firms.
6. Bidding will allow the best of firms to charge even more as it forces them to spend more on marketing in order to position themselves correctly in the marketplace and to avoid the necessity of bidding.

Stay Away from "Lowballing"

There are so many firms out there who fall into this trap that you should understand very clearly why it is a trap before you open for business. The trap is "lowballing."

"Lowballing" is a practice in which a project is taken at a fee lower than the cost of doing the work, in the hopes of obtaining fees for a future project or change orders. Consider the following example of lowballing on a typical time-and-expense project:

Total estimates cost =	$80,000
Proposed compensation =	$50,000
Estimated loss = $80,000 − $50,000 =	$30,000
Anticipated additional fees from change orders =	$50,000
Anticipated profit =	$50,000
	+ $50,000
	− $80,000
	= $20,000

Because the practice of lowballing is a gamble, let's evaluate the above example in gambling terms. You have taken a bet that you will be able to double the originally negotiated fee without suffering any additional costs. You have laid 3–2 odds that you will succeed! If you really want to gamble, play the stock market; if you want to be profitable, avoid lowballing when budgeting projects.

When the Client's Budget Is Less Than Cost

No matter how well a scope is defined, there are situations in which the client simply cannot (or will not) authorize enough money to cover all your costs, let alone a reasonable profit. Don't try to offer more for less—your fees go down and so does your reputation. Instead, considerable ingenuity is required to avoid the dilemma of: 1) taking the project at a loss or 2) declining to accept the project.

Use a combination of the following tips to overcome this problem:

SAVE INTEREST COSTS BY IMPROVING CASH FLOW

One way to accept a project at an apparent loss is to specify the proper invoicing procedures in the contract to improve cash flow. One such procedure is to include payment of a substantial retainer by the client upon project initiation. The entire retainer should be held until the final payment.

Another way to improve cash flow is to establish a weekly billing cycle based upon a pre-established billing schedule. For example, if a $130,000 project is scheduled to last thirteen weeks, the contract can specify a billing amount of $10,000 a week. It is also useful to include a clause in the contract *guaranteeing* that interest be paid for late payment.

These approaches can cut the overhead rate substantially by reducing or eliminating the cost of interest to finance project expenditures. It may even be possible to create a positive cash flow, thus actually generating revenue from the earned interest.

REDUCE NORMAL OVERHEAD COSTS

Another way to accept a project at an apparent loss is to reduce or eliminate costs that are normally built into your overhead rate. For example, if your firm allocates accounting costs to a general overhead account (as do most design firms), these costs can be reduced for a specific project by obtaining agreement from the client on a simple billing format with no backup documentation of expenses (such as copies of time sheets, phone logs, or receipts). Under this kind of arrangement, the client can still audit invoices on a random basis, but this saves you and them money.

WORK OVERTIME

Another approach is to take the project at a compressed schedule and work overtime. As long as the client agrees to pay for overtime hours at the same rate as regular hours, this can be an effective way to reduce the overhead rate, because overtime hours generally do not carry the same burden as straight-time hours. For example, once the office rent is paid, it costs little more to occupy the space sixteen hours a day than it does for eight hours.

LOWER YOUR MULTIPLIER

If the client feels that your multiplier is too high, it may be possible to lower it by extracting some of the items as direct project costs. For example, professional liability insurance can be obtained on a job-by-job basis, with the premium costs being paid as a reimbursable expense by the client. Another example would be to charge all labor and expenses associated with your firm's job cost control and billing system directly to the project. These kinds of measures, while not affecting the bottom line project costs, can overcome the psychological effect on many clients of paying a high labor multiplier.

PERCENTAGE OF CONSTRUCTION COST SAVINGS

Finally, if your client simply does not have enough money to cover your costs for a design project, you can offer to take the job at a loss, but include a provision that you will receive a percentage of the savings if the construction cost comes in under the estimate, and/or include a contract "royalty clause" whereby your firm receives 5% of the sale of the structure for a fixed number of years. If the client responds with a request that you also pay a percentage of any construction cost overrun, point out that you have already taken a financial risk by accepting the design contract at a loss.

19 YOUR IMAGE AND YOUR PRICE

> "Mirrors should reflect a little before throwing images."
> —*Jean Cocteau*, Des Beaux-Arts

WHY SET THE HIGHER PRICE?

Twenty-five years ago, architects and engineers priced their services based on a national average, and they obtained those prices from a little publication called the "Blue Book." That method of pricing services was determined to be price fixing and therefore illegal, and so architects and engineers now must set their own price. The problem is that oftentimes we set our prices too low, and there is not enough encouragement for professionals to place a higher value on the services they provide. But when you consider the work involved in making sure a building is structurally sound, environmentally safe, or emergency-equipped, you must realize that all of the services related to design enhance the quality of human life. For example, engineering sometimes saves lives, as in the World Trade Center bombing of April 1992, when the building did not fall apart and crumble. Your design also creates atmosphere that can enhance a business. For some reason, engineers fail to see the value in these factors, and often charge too little. When you consider your liability risk alone, you must understand the complex structure that goes into setting your price.

Basically the price you set and your pricing policy communicate your image. When you underbid projects and you continually perform work for less than the going rate, you get yourself deeper into debt trying to run operations, and deeper into a spiral of ineffective work habits. Why? Because when you underbid yourself you are trying to please the customer, but you are really hurting yourself, and not allowing yourself enough time or money to perform the work correctly. When you charge an adequate price, you have ample profit to spare and to get the job done, you are satisfied so you create better work, and the client respects you more. Believe it or not. With money, comes respect. But no one is going to give you more money, unless you ask for it.

In design work, it is best to perform all services using a lump sum contract. Basically this is because you can state a lump sum for each portion of the project, and get away from time and materials agreements or other nonproductive arrangements. When you have a lump sum, you can allocate a certain figure for profit and the rest for production. For example, Engineering-Science in Atlanta budgets all of its projects at 80% of the project cost. Allocating a specific figure to completing a project is probably one of the best ways to control costs and make sure that you meet the client's budget requirements and your profit requirements every time. That's right, even the smallest design firm must allocate separate portions of a project cost for overhead, profit, and salary. The following sections show you how to set your price, so that you are placing value on your firm.

FACTORS IN SETTING YOUR PRICE

A number of factors influence that way in which you set your price. The challenge you face is in determining an appropriate role for the price, understanding the factors that affect it, and raising or lowering it when necessary to achieve your objectives. In other words, pricing is a marketing issue, and should be treated as such.

The first step is to take a look at your overall goals. If you are planning on starting up an average firm, you will seek to recover the costs of all the elements of marketing plus the production of services. In addition, you want to generate some profit. The first two are easy—getting to the profit goal is the hard part. But there are ways in which you can set up your pricing structure to automatically build in higher prices.

Here are some of the factors that affect your price. Weigh them carefully before setting your price.

1. *What are your objectives?* Before setting your pricing structure, be sure you have thoroughly thought out and written down your complete strategic plan. With regards to pricing, consider your overall philosophy and convert that into a one-year action plan. Include objectives for management, marketing, finance, human resources, and production. No pricing philosophy can be set without this commitment.

2. *What is your firm's cost structure?* Consider in advance the cost of delivery of services, because this sets the floor of your pricing structure. Don't just look at the minimum you can charge—consider what the maximum is. Some projects can be priced significantly above cost because the *value* of the service you provide is higher than the value of routine design services that you provide. In addition, your firm's current work mix affects project costs. If you have a significant backlog, then you can afford to charge higher prices. If you have no work at all, you may forego profits in order to maintain a break-even level.

3. *Each service your firm will provide should have a separate pricing philosophy.* This policy should be based on the characteristics of the service, not just on the cost to produce it. For example, perhaps you are planning to provide architectural services for small residential units. Another service may involve the renovation of strip shopping malls. Obviously there is more value placed on shopping mall design, because the design you produce will affect the income of the stores in the mall. In a sense, you are creating an image for the store owners that will help their business. This type of business requires an entirely different approach and pricing structure than that of small residential architecture. In setting your price for each individual service, take into consideration how specialized the service is that you provide, the location of the service, marketing and production costs, and the competition.

4. *How "hot" is your service?* Demand set the final ceiling on price, just as cost sets the floor. Be sure to understand that demand for a service differs from that of demand for a specific firm. Demand for a specific service from a specific firm is known as *selective demand*, and depends on the value your clients place on that service, the existence of substitute services, and a variety of other factors.

5. *Don't focus on price when you prepare proposals.* Although a client asks for a price, he or she is really asking you what kind of scope you recommend and the price for that scope. All too often, and in this economy especially, design professionals respond to a price proposal by assuming the client is looking for the best price. Show the client why you are providing the best service, technically, first. Then give the price.

6. *Analyze the competition.* The number and quality of firms offering the same service to the same client group will directly affect your pricing policy. You have little leverage, for example, if there are 100 other design firms in the area providing the same service you provide. In this case you have no choice but to price according to the marketplace, or even to underprice. When developing your list of services (which should not be very long!), be sure to include at least one highly valued service.

7. *Convince clients through image management that they should select you.* If you can convince them to select you on the basis of your design, your expertise, or your unique experience, you are less vulnerable to competitive attack. Don't allow the price to be the deciding factor. If price is the deciding factor and there is no way around that, then be sure you can always support your higher price, if that is the case. In the end, clients want to know whether or not they are getting their money's worth. Prove to them why, in choosing your firm, they will be.

8. *Client Perception Is Reality.* Consider it this way: a client measures the appropriateness of a price by weighing the benefits offered by the package of services. Any difference in the nature of the package *you* offer obviously affects the amount the client is willing to pay for the service. The client expects to pay more when he or she perceives that a desired service is available from only a very few sources. Different clients have different views on prices and services, and it is critical that you understand what the particular clients' view when going into a presentation. The client may or may not be using price to eliminate competitors in the selection process. The client may be using it to help set total project budgets, or to ensure that a limited budget can be met, or to justify his or her own actions to someone higher in the organization. The client's view of price is affected, then, by his or her perception of supply available and of value being purchased. Don't get trapped by the bidding process!

Here's a list of questions to ask before setting a price on any job:

1. What are our overall firm objectives?

2. What are our current and projected mixes of work, fees, and projected profit?

3. Do we want price to convey a specific message or support a given image? Do we want to be viewed as a firm that offers "value for money" or "high quality"?

4. What will it cost to produce this job in terms of salary and overhead?

5. How does our cost structure compare to the cost structure of competitive firms in this market segment? Can we quote our price in such a way as to appear to offer the client a better value?

6. What proportion of our costs for this project is fixed?

7. How much will raising or lowering price affect demand for our services by this client? How important is price on this job to this client?

8. How much selective demand have we or can we create with this client? Do we have any unique competencies for this particular job (i.e., 20 years of experience with this zoning board or 20 years of survey records, etc.)?

9. Where is this service on the service life cycle? (For an explanation of service life cycle, see *Value Pricing for the Design Professional*, Wiley, New York, 1993.) What nonprice promotional strategies can we use to redefine this service to changes its life cycle curve or to create a competitive advantage?

10. How many other firms can offer this same service to this same client right now? Is this a "me too" service?

11. How much will raising or lowering price on this job affect its profitability?

12. Where is the location of this project and the client in relation to our production centers?

13. Does provision of this service increase liability exposure or risk to the firm?

14. How much will it or has it cost to get this job? Is the marketing expense worth the effort given the probable price range we can expect?

15. How sophisticated is this client? How familiar with this type of project is he or she? How much experience has the client had in dealing with our type of firm?

16. Are there economic or other factors that might affect production or completion of our payment on this job?

17. Do we have the financial resource to sustain a loss on this job?

18. Are we trying to enter a new service or geographic market? Are we in a growth mode or trying to maintain the status quo?

Here's one final tip in setting your pricing structure: regardless of whether you quote a price to clients that reflects your costs to produce any job, never share your costs with the client!

VALUE PRICING PAYS

The pricing concept described in the previous section is known as "value pricing" and has been gaining popularity among design professionals as a way to make higher profits. It is described in much more detail in my recent book *Value Pricing for the Design Professional* (John Wiley & Sons, 1992). However, the discussion here is sufficient to allow you a basic understanding of why you should set up your pricing structure based on the value of your services, and not just on the cost of services. Here's a list of the "pros" of value pricing.

What is value pricing? It's a win-win alternative to bidding that allows you to charge for unique services based on their perceived value.

Why is it win-win? There's simply more bang for the buck. Although the services may cost more, the costs may be up front, which can reduce the client's life cycle costs. At the same time, value pricing allows you to cover your risks, provide superior service, and raise your potential profit margin.

What does it take? Value pricing requires you to position your firm ahead of the pack, by creating new services that are perceived as being so unique that they're worth the extra money. As an example, delivering a CADD or GIS database that can be used for facilities management, rather than just delivering a CADD drawing.

What are the steps? I recommend the five P's: product research, packaging, promotion, positioning, and pricing. You can't go wrong if you follow through on all five points.

Position for Value Pricing Now

Follow these simple rules to position your firm so that the client will pay you based upon the value of your services, not their costs:

1. Research and develop your clients' needs. If they don't need architecture, how about financial analysis, market analysis, site investigation, regulatory approvals, lending negotiations, presentation materials, or systems management?
2. Package existing services into mini services or unique product "bundles." Don't forget to set a pricing structure for the extras you normally give away, like construction and facilities management.
3. Package your identity. Forget about the traditional words "architect" and "engineer" and be creative—use titles such as "Facilities Management Consultant," "Program Manager," or "*XYZ* Specialist."

COMPENSATION FOR EXECUTIVES OF DESIGN FIRMS

To begin a design firm, you will take whatever salary you can get for the first few years. However, it's a good idea to understand the typical compensation levels for design firm executives.

Figure 19.1 is a tabulation of compensation levels for every executive position in a design firm. As you can see, the median base salary for a design firm CEO is $94,336. The typical salary for partners/principals is $65,000. The director of finance typically receives $54,215, the business manager $39,000. The marketing director receives a median of $55,000.

These figures were extracted from the 1993 *PSMJ* Executive Management Salary Survey.

Billing Rate Per Hour

In determining your billing rate per hour, consider the national averages. Billing rates are shown in Figure 19.2 for each management position in a design firm today. As can be seen, the median billing rate for CEO's is $102 per hour. Median rates for project managers are $75 an hour for senior project managers and $65 an hour for junior project managers.

COMPARISON OF DIRECT COMPENSATION WITH 1992 SURVEY RESULTS

Title	Base Salary (Median) ($)		Bonus (Median) ($)		Total Direct Compensation (Median) ($)	
	1993	1992	1993	1992	1993	1992
Chairman of the Board	102,231	94,336	45,000	27,551	123,603	112,495
Chief Executive Officer	100,000	93,450	45,682	37,218	115,000	114,538
Executive Vice President	92,000	85,000	32,011	27,030	110,000	100,000
Senior Vice President	84,364	75,000	25,000	20,000	95,576	82,636
Other Principals	71,909	65,000	14,389	14,289	80,000	72,100
Director of Finance	75,000	69,800	14,000	13,500	77,673	74,135
Controller	49,906	46,000	5,800	6,000	51,650	50,000
Business Manager	38,129	39,000	3,876	1,571	38,582	40,900
Director of Administration	65,000	46,000	9,505	4,000	66,612	56,365
Director of Operations	70,000	65,000	12,050	14,298	84,000	74,900
Director of Quality Control	67,860	60,022	8,000	12,740	76,200	66,021
Director of Marketing	63,960	55,000	8,364	5,000	70,000	56,169
Director of Personnel	52,000	48,000	3,000	2,000	52,500	50,000
Director of Computer Operations	46,800	45,000	3,000	2,337	47,300	47,500
Branch Office Manager	66,625	66,947	12,755	12,067	70,852	70,378
Department Head	60,898	58,247	7,602	5,432	66,101	61,000
Senior Project Manager	55,158	52,000	4,786	4,700	57,381	55,000
Junior Project Manager	41,600	40,560	3,000	2,952	44,000	43,000

Figure 19.1

Of course these rates must be adjusted according to geographic region. Regionally in the United States, the southwest and mountain regions reported the lowest billing rates, while the west reported the highest. In terms of firm type, engineering firms in general have higher billing rates than other firm types. In larger design firms (a category dominated by engineering), billing rates for lower level managers still fall below other firm types.

The information provided here was taken from the 1993 *PSMJ* Executive Management Salary Survey.

SET A POLICY FOR CHANGES

When setting your pricing structure, don't neglect to set up a system for handling changes right from the start. Richard

BILLING RATE PER HOUR

Title	25%	Median	Mean	75%
Chairman of the Board	100	115	127	148
Chief Executive Officer	90	114	119	140
Executive Vice President	90	114	115	136
Senior Vice President	90	100	113	135
Other Principals	82	99	106	124
Director of Finance	62	103	105	142
Controller	43	50	66	75
Business Manager	35	40	52	60
Director of Administration	100	100	111	115
Director of Operations	76	95	104	115
Director of Quality Control	72	95	100	107
Director of Marketing	57	76	84	105
Director of Personnel	41	63	77	90
Director of Computer Operations	50	65	74	82
Branch Office Manager	75	90	97	114
Department Head	65	80	86	100
Senior Project Manager	70	80	82	94
Junior Project Manager	55	65	66	75

Figure 19.2

Roedigger, of Lorenz & Williams Inc. (LWI), Dayton, Ohio, has a changes system. His firm uses a cute acronym for their changes form—they call it the DARN, or the Design Adjustment/Revision Notice. Typically the form is filled out when there is a change in the scope of the job, and LWI charges hourly for changes.

A fitting name for an inconvenience, the DARN injects a bit of humor into the process. The form includes space for:

1. A description of the change.
2. Source for the change.
3. Document reference.
4. Affected departments.
5. Remarks.
6. Distribution.
7. Signatures.

If you do not have a form for your change orders, you are

asking for trouble. The client should always be informed of changes *in writing* and be asked to sign off on those changes. Introduce the client to the concept that changes are inevitable, and show them a copy of your changes form up front, at contract signing time.

Realize that changes cost you money, and that they are disruptions to the process. You may choose to inform the client that they will receive ten free changes and will be charged full price for any changes thereafter. Full price for changes, by the way, is higher than the norm. Here is your justification for using a standard, firmwide markup percentage for changes:

1. Where else will they go?
2. Changes negatively impact other clients by taking up additional time.
3. Liability exposure increases because chances are greater that the changes won't be made on all your drawing.
4. If you are working overtime, staff morale goes down.
5. Changes disrupt the project flow.
6. Each is its own small job—there is more overhead for small projects.
7. You are saving the client money in the long run. Building maintenance costs are reduced.
8. The change improves the quality of the job.
9. You are the most capable firm to perform the change.
10. Other clients get shunted—there is potential damage to other projects.
11. Charge more to cover overtime rates.
12. Use the markup as a penalty for client-initiated changes, to discourage them from making too many.
13. Schedule impact—what is the cost to get the change completed and still maintain the schedule?

AN EXERCISE IN PRICING YOUR SERVICES

The following is a suggested process to use in setting the price of your design services. Go through this exercise in order to determine the price you need to establish for your firm. Then take a look at the firm profiles in Figures 19.3 and 19.4, and their respective pricing levels.

Firm name   LaSalle Associates Engineers and Architects
Size   6
Principal   Samuel LaSalle
Focus   Commercial office/industrial
Address   17 Boston Street
                Concord, MA 02131

Samuel LaSalle started his firm in 1985 after he was terminated from a firm and, "Had no desire to join any other firm." His objectives in starting the firm were to hit three markets:

1. Developer/industrial market.
2. State projects.
3. Institutional projects.

LaSalle's objectives included making a 15–20% profit each year, and growing to a staff size of 45 to 50 people. When asked what he has accomplished of those objectives, he answered:

> We've cornered target market #1, even in today's bad economy. How? Service, service, service! We've accomplished a large chip of market #2 and are still looking to do more work in that arena. And we've basically had one institutional job—very frustrating. As far as profit goes, we've made a little profit each year (but one) since we've been in business, but never made more than 5 to 10% profit. But I'm not giving up on my original goals. Just got to bear down on this and read the staff the riot act!

As far as size goals, LaSalle's objectives have changed: "We made it to 16 in 1989, and would like to grow back up to 14 to 16 people ... 45 to 50 was too big for one leader. Maybe I could get that big if I had a strong partner, but I haven't seen many people I could go into business with."

LaSalle suggests the following advice to anyone starting a new design firm: "Be sure you know how to find work! Be sure you know how to justify your fees. Charge more, not less! And the give the customer (not the *client*, the *customer*) service, service, service. And don't always look for what they want ... it's your job to analyze what they *need*." (LaSalle Associate's price list is included below.)

How long did it take LaSalle to build his practice and how much money? LaSalle says he spent only about $500 to $1000 in setting up the office, and a month's worth of time. But he says he spent "Enough energy to light up one small city for a week" to get things rolling. And he feels it has been worthwhile "If we hadn't had the depression of 89–92, I'd be more enthusiastic. But as far as glorification of the ego goes, gratification is great, as is the satisfaction of having survived the recession while others have sunk out of sight."

LaSalle strongly feels that the "Bubble's going to break" on the beliefs about the medical market, and feels that "Long-term industrial investment will return after NAFTA gets straightened out. Some office space will still be created. Transit will be a big market, especially public ground transit." LaSalle also feels that, "The EPA's clean air regulations are a bomb about to hit private auto industry."

LaSalle's vision for the future of his firm is: 1) to regrow to at least 12 people, 2) to produce quality design of all projects including the nonglamorous ones, 3) to do some "glamorous" projects that are publishable, and 4) to crack the public transit market.

Figure 19.3

LASALLE ASSOCIATES' PRICE LIST

Space Planning

Area (square feet)	Fee
0–2,000	Hourly @ $60.00 per hour maximum
2,000–4,000	$ 600.00
4,000–6,000	$ 750.00
6,000–8,000	$ 850.00
8,000–10,000	$1,000.00
10,000–15,000	$1,200.00
15,000–25,000	$1,500.00
Over 25,000	$.07 per square foot, or a negotiated fixed fee

Hourly work charged at 3.0 times direct salary expense, maximum $65.00 per hour. Full-floor tenants may be subject to a discount from the fees shown above. Our travel expenses to both meetings with the tenant are included in these fees, assuming they are within Route 128.

Construction Documents

For the Design Development, Documentation and Construction Administration phases, our fees are:

Area (square feet)	Fee (per square foot)
less than 3,000	Hourly at $65.00 maximum
3,000–5,000	$1.30
5,000–7,500	$1.20
7,500–10,000	$1.05
10,000–15,000	$ .95
15,000–25,000	$ .87
Over 25,000	$.80 or a negotiated fee

In no case shall the fee be lower than the maximum fee possible in the next lower bracket. The foregoing proposal is based on "tenant standard" interior development. Should the tenant desire elements normally considered above building standard, such as custom millwork, glazed walls, computer rooms, or other specialty areas, we will be pleased to provide the required design services. Once the scope of the work is clear, we will provide a fee quotation for the extra services required.

Figure 19.3 (Continued.)

Firm name	J. H. Associates
Size	1–2
Principal	John Healy
Focus	Contract facilities management and engineering
Address	3 Duke Road
	Cumberland, RI 02869

John Healy, principal of J. H. Associates in Cumberland, Rhode Island, started his practice in 1983 because, "I felt that I knew as much or more than the consultants that the firm I worked at was hiring. I was looking for greater income, freedom from status reports, and corporate bull."

Healy's objectives were to make over $100,000 a year, and to have five to ten engineers working for him. So far Healy has made from $50,000 to $125,000 a year, and only grown to a size of 3. "Due to the poor economy, my long-term plans have not yet materialized."

His advice to design professionals starting their own practice is to: "Network. Build a customer base, and aim for multiple customers with small projects rather than one large customer with one large project." He also advises that you learn several CADD software packages, and be willing to take a pay cut, initially. "Once you establish a good relationship with your clients and have their facility in your CAD system, you can outbid anyone and continue to provide excellent service." Healy says you should "Expect to work 10 to 14 hour days and pay for lots of business lunches." He sees opportunities arising for engineering in building renovation and specification preparation.

J. H. Associates' vision is to get more customers, more jobs, and to hire engineers to perform the work, while Healy continues to sell the services. Has it been worthwhile? Healy says yes, it has, "I have my freedom, I am paying my bills, and I am not bored. There is always something new I am learning and working on." Healy feels there are growing opportunities in building renovations and specifications.

Figure 19.4

J. H. ASSOCIATES' BILLING RATES

Position	Billing Rate per Hour	Overtime Rate per Hour
Project Manager	$75.30	$75.30
Project Manager's Assistant	$31.00	$31.00
Engineer I	$35.00	$35.00
Engineer III	$46.70	$46.70
Engineer V	$62.80	$62.80
Planner V	$59.90	$59.90
Senior Designer	$49.40	$49.40
Technician I	$19.30	$23.80
Technician III	$30.20	$38.10
Technician V	$41.60	$51.40
Secretary I	$15.60	$19.80
Secretary II	$21.00	$26.70
Secretary III	$23.80	$29.50
Secretary V	$27.50	$27.50
Survey Crew	$65.00	
Survey Computations and Mapping	$50.00	
Legal Descriptions and Deed Research	$45.00	

Figure 19.4   (Continued.)

1. What are your profit objectives (as a percent of total gross income)? _____

2. Define the dollar amount of your expected profit for the next one year period. (This may simply be your desired salary plus a 10% bonus you'll designate as profit.)

3. Define the number of projects necessary to achieve your gross income company goal. Divide your expected profit from #2 above by the number of anticipated projects, so that you come up with a flat figure per project for profit. (For example, if you expect to do four $20,000 projects, and you want to make $8,000 profit, then that means you must make $2,000 profit per project.) Of course this example is assuming, for simplicity's sake, that all of your projects are the same size. But it gives you an idea of how much profit you need to make on each project.

4. What is your anticipated billing rate? _____
   Why? _____

5. Next, calculate the average number of hours left in an
   $18,000 project ($20,000 minus the $2,000 profit fig-
   ure) based on your anticipated billing rate. You now
   have the average number of hours that you must spend
   on a $20,000 project in order to make a $2,000 profit.

If you approach all of your projects by defining your profit
expectation (not to the client, only for your own information!), then research has proven that you have a higher
chance of reaching your goal. Remember that in setting up
your own business, and your price, you are communicating to
the world what you feel is your worth. How much are you
worth?

20

WHAT YOU NEED TO KNOW ABOUT PROJECT DELIVERY

"You never get it right, if you never write it down."—Anonymous

GETTING IT ALL DOWN: THE DATA COLLECTION PHASE

The most important part of project delivery is the beginning, and that gets back to honing client requirements. Not enough can be said about focusing on the client's requirements and giving the client what he or she wants. Your requirement is to listen, and to question.

Jeff Floyd, Principal of Sizemore Floyd Architects in Atlanta, recently discussed collecting data and beginning a project. Floyd says that in one form or another, you must always perform programming and data collection to begin a project. There must be a written program of requirements, including the data necessary to begin a project. If there is no such written program, the project manager should make sure that writing one gets added to the scope of services.

Moreover when the owner does provide a program, it is *always* necessary to go through a program verification phase. Quite frankly, preparing and/or verifying a written detailed program is the only way to ensure that you know what the owner wants and needs—and to ensure that you have a fighting chance to make a profit on the job.

Contrary to new ideas on fast tracking and project delivery, Floyd does not feel that construction should begin before the design is complete. "A good manager will schedule a specific, separate pre-design, programming and analysis phase before design begins. Every time we have thought we could get a head start by not programming, or moving too quickly with an incomplete program, we—and the owner—have been unpleasantly surprised and disappointed by false starts, or big problems that could have been avoided."

To improve data collection and programming skills, Floyd has the following advice:

We are great believers in the problem seeking methods and techniques pioneered by William Pena at CRS years ago. For anyone starting a design firm or trying to improve data collection skills, get Bill Pena's book and read it, then read it again. The key word index is an excellent opening matrix for data collection and analysis. We've built upon and modified those concepts to include: establish goals, collect and analyze facts, uncover concepts, and test needs. We do this in the matrix categories of: function, form, economy, time, and energy.

The biggest mistake inexperienced programmers make is in assuming that a list of rooms or spaces and necessary square footage constitutes a program. It does not. A program must build upon these basic needs, set project goals, and establish the priorities that will be used for trade-offs in subsequent design phases.

Be sure you choose the right person for data collection. It takes a special kind of professional to successfully complete the necessary data collection and programming. It is definitely *not the designer*. Designers are geared to solutions, rather than setting up the questions and defining a problem to be solved. A special sensitivity is required to ask the right questions, and not give answers at this pre-design stage of the project.

The pre-design effort is not a passive activity of just asking questions and recording facts, says Floyd. On the contrary, pre-design work is tough, and it requires a confident individual who will not be afraid to deal with conflict. "You cannot accept the motherhood and apple pie goals and objectives statements that so many want to rely on. All goals must be quantifiable, and they must be tested." Floyd feels that a good data collector/programmer will push the entire team, including the client, to the brink of dynamic tension to get priorities established, goals understood, and evaluation criteria quantified.

It is absolutely essential that the tough decisions get made in the pre-design "analytical" phase before the owner and the designer enter the "emotional" phase of design. Once individuals begin to identify with and chose concepts, images, and solutions, it is exponentially difficult to make necessary trade-offs.

In a sense, the "data collector" becomes an aggressive investigative reporter. Don't ask questions that can be answered simply "yes" or "no." Rather, use a continually probing dialogue of open-ended questions and comments. Floyd's firm accomplishes data collection through a combination of face-to-face and arms-length work with the client. "Begin with an orientation and kick-off meeting or discussion. Then collect data via a questionnaire. Build upon these data by using the questionnaire as an outline for a face-to-face interview." Finallly, coordinate and test the program data by presenting a written summary, reviewing it, and having a final face-to-face work session to ensure agreement, commitment, and common understanding.

One thing to be aware of is that you should get paid for data collection! Generally professional fees for data collection and programming are directly influenced by the complexity of the building or project type, the degree of sophistication and experience of the owner's staff, and the size of the project.

CHECKLIST FOR SUCCESS

"If it ain't broke, you just haven't looked hard enough."
—Tom Peters, *Thriving on Chaos*

Tight budgets, schedules, and other constraints impede success in a market where there are fewer and fewer opportunities to recover from mistakes—that's the chaotic environment in which we work. Projects have to be tightly controlled and monitored in order to achieve the high standards of excellence you have set for yourself. You need all of the help you can get—and help in business management comes with practice and structure.

The following is a checklist of the elements that contribute to project success:

1. Know what you are doing before you start.

2. Carefully choose the team.
3. Participate in proposal writing.
4. Obtain full authority to manage and control the work.
5. Use your people skills.
6. Set sensible, achievable goals.
7. Document each significant project event clearly and promptly.
8. Produce project documentation efficiently.
9. Pay close attention to schedules, budgets, and negotiations.
10. Use a simple scheduling method.
11. Remember that speed is critical, but double-edged. Instill a sense of urgency in your staff, but stress quality.
12. Quality assurance is inherent in a well-managed job. Have a total quality project management program and use it.
13. Control the project budget with an easy system using the man-hours and the hourly cost (to client).
14. Don't just track overspending, cut the budget! Look for ways to save money.
15. Beware of excess perfection. Too much quality, as well as too little, is not cost-effective.

Choose the techniques that work for you to achieve the above results. You have the authority to manage, so hold yourself responsible for the results.

PRODUCTIVITY NO LONGER AN OPTION

"Productivity improvement for design firms is no longer an option—it's a necessity."
— David Burstein, Vice President, Engineering-Science

Productivity has become one of the last resorts for making project profits, since the days when time and materials work actually paid off have gone by the wayside. These days, you negotiate a lump sum, and then it is up to you to get the job finished and not dig into the profits while completing the work. This poses an age-old question in design, and if you are starting a firm you will soon find out that this is one of the most pressing, and most perplexing concerns in design firms throughout the world.

David Burstein, Vice President and Regional Manager of Engineering-Science, Inc., shares his perspective on productivity. The biggest trend in the design industry today, according to Burstein, is the dissolution of the old axiom that a client could have the work done fast, cheap, or good; pick any two. Today's clients are demanding all three. They won't put up with just two.

That means you can no longer trade off higher costs in order to get quality. You have to somehow figure out a better way to get higher quality and faster turnaround, at a lower cost. For example, Engineering-Science started a program in its office last year where it sent a questionnaire to each client at end of each project and asked him or her to rank its design performance in each of eight categories: technical quality, documents, timeliness, costs (both cost of design service plus cost of project), dependability, cooperativeness, and communication. According to Burstein, "While we had 90% return, and our overall report card was very good, what was interesting was the sensitivity of clients to cost and timeliness. That's the hot button."

How does this all boil down to productivity? Your goal should be to accomplish all three objectives: to provide a quality product, delivered on time and at a reasonable cost. You won't get there by extra quality control. Checking and rechecking does nothing but drive up the cost. The only way you can get there is by preventing problems from creeping into designs or studies in the first place.

This boils down to total quality project management (TQPM). Productivity is an inherent part of TQPM. The whole concept is to prevent errors, thus giving you your only hope of getting things done faster, cheaper, and better. Productivity must be procedural. It involves looking at TQM, and it also involves looking at quality and production as a family, as going hand in hand. (See the following overview on total quality project management for a better understanding of how to rethink your work processes in order to improve them.)

HOW TO INSTILL TOTAL QUALITY PROJECT MANAGEMENT IN YOUR FIRM

How many times have you asked yourself or heard others asking this question: "What we going to do about total quality project management?" As Director of Business Development and Marketing for Sumner Schein Architects and Engineers, Amy Enfield reiterates, "We have targeted total quality project management (TQPM) as an issue that needs to be addressed." The big question is: How long are *you* going to wait before *you* address TQPM?

In starting your own firm, it is best to think about total quality project management in advance—and to review the project management process you plan to implement in light of the subject. Of course, this section alone is not going to teach you everything you need to know about total quality project management, but is will give you the basics. For a more thorough treatment of total quality project management, you should obtain a copy of *Total Quality Project Management for the Design Firm*, by David Burstein and Frank Stasiowski (John Wiley & Sons, 1993).

You may be well aware that there is a feeling going around that TQM is a moot topic, a passé term, another one of those hyped up buzz words that you can't really define. This is basically because, unlike good old "QA" or "QC," total quality management is not one set of checklists you can apply to your operations! Instead, it involves a rethinking of your firm's work processes in light of the total quality management philosophies first introduced in World War II.

That's right, total quality management is nothing new. The concept of controlling quality by using measurement techniques, conforming to requirements, and targeting zero defects was developed in the United States during World War II. After the war, General Douglas MacArthur sent Dr. Edward W. E. Deming to Japan to help that defeated and largely destroyed nation rebuild its economy. Deming's approach was simple: you look for waste, measure its cost, determine what caused it, and get everyone involved to fix it so that it doesn't happen again. Japan's industry leaders listened to Dr. Deming and heeded his advice; the rest is history.

By the early 1980s, it had become apparent to U.S. industrial leaders that the Japanese were beating them at their own game—producing high quality products at reasonable prices. They therefore consulted Dr. Deming as well as other experts, such as Dr. J. M. Duran and Philip Crosby. They read Japanese TQM manuals. The result? A dramatic improvement in the quality of American manufactured goods, faster cycle times in getting new products to market, and reduction of costs resulting from waste and rework.

To date, professional service firms have remained on the

sidelines of total quality management, seeing no reason to change traditional business practices. But those who fail to adapt to the following changes in the marketplace eventually will fall by the wayside:

1. Clients are insisting on a higher standard of quality than ever before.
2. They are more eager to sue if they don't get it.
3. At the same time, they are pursuing lower costs.
4. Foreign firms are entering the market, particularly from Europe and Japan, increasing competitive pressures.
5. Capital requirements for CADD and other major investments require design firms to become more profitable in spite of these obstacles.
6. There are not enough qualified technical professionals available to meet the needs of growing firms.
7. Employees are becoming less willing to dedicate their lives to their companies and are demanding more from their employers.

"As businesses become more and more competitive, the issue of quality becomes an absolute necessity to keep your clients," says Enfield of Sumner Schein. What are you doing to address these market changes? The answer, although you might not know it yet, must be total quality *project* management (TQPM).

Do either of these scenarios sound familiar?

A representative of an engineering firm visited a textile plant and promised to send the client a report on the findings. The report was sent late and the client refused to pay for the costs of the visit. The engineering firm lost $8,200 in uncollectible fees plus loss of reputation with a long-term client.

An architectural firm contracted with a client for a small project that was scheduled to last 3½ months. Midway through, the project was delayed by the client. By the time it was restarted, the personnel had been diverted to other jobs and had lost interest in this project. Agreed-upon completion came and went without any information to the client from the design firm's technical manager. Result: though the client was satisfied with the work, the design firm's numerous delays precluded the firm from working there on any future jobs.

Total quality management (TQPM) can solve these types of problems. But how?

What Is Quality?

In setting up a total quality project management system it is important to first define quality—and those aspects of quality you wish to focus on. Basically you focus on the aspects of quality that the client specifies. "Quality is a huge area to address," says Enfield, "you may expend a lot of energy on what the client considers to be quality in one area, but not enough in the areas that matter to them. If you're not addressing quality from the client's perspective, then you're missing the boat."

There are many points on the axis of quality to consider: traditional aesthetic qualities, psychological impact, concept, functionality, and structure. As well, there are legal liability aspects of quality, including negligence, errors and omissions, damages, warranties and guarantees, consequential damages, indemnification, and so on.

How and when do you address each of these issues, how important are they, and how do you define your quality requirements for each one?

The Rudiments of TQPM

Understand that total quality project management is not another review method. It is a total firm commitment to rethinking the way in which the work has been performed in the past, down to the smallest detail. This is what TQPM is all about. Consider the following story about an egg farmer:

Several years back, a midwestern egg farmer had a control problem: he couldn't keep up with egg production fast enough. Everywhere he turned, it seemed, he'd find broken and neglected eggs, eggs he could have sold. To attend to this problem, he called in an expert—his 77 year old neighbor, who had sold eggs for half a century. This guy, he knew, had a system.

The neighbor suggested a simple solution that had never occurred to the farmer: first he was instructed to line up his chickens' nests in pens that were side by side. His nests were everywhere, wherever the chickens had chosen. Second, he was told to begin checking the eggs three times a day, at 10 am,

1 pm, and 4:30 pm. His previous schedule was simply once in the morning and once at night.

The result? By controlling the collection system, he was able to sell 10% more eggs in a one-year span. But he had to completely overhaul his system of collecting eggs.

Obviously the above example is very simple, but it makes a point. The same principle applies to TQPM in design firms—you must rethink every work process in order to find a better, faster way. Here is a basic program to begin planning total quality project management in your firm today:

1. *Define requirements.* Designing client requirements should be an exhaustive process. Rethink the way in which you traditionally define client requirements to better understand what "quality" means to them. Here are some tools to use to better define client requirements:

1. A pre-design questionnaire to determine the basic project requirements.
2. A list of questions that should be asked by the designer to determine the scope of services desired by the client.
3. A checklist of typical services provided by the design firm for a particular type of project.
4. A project requirements plan that documents the design firm's understanding of the project's technical requirements.
5. A drawing list and specification index to establish the scope and level of detail to be provided in the design.

2. *Organize the team for quality.* The next step is to identify the strengths and weaknesses of each team member, since the ideal project team is always impossible. Tabulate these evaluations on a one-page profile, and use that profile to make the most effective use of each person's strengths while mitigating the impacts of his or her weaknesses.

3. *Plan the work process.* All work is a process that can be represented in a flow chart for each project. This should be done for your design process using task precedence diagrams. The diagram should allow for changes, and anticipate problems.

4. *Use the single statement principle.* The principle of single statement is a simple concept described by Mr. J. J.

Reichenberger, a Vice President of Engineering-Science, Inc. The concept holds that each dimension, coordinate, elevation, callout, and so on, must by shown only once in a set of drawings. Resist the temptation to repeat yourself and open up the margin for error!

5. *Anticipate problems.* At the outset of the project, the project manager should assemble the team and ask, "What can go wrong with this project?" All of the responses should be recorded, and ideas for prevention or mitigation developed. This list should be distributed to all team members as a Crisis Prevention Plan. This plan takes only a few hours to assemble and can save many times that cost in reduced rework alone.

6. *Prepare a QC plan.* Next you prepare a plan for reviewing the quality of your documents. This should spell out which documents are to be reviewed, by whom, when, what kinds of errors are sought, the allotted budget for the review, and the schedule and allotted budget for corrections. But beware of the good ole' smoking gun—your own formal QC procedures: if you have any published manuals, memos, or other documentation for a QC program, you are legally required to use them!

Making a Management Commitment

The following 14 points were outlined in Dr. Edward Deming's book *Quality, Productivity, and Competitive Position.* All levels of management must provide hands-on leadership in quality management by taking on their own quality projects. A breakthrough concept starts with a breakthrough attitude. The following 14 points are geared toward bringing about this breakthrough attitude.

1. Create consistency of purpose for improvement of product and service.
2. Adopt the new philosophy of refusing to allow defects.
3. Cease dependence on mass inspection and rely only on statistical control.
4. Require suppliers to provide statistical evidence of quality.
5. Constantly and forever improve production and service.

6. Train all employees.

7. Give all employees the proper tools to do the job right.

8. Encourage communication and productivity.

9. Encourage different departments to work together on problem solving.

10. Eliminate posters and slogans that do not teach specific improvement methods.

11. Use statistical methods to continuously improve quality and productivity.

12. Eliminate all barriers to pride in workmanship.

13. Provide ongoing retraining to keep pace with changing products, methods, and so on.

14. Clearly define top management's permanent commitment to quality.

The above is only a brief discussion of the ways in which to rethink the processes you use to perform work functions. However, it is enough to understand why TQPM is essential. Figure 20.1 contains a listing of the rules to follow in implementing a TQPM program.

PROJECT ACCOUNTING MADE EASY

Four Ways to Evaluate a Project's Progress

In setting up your project management program, you should establish the following reports to monitor your project progress—for each project. The key in setting up any reporting system is to keep it simple, and keep it to one page!

1. *Weekly Man-Hour Reports.* This is a computer printout that reports all time recorded under your project for the previous week. Review this each week to:
   a. Check for errors.
   b. Understand in man-hours what is going on with your project.

2. *Project Status Report.* This is a computerized man-hour and expense report on which you are required to provide information related to the status of each job and a description of the month's activities. Information

THE RULES OF QUALITY MANAGEMENT

1. Quality is defined as "conformance to requirements"—all requirements including budget and schedule.
2. Requirements must mutually agreed upon with the client and among the entire project team.
3. Requirements must be defined quantitatively so that nonconformances can be measured and made visible to everyone involved.
4. The traditional concept of the "project team" must be expanded to include all "suppliers" (people who provide input) and "customers" (people who use the products of our work).
5. Solving quality problems requires the efforts of a broad cross section of this extended project team.
6. There must be firmwide system to seek out nonconformances that recur from project to project.
7. Nonconformances should be expected, but not tolerated. In striving for "zero defects," everyone must continually reduce the number of nonconformances.
8. Nonconformances that affect client satisfaction are the most serious; they should receive highest priority.
9. Prevention is cheaper than damage control; the earlier you catch a problem, the less costly it is to fix.
10. There must be a firmwide commitment to quality from the CEO all the way down to the most junior clerical assistant.
11. Everyone in the firm must be trained so that they understand the new ways of looking at quality.
12. Individuals and groups who achieve the goals of quality improvement must be appropriately recognized and rewarded.
13. TQPM cannot be view as another program in addition to the firm's "normal" business; it must become the way the firm does its business.

Figure 20.1

you put on the PSR must be accurate and complete. Prompt completion of the PSR is your top priority.

3. *Project Team Meeting.* Good communication is the key to an efficient team. Frequent team meetings foster good communication. Do not hesitate to call meetings as often as you feel they are necessary. They can be brief, stand-up meetings to discuss one particular aspect of the project. You must know what work is being done on your project at all.

4. *Project Reviews.* Project reviews are team meetings to review your project at key milestones established at

your orientation meeting. Other staff with quality control responsibility for your project should also attend these meetings. The purpose is to see that the project's goals are being realized in terms of schedules, budget, and quality.

DON'T LET THAT BUDGET UNRAVEL!

"Don't fool yourself."
—Scott Braley, Vice President, Heery International, on the subject of budgeting

Scott Braley, Vice President of Heery International, shares his insights on ways to avoid a creeping budget. As a start-up firm the last thing you can afford is the budget that continually grows out of proportion to its original estimation. This is the fastest way to lose a repeat customer—your first projects must be delivered on time and within (or even under) budget!

First, let's define "creeping." Creeping is the slow erosion of the design fee budget by those small extras that don't seem to do much harm individually but that, when added up, amount to a blown budget. To avoid creeping budgets, Braley offers the following advice:

Set realistic initial budgets. Don't fool yourself. Make initial budget allocations compatible with the scope of work expected.

Include a contingency plan. Don't be too optimistic. Recognize that there are going to be unforeseen conditions and minor changes for which you can't request additional compensation. Plan for them. We suggest 5% of total fee.

Talk man-hours and fee dollars. Don't focus on only one. Advise all team members of both the man-hours and dollars allocated for their tasks. Insist they plan their work to complete it within both budgets.

Make candid percent-complete estimates. Don't rely on job-cost reports. Require each discipline to candidly advise you of percent complete. Double-check their estimates yourself. We suggest checking at every "additional 10% complete" milestone.

Use trend analysis. Don't depend on today's status; look ahead.

Consider "what if" options based on current or revised staffing, schedule, design objectives, quality requirements, and client expectations.

Take corrective action immediately. Don't think the problem will correct itself. Take corrective action at the first sign of trouble.

Revisit the project plan. Don't believe the initial work plan will suffice for the entire project. Periodically revisit the work plan. We suggest review and updating at every 20% complete. Keep the level of detail consistent. Don't be disproportionate. Make sure all disciplines have a consistent level of detail and volume of material to be included in the final documents.

Start only what you can finish. Don't overestimate what you can get done. Prepare a work plan. Be candid about what it will take to finish the tasks. If you can't complete within budget, don't start. If you've started drawings or specifications which can't be completed within budget, find an alternative way to complete them.

Have a strict additional services procedure. Don't give away services. Establish an additional services review and approval procedure. Inform all team members that there will be no compensation for additional services performed without your prior approval.

Following is a "get tough" checklist you should use to ensure that your project delivery method meets the client's needs.

Get Tough Checklist

1. For every project write a list of assumptions about what the client's expectations really are.
2. Meet with the client to clarify which of the assumptions are correct and which are not, especially assumptions pertaining to the schedule and budget.
3. After clarifying all assumptions, communicate them to your team so they will clearly understand their role in performing for the client.
4. Build into your schedule/budget a 90% factor to allow for unexpected problems. In other words, plan to finish 90% early and 90% under budget, to allow leeway for changes and other unexpected problems.
5. Allow sufficient time to implement changes after every review of the schedule and budget.

6. Recognize that there will be, on every project you have, some slippage—within the firm, the review agency, the client. Explain to the client that there are always some changes on a project.

7. Plan for team member changes, on your own and your client's team.

8. Plan for massive financial changes—could the client refinance the project if necessary?

9. Establish a team center in the office where the group can meet physically, where you can leave progress, status, and changes reports.

10. Have a "To do" list for every project that clearly lists what needs to get done for each task.

11. Set weekly, biweekly, and/or monthly meetings with your clients to review project progress.

12. Establish a time to call your clients each week so that you understand where your clients are moving and so that you are not interrupted by unnecessary client calls when you are otherwise unprepared.

All of the above are ways to take charge of your projects—to get tough. Remember that today's clients want leadership, someone to take charge and get the job done right.

TEST YOUR PROJECT MANAGEMENT CHARACTERISTICS

Take the following test, and see how you score on the project management continuum.

1. *Decisiveness.* You solicit information from team members and collect data from all appropriate sources, but ultimately are prepared to make a decision and stick with it. Once decisions are made, you follow through.

2. *Reliability.* You make realistic commitments, and stick to them. When you say yes, you can be counted on.

3. *Pragmatism.* You know what is achievable, and what is not. You and your team members establish realistic goals. You do not build false expectations.

4. *Organizational Ability.* You not only plan your pro-

ject, but also plan your team's and your own activities. You are prepared and are situated so that you work both efficiently and effectively.

5. *Goal-orientation.* You never begin a project or task without knowing what the final outcome and expectations are. You always establish a goal and work to achieve it.

6. *Ability Take Ownership.* When you begin a project, you act as it you own the project and you and your team members own the firm providing the services. You are fully accountable.

7. *Stability.* You don't have wide mood swings and erratic behavior. You can be counted on to be true to a pattern and predictable in a positive sense.

8. *Communication Skills.* You work hard to keep a team informed. When referring to you, they would say you were on the side of "overcommunicating" rather than "undercommunicating."

9. *Delegation.* You select the appropriate resources to get the job done. You would rather control and achieve than complete every task yourself.

10. *Ability to Motivate.* You create an environment in your firm where your people are encouraged to excel. You find out what people are strong at, and you assign them work that challenges their limitations. When people work with you, they are motivated.

How Do You Rate?

Give yourself 1 point for each "yes" answer to the above.

8–10: You are a good manager, and if you consistently answer "yes" to these questions you are on your road to a successful practice.

6–8: You have the foundation on which to build great managerial skills, and with hard work and diligent self-improvement, you will be a good manager. Work on consistency.

5 or Fewer: You may have the interest and the inclination, but you are not yet exercising your full management potential. Invest considerable time and energy in improving your management skills and you will be successful.

21 A BEGINNER'S GUIDE TO USING CONSULTANTS

"Delegation is a good thing—but it doesn't mean abdication"
—Michael J. Kami, Trigger Points

WHEN TO USE A CONSULTANT

There comes a time in any organization when you must deal with the hiring of specialized consultants to assist you in your business functions. This is especially and immediately true for the smaller, one to three person, firm, which needs the advice but cannot afford full-time staff to perform accounting, spec writing, marketing planning, and other such tasks. The first thing to understand is to WATCH OUT! There are a lot of consultants out there promising the world and delivering next to nothing. In addition, consultants are not always a cure-all for solving your problems and improving your organization. They can only make recommendations to you. Only you have the power to act within your organization, or to take their advice.

Basically, consultants and subconsultants should meet all of the following criteria before being hired:

- *The specialized expertise is not available in-house.*
- *Time is of the essence.* Your in-house staff cannot accomplish the assignment within the required time frame.
- *You need a different perspective.* Ask yourself the following question: "If a client was paying for this project, would we add a sub to our team?" If the answer is "yes," using a consultant will usually prove beneficial.

Use the following evaluation checklist to be sure you're choosing the right consultant for the right job.

1. Are the professionals with previous relevant experience still with the consultant firm, and will they be assigned to your project?
2. Does the client know the proposed consultant?
3. Does the consultant have experience in the project type *and* client type?
4. Does the consultant have prior working experience with your firm?
5. Is the consultant's proposed fee range competitive?
6. Will the consultant give you an exclusive agreement to pursue the project and work only with your firm?
7. Are there any special considerations such as MBE (Minority Business Enterprise), WBE (Women's Business Enterprise), Small Business, or other intangibles?
8. Does the consultant have any conflicts of interest—either actual or perceived?

Be a skeptic when it comes to believing consultants will give you what you are seeking. Give them as much scrutiny as your clients give you. Here's a list of specific questions to ask potential consultants before you hire one.

- *Why did you go into consulting and out of the mainstream of practice?* Watch for cases of the old saying: "Those who can, do; those who can't, teach."
- *Which firms have you consulted for?* Develop a profile of each potential consultant's clients and assignments. Is the experience profiled generic, or does it represent a range of sizes and special requirements.
- *How long have you been in practice as a consultant?* Look for an endurance and experience level covering several economic cycles.
- *Do you have all the answers as soon as you walk through the door?* If they do, send them back out; they haven't even heard the questions.
- *Are you known to the professional associations?* Do they endorse their credibility and what they have to say?
- *What's your level of creativity?* Do they challenge you

and ask hard questions and are they prepared to suggest nontraditional tactics?

- *Are you published?* Have they written any books or articles? Does the writing challenge your assumptions?
- *How many years did you spend in the trenches?* What range of positions did they hold? How successful were the firms and projects they managed?

The recession has left a lot of good people in the street, but the best ones are still working. Beware. It's too easy to hang out a consulting shingle in times like these.

HEAR IT FROM THE HORSE'S MOUTH!

Consultant Richard Burns, President of the GNU Group, provides excellent advice from the consultant's perspective based on his successful involvement in consulting for over 20 years with dozens of design firms.

Recognize that you're now the person in the selection position. You have a tremendous number of options. It's equivalent to describing the challenges of getting someone to buy your services.

What you're buying can be perceived as a parity service or product. Hence the selection process must be one of sorting out one consultant over the others.

This breaks down into two basic considerations: expectations and credentials. What are their credentials and is there credibility behind what they say they're going to be able to do for you? Can they prove their past effectiveness? Most important, what do you expect from the consultant?

Recognize the importance of chemistry. The success of everyone's ability to deal with each other depends upon it.

Ask yourself some basic questions. That's the straightforward way to go about this. Question one should be your expectations.

Work backwards. Establish the criteria against which to judge the success of the relationship first. This can be measured in terms of the creativity of the solutions, innovation of the solutions, predictability of the solutions, or the personality of the people.

Quality of the service can be measured in various ways. It can be measured in terms of hassle factor, attentiveness, efficiency, and eventually price. The rules are simple: it's your criteria.

Establish the pricing parameters up front. This is because price is the issue that ultimately kills most consulting relationships. Include in your discussions: meeting the price, coming in under budget, and how the consultant deals with changes and charges for extras and reimbursables.

Don't overlook the effectiveness of the solution. What is the long-term value? The viability of the answer? Does it solve the problem? How valuable is it to you? That's value pricing.

You need to understand the way consultants work. All consultants have their own personal style. You can get people who can give you anything from very definitive prescriptive answers, to options, to broad generalizations, to the process becoming a product in and of itself. Know what you are buying.

Define the duration of the relationship. Is it a one-time situation, or is it ongoing? This factor alone may affect your answers to the other questions.

Now check the references. Consider how (and if) they relate to your expectations.

BENEFITS OF REPEAT CONSULTANTS

Many design firm owners report that the use of the same consultants on a continuing basis saves time, money, aggravation, and man-hours. They also feel the choice relationship is one where there is a good rapport between the consultant and the project manager. Here's what one firm owner had to say. Bob Habel, Principal for Baxter Hodell Donnelly Preston Inc. (BHDP) in Cincinnati, says the key to good quality and coordination is to use the same old consultants on every job.

Habel and BHDP identified the best of their consultants, and selected a limited number of firms with whom to work. By using the same consultants on multiple projects, the mid-sized architectural firm has improved engineering quality, co-ordination, client satisfaction, and project profits.

Habel says that BHDP project managers have conducted work sessions with the consultants to develop a common and consistent vocabulary. He says that by becoming very specific with terms and design vocabulary, such as exact sprinkler head types and hardware selections, architects and engineers have become much more efficient.

Because a project manager spends relatively more time with consultants and the clients than with the individual project team members, this "inherent understanding" of what is wanted goes a long way toward ensuring project success.

Finally, Habel notes that because the learning curve is already behind them, BHDP project managers can spend more time and effort on client satisfaction, and an integrated, all disciplines concentration on a total quality project management.

HOW AND WHEN TO USE MARKETING CONSULTANTS

Often, design firms look to outside marketing consultants to supplement their in-house marketing capabilities. Each firm's situation is unique, however, so identifying the type of help needed, and matching it with the correct type of marketing consultant is a critical first step.

You also need to consider your own marketing experience level when selecting an outside consulting firm. Firms with well-developed marketing programs will generally need to contract for outside activities. Firms with the lowest level of marketing experience will simply require training from outside consultants. Firms in the middle range will require consultants that can provide planning resources.

When consultants work primarily with a firm's principals, the assignments are generally strategic (the "why" of marketing). When working with technical managers, the consulting assignment focuses on skills development (i.e., client presentations, client relations). When working with the firm's marketing staff, the assignments are implementation-oriented, and include assistance with brochures, publicity, and marketing database development. Determine which kind of consulting you require before you sign a contract.

The most common types of assistance that design firms require include:

Strategic Planning. An outside perspective is helpful for a number of reasons: wider views of the marketplace, objective assessment of the firm's capabilities, facilitated planning with reduced in-house political pressures, a more efficient planning process, and realistic budgeting and planning of the marketing implementation program.

Consultation. Firm principals can benefit from regular and long-term input from seasoned marketing consultants, who can help them monitor their market focus, improve marketing skills, gain access to additional marketing opportunities, develop strategies and action plans for pursuit of specific projects, and identify external trends and make the marketing operational adjustments needed to deal with those trends.

Organizational Development. Consultants can help identify the capabilities and training needs of management and staff. In-house training programs can be developed and delivered to in-house staff to meet those needs.

Publicity. Outside public relations specialists can have a major impact on the public awareness of the firm. These specialists can define a firm's features and help craft them into an image. They can pinpoint the most effective media to deliver the message, provide access to the media, and present the activities of the firm in a manner that's appealing to editors and subscribers.

Public Relations. In addition to publicity, relations with the firm's public can be extended through participation in special events such as project milestones (groundbreaking, topping out ceremonies, etc.), participation in conferences and tradeshows, open houses, anniversary celebrations, and so on. Specialists who can plan such events, help stage them, and train in-house personnel to do the same are another valuable outside resource.

Market Research. Outside research organizations can provide assessments of new geographical markets, new services, general preferences of those who buy professional services, clients' perception of the firm and its competition, and the firm's overall image.

Communications Tools. The tools that a firm develops to communicate to its clients, target markets, consultants, public agency staff, and contemporaries require other experts. These tools may include corporate identity systems (logo, letterhead, etc.), brochures and annual reports, newsletters, article reprints, tradeshow exhibits, photography, and video. Outside specialists exist for each of these tools.

When selecting consultants, be sure they understand your firm's professional practice area, know the local market, have experience with the particular type of assignment, and can supply references.

Frank Barrett, CEO of the Barrett Consulting Group, shares his insight on hiring and utilizing a marketing consultant.

Use the same basic process that your clients use. Establish selection process where you invite several firms to submit proposals and then hold interviews in their offices.

Examine their qualities. Do they ask the right questions, such as "What are you trying to accomplish?" Do they listen and are they responsive? Are the same qualities reflected in their staff? Will they help you through the process with your own staff by acting as facilitator?

Recognize that there are risks. It's like a crapshoot, but the amount of risk depends upon what you're looking for. If it's something tangible, like a brochure, you can contact the firms that have the best looking ones in a format that fits your needs, and then find out who did their work. Then the trick is being able to work with that consultant.

Involve your staff. This is particularly true if it's a marketing issue. While you can't get everyone involved in each and every meeting, make sure you have involvement from each of the parties that serves a specific market. There are not only different markets, but different cultures.

Don't be afraid to spend the dollars. Establish a budget up front, and adhere to it. Work with the consultant in getting what you want within that budget, not by increasing the budget. Have a contingency plan that will allow you to add the bells and whistles that separate your brochure or marketing piece from the others.

Remember, it's a relationship. Like any relationship, it's a matter of trust. Make sure you're comfortable with the players before you say "I do."

GETTING THE MOST OUT OF YOUR ACCOUNTANT

Your financial status may only be as good as your accountant—so watch your step in hiring an accountant. What is a good accountant? Someone who is geared toward improving your net worth and your profits, the most valuable resources you'll create. You need someone to confide in about your plans, not just a "yes man" but someone who will challenge your ideas and push you to better ones.

Following is a list of criteria by which to measure a potential accountant or accounting firm:

1. Hire an accountant who has a good understanding of the design business. As was stated previously in the section on banking, design businesses differ significantly from most service businesses and from manufacturing or inventory-based businesses. For this reason be sure your accountant has previous experience with four or five other design firms. You cannot afford to be someone's learning curve project. (The *Professional Services Management Journal* publishes an annual list of recommended accountants, which can be obtained by contacting *PSMJ* at 10 Midland Avenue, Newton, MA 02158.)

2. If you are contracting the services of an accounting firm, be sure that you will get the principal's involvement in your work. Just as your clients will prefer you, the principal, to be involved in their projects, you should expect the same from your accounting firm.

3. Ask the accountant if he or she is knowledgeable in both tax and business strategy. Do not hire an accountant who can only fill out your forms for you—and there are plenty out there who will do only that. Look for an accountant who can act as your advisor on business decisions.

4. The accountant should understand your tax situation and banking relationships within the local area. Most importantly, an accountant should be from your geo-

graphic region, in order to fully understand the nuances of specific banking and tax regulations.

5. Hire an accountant whose business is located nearby. If your accountant is one or two hours away, you won't seek advice as often as you should.

6. The accountant should be willing to visit you in your business once a quarter—this is essential in gaining a true understanding of your management procedures.

7. Make friends with your accountant. Having a personal relationship helps ensure that they are concerned about the progress of your business. You don't want to be considered "just another client."

8. Make sure the accountant/accounting firm is not overburdened with to the extent that you get short shrift. Be certain the staff is competent, that they can handle your work expeditiously, and that they respond swiftly when you call.

WHEN TO HIRE OUTSIDE SPEC WRITERS

As a start-up firm, you have two choices for preparing specifications—you can either prepare them yourself or contract the services of an outside specifications writer.

Frankly, no one can produce better specifications than the project team member who designed or selected the item being specified. This person knows the design intent, and knows the most about how the item will fit into the overall project. However, there are times when you must use an outside specifications writer, as in the following cases:

- You or your project team members do not have the time to do a first-rate job yourself.
- You or your team members do not have the special expertise required for a particular item, system, or installation.
- You have had problems with specifications prepared by your team in the past.

When you chose to use an outside specifications writer, look for the following:

1. Hire only individuals who are members of the Con-

struction Specifications Institute (CSI), as well as being a Certified Construction Specifier (CCS).

2. Ask for references and lists of previous similar projects.

3. Verify the writer's other time and project commitments.

4. Find out how long the person has been writing specifications, and how long he or she has been CCS certified. Ask whether he or she is a registered professional architect, engineer, or other professional.

5. Allow (or require) the specifications writer to work in your offices with your project team.

Finally, remember that because you will seal the drawings and specifications, you—*not the specifications writer*—are liable for the quality of the work. Given their relatively low fee compared to total project fee, most specifications writers cannot and will not assume professional liability for specifications they prepare. However, if the writer is a registered professional, you may have a better case for shared liability and responsibility. To protect your liability, consider including some liability requirements in your contract with the specifications writer.

SELECTING PROFESSIONAL TEMPS

Professional service firms occasionally face client pressures to increase services for a fixed period. The prevailing answer to this apparent paradox is to use a professional temporary service agency. This new breed of temporary, professional placement agency matches specialized experts and sophisticated technical candidates with exact job requirements. And the scores of layoffs in the design field have left thousands of qualified professionals looking for work. Learn how and when to take advantage of these new agencies.

If you have a busy period and are considering hiring temporary professionals, be sure to choose an agency that:

Specializes in your professional field.

Has sales coordinators that are familiar with your profession.

Offers project planning services to help coordinate manpower requirements of your project.

Will interview, screen, and recommend several candidates.

You should also get answers to the following questions, to determine if the agency meets your firm's specific needs:

Does the agency assist in the development of a job description?

How much lead time will be required to find an appropriate candidate?

Does the agency maintain a database of candidates?

How are references and backgrounds verified?

The kind of temporary professional placement agency to seek is one that will be a partner in planning your staff needs. The agency should understand your firm's internal capabilities, limits, and resources, so as to best recommend those candidates who will truly meet your firm's needs.

Below are some important points to consider when using a temp agency:

- They cannot read your mind! Clearly communicate your project requirements, cost limitations, and schedule.
- Don't expect the cost per hour to be less than that of permanent staff (although significant savings are realized when adjusted for improved efficiency, fringe benefits, employment taxes, and administrative overhead).
- Quality is a perceived issue. Details concerning qualifications and professional background will set the quality level you'll receive.
- Allow enough time. Pressuring an agency for immediate turnaround can affect its ability to address your specific requirements.

Proper use of a temporary agency can be an important tool in improving service while reducing personnel costs.

22

THEN THERE'S THE MATTER OF GETTING PAID

"The difference between profit and loss on a project depends on the time it takes to get paid." —*Anonymous*

PLANNING FOR FEE COLLECTION

Obviously all the great work and project management in the world will get you nowhere unless you can collect your fees. This section is devoted to outlining the process of getting paid. Not getting paid can be the end of the line for any design firm—so make sure you build into your contract a very structured process for collecting your fees. This process requires constant attention; therefore it is best to outline a firm policy on fee collection while you are setting up your firm.

Here are a few tips for collecting your fees on time.

First, all accounts receivable calls should be made by one individual. Preferably this is not the designer or project manager. If you have only one administrative staff member, designate that person as the accounts receivable caller. *Here are the reasons why*:

1. With only one person making accounts receivable calls, clients are not subject to more than a single call in a short period over one outstanding invoice. It also builds the relationship. Misunderstandings and ill-feelings can be avoided by forging a personal relationship with the client's accounts payable person. This also guarantees

that at least one call will be made because there will be no dispute as to who is making the call.

2. It communicates professionalism. The reason you make an accounts receivable call is to remind the client of his or her debt and to secure payment. Small talk is minimalized and time saved if you assign one individual, preferably not someone who has worked on the project in the past.

3. Having a person call who is not related to the project focuses attention on what should be paid, rather than on percentage of completion. If the individual calling the client knows nothing about the past project, there need be no conversation about how much work has been completed and whether payment is justified.

4. The accounts receivable person can anticipate excuses and be ready to counter them. A trained collections person knows all the usual excuses and can respond to them in such a manner as to secure payment.

Here are a few standard excuses. Study them and be ready for them:

1. *The check is in the mail.* Great. Ask for the mailing date so you can immediately notify the client if the check does not arrive within a reasonable time period.

2. *The invoice was given to someone else.* Find out precisely whose approval is needed for payment and who authorizes that checks be written. Call those people immediately.

3. *The bill was not received.* Fax them another copy right away!

4. *We have no money.* Try to negotiate a partial payment. Arrange a payment schedule for the balance. Stop all work until you know exactly when you're getting paid.

Don't extend credit and payment time—design firms all too often develop a reputation for being "the cheapest lending institutions in town." Don't let your firm be one of them!

ARE YOU READY WITH AN ANSWER?

Most prime contractors tell their consultants, "You'll get paid when I get paid," a fact of life in the design industry. What's your response? Have you thought this out in advance? When you work as a consultant, you can protect yourself from collections problems by following these suggestions:

1. Negotiate a retainer up front to cover the cost of carrying invoiced amounts until your prime has funds to pay you regularly. If a retainer is not possible, get agreement that your first invoices will be "front-end loaded" to accelerate cash flow on your project.

2. Find out when the prime plans to submit invoices to the client. Develop a schedule that ensures that invoices are submitted monthly.

3. Submit your invoices to the prime at least seven days before the prime is scheduled to invoice the client.

4. Submit separate invoices for basic professional services, additional professional services, and reimbursable expenses.

5. Add provisions to your contract that require the prime to bill promptly and to include your invoices, or your invoiced amounts, with each prime invoice.

6. Also add contract provisions that you will be paid within five days of the prime's receipt of payment from the client.

Don't wait a day longer for payments than you have to.

Here are some additional tips to help you make sure you get paid:

1. Ask before you contract work if your client has financing in place for the project or at least for your phase of the project.

2. Review your firm's standard invoice format with your client to make sure there are no problems with the details.

3. Ask for the name of a contact for your financial department in their accounting department.

4. Check and see if the invoice should be addressed in any special way and to the attention of any special person.

5. Don't delay any billings. A delayed billing usually indicates a problem not being addressed.

6. When the project schedule and budget are prepared, develop a cash flow plan for your client, present it, and ask if there are any problems.

7. Utilize your accounting department's standard collection procedures: telephone calls, statements, and letters.

8. Review your account status at project/client meetings and secure commitments for payment.

9. Ask for retainers and apply the retainer to the last invoice.

The mark of a professional is getting paid for services rendered. On a separate sheet of paper, list five things you could do today to improve your collections process.

23 TACKLING THE FEDS

"...Don't say in Power what you say in Opposition;
if you do, you only have to carry out what the other fellows
have found impossible."—*John Galsworthy,* Maid in Waiting, *1931*

DOING WORK WITH THE FEDERAL GOVERNMENT

In evaluating your marketing possibilities, you may be considering whether or not to embark on public sector projects. Here's a simple do-it-yourself checklist to help you evaluate your options and make your decision:

1. Assess the government contracting environment.
2. Do you understand the general nature and provisions of the Brooks Bill?
3. Are you familiar with the nuances of the financial system controls and record keeping that may be required to pass a government audit?
4. Are you willing to make an attitude adjustment, if necessary, to work within the "government" system?
5. Assess the market opportunities.
6. Do you understand the nature and importance of indefinite delivery or open-end contracts?
7. Are you willing to take a back seat as a subconsultant?
8. Have you targeted a specific agency based on your firm's capabilities, or are you thinking in terms of a shotgun approach?
9. Assess your capability to capture the opportunities.
10. What is your marketing style? Is it more than just reactive?

11. Do you have staying power and are you willing to make a long-term marketing investment?

12. Do you understand the nuances of the Standard Forms 254 and 255?

13. What's your firm's culture flexibility ratio?

MANAGING PUBLIC-SECTOR PROJECTS

About to manage your first public-sector project, but overwhelmed by the rules and regulations that came with the contract? Don't panic. Here's a common sense approach that will see you through: Understand the totality of the project. This includes the program the project supports, its genesis, its funding, its mission, and its relationship to other projects. Your marketing people probably understand this; make sure you do too. Understand and adhere to the chain of command. There are many players, with many interests. Make sure you determine the individual that issues the orders. Once established, never end run.

Organize information. There's an enormous amount of information inherent in the building process itself, only to be impacted by an equally enormous amount of bureaucracy. Look to technology to give you a hand. If it's a federal project, the Construction Criteria Base published on CD-ROM by the National Institute of Building Sciences is an important tool. It contains design criteria, standard drawings and specifications, and a host of other essential information, including sections of the Federal Acquisitions Regulations (FAR). You'll also need an automated project management program. Choose carefully as there are many on the market. Make sure the one you choose suits your client's needs, as well as your own.

Think in terms of systems. Again, use automation and look at totality. An example, think cost engineering, not just cost estimating. This also applies to your automated project management program. Think in terms of resource management and control: cost and time. And don't forget people. They're your most important resource, and the key to your success. Communicate and care. If you don't understand why you're doing something, then stop and ask. If you have a design problem, talk about it and work it out. Above all, remember that it's a partnership between you and the client, and it's the people skills and enhanced customer care that will see you through.

OPPORTUNITIES IN THE FEDERAL BUDGET

What's 8½ x 11 inches, 2¼ inches thick, weighs 6 pounds, and has a red, white, and blue cover? No, it's not a laptop computer on Amtrak; it's another moving train, the 1993 Federal Budget. Some opportunities within its 1,653 pages:

Defense. Lots of dollars for pollution abatement and environmental restoration, closing bases, maintaining and repairing existing assets, and improving the family housing stock. Missing are the big ticket design projects.

Commerce. Limited opportunities in the United States, especially since it takes away $100 million in funding for the Economic Development Administration. Numerous opportunities through the International Trade Administration and the Consortia of American Businesses in Eastern Europe.

Energy. $5.5 billion, or one-fourth of the Energy Department budget of $19.4 billion, is for management and cleanup of contaminated waste. Also $181 million for solar energy research and $650 million for the Supercollider.

EPA. Nearly $2.7 billion of the $7 billion total goes for day-to-day agency operations. $1.75 billion for the removal of toxic waste.

Health and Human Services. Opportunities may be limited, since all but 5% of the $585.2 billion goes for entitlement programs including Social Security, Medicaid, and Aid to Families with Dependent Children. Look for laboratories and other research facilities in the $2.1 billion dedicated to combating AIDS.

HUD. The focus is on homeownership. Nearly $3 billion for the HOPE program, including $1 billion to help residents of public housing and privately owned, government subsidized housing become owners.

Justice. $11.3 billion budget, with $353 million to expand the federal prison system.

State. $140 million for a new embassy in Moscow. Watch for emerging opportunities as aid priorities shift.

Transportation. $33.7 billion budget with increases in aviation and highway spending on top of the November highway–mass transit bill. Watch out! Defense contractors and technology companies have discovered this one.

Note: These figures were compiled in 1993 and meant only as estimates. As more specific legislation is passed, budgets will change.

LONG-TERM DEFENSE OUTLOOK

Army, Navy, and Air Force have historically held the lion's share of federal government opportunities for design firms. With the downturn in defense spending, here's what's in store:

NAVFAC

Construction in Support of Base Closures. Anticipate $531 million in FY 93 and $491 million in FY 94 to support the ripple effect of Navy and Marine Corps base closure actions.

Integration of Environmental Cleanup, Real Estate, and Disposal in Support of Base Closures. Closure and realignment actions must start in 1992 and be completed by 1998. Environmental restoration, however, may take as long as ten years.

Environmental Programs. Over $500 million has been invested in the Navy's Installation Restoration Program. Look for over $3 billion more to complete the job. Not counting the 24 NPL sites (EPA's National Priorities List), there are more than 2,000 sites at 240 installations under investigation.

Family Housing. There's a 73,000 unit inventory with an average age of 30 years and a validated repair and improvement backlog of $1.8 billion. There's also a projected shortage of 35,000 units by 1997.

More Public Works Centers. Super-base organizations that cover more than one installation. Look for new ones in

Washington, DC and Jacksonville, FL in FY 93 and Charleston, SC in FY 94. Their mission, like public works departments at all other installations: take care of what's already there.

Less Engineering Field Divisions. Look for consolidations on the east and west coasts. Stateside survivors will be LANTDIV in Norfolk, SOUTHDIV in Charleston, and SWDIV in San Diego. Philadelphia and San Bruno remain as satellite operations.

The above analysis was compiled by Richard Bilden, former editor of the *Professional Services Management Journal.*

In addition to the general laws, there are opportunities within each government project that you can capitalize on. The following is a partial listing of nontraditional services that government agencies can procure through contract, also prepared by Richard Bilden.

Budget preparation.

Reorganization and planning activities.

Analyses, feasibility studies, and strategy options for policy development.

Development of regulations.

Evaluation of another contractor's performance.

Strategic acquisition planning.

Assistance in contract management.

Technical evaluation of contract proposals.

Development of statements of work.

Arbitration or alternative dispute resolution.

Corps of Engineers

Revitalization of Enduring Installations. Only putting dollars into critical health, safety, and environmental projects and taking care of existing infrastructure at bases that are not affected by base closure. Dollars for new construction: only $369 million in FY 93, of which $185 million is for chemical demilitarization.

Reduced Inventory. The Army plans to dispose of 35,535 million square feet of facilities from FY 92 to FY 96, and plans to demolish one square foot of temporary facilities for every square foot of new construction.

Strong Civil Works Program. Over $3.7 billion in FY 93 budget for nationwide water resources development and management and environmental restoration of everything from design to construction to maintenance and operations. Several long-term projects will continue into the year 2000.

Support for Other Agencies. Increased support to the Department of Energy and EPA for environmental program management. Also support to developing nations in Eastern and Central Europe, Latin America, Southwestern Asia, and the Pacific.

AIR FORCE

New Name, Organizational Structure, Mission, and Operational Concept. The old Air Force Engineering and Services organization is now the Air Force Civil Engineer, or AF/CE. In addition to traditional base development and operations, housing and environmental protection, they've picked up the responsibilities for explosive ordnance disposal, disaster preparedness, and air base operability. Gone are nonengineering services (billeting, food services, etc).

Environmental Everything. The new Air Force Center for Environmental Excellence, or AFCEE, at Brooks AFB, Texas is the key to where the Air Force is placing its emphasis. AFCEE will provide in-house and contractor support for everything environmental from planning and design for pollution prevention to environmental impact analysis to construction management for hazardous waste cleanup for the Air Force Installation Restoration Program.

GET SMART ON INTELLIGENT VEHICLE HIGHWAY SYSTEMS

What's an IVHS? It's a mission-oriented program sparked by the Intermodel Surface Transportation Efficiency Act of 1991 (ISTEA) that brings opportunities far beyond the traditional transportation planning and highway design project.

What will the program do? Look at IVHS as the redirection of Aerospace and Defense technologies and energies to solving transportation problems. Instead of putting someone on the moon, we're going to move people across town and around our cities.

What are the technologies? Advanced concepts in communication, navigation, and information systems applied to highway safety, traffic congestion, and environmental concerns.

Who are the players? DOT agencies including FHWA, state and local transportation agencies, universities, and a wide assortment of private sector participants. There's also IVHS America, a nonprofit educational and scientific association that serves as a technical clearinghouse and advisor to DOT.

How is it funded? Congress has already authorized $600 million over the next six years. Included is a corridors program to provide operational tests under real world conditions. Priority corridors include the Northeast/I-95, Chicago, Houston, and Southern California.

Are there other provisions? Yes, including a fully automated prototype highway and vehicle system that's to be operational by 1997. The ultimate goal is full deployment of proven IVHS technologies throughout the United States.

What are the business opportunities? There will be a major focus on contract awards to diverse teams of public, private, and academic consortia. IBM, EDS, and TRW may be experts in technology and systems integration, but they need help on civil engineering, environmental planning, and infrastructure management. Don't abdicate your bread and butter skills to the universities and government laboratories.

How do you become a player? Begin by sending for an executive summary of the program's Strategic Plan. Contact IVHS America, 1776 Massachusetts Avenue, NW, Suite 510, Washington, DC 20036-1993, (202) 857-1202. Also ask for their annual report. Then think consulting, stake out your niche, and begin to develop your strategic plan.

PILOT PROJECTS

Start-up firms with little experience in government work may have a disadvantage, but there are ways in which you can gain access to experience. One such way is to participate in pilot projects. Many government and public entities sponsor projects that enable firms to gain experience in a new arena.

For example, water districts hire landscape architects to design demonstration gardens, which may focus on issues such as drought-tolerant plant materials and alternative irrigation systems. Several local government entities in Japan sponsor development projects in which they mandate international participation. Participating in these projects can help in establishing your firm as an expert in a new project type and are a paid means of gaining exposure.

Review your list of targeted, potential client organizations. Contact decision-makers to determine if they are planning any pilot projects and/or promote the idea within the organization. In some cases, you may be able to create a project for your firm.

IT'S NOT ALLOWED

When you have to negotiate a public sector contract realize that the federal, state, and most local negotiators will single out certain actual cost items and disallow them from your calculation of overhead rate. Many large private corporations are now using the same approach to negotiate lower design fees.

The most frequently sighted targets include:

Interest expenses.
Company-owned or leased automobile expenses.
Charitable contributions.
Entertainment.
Advertising or promotional material expenses.
Bad debts and uncollected receivables.
Marketing and business development costs.

Travel costs in excess of federal, state, or local per diem rates.

Payments to team members who are on leave of absence or sabbatical.

Know your firm's costs for these items before beginning any negotiation. And be sure to find out what costs you can charge for and which ones are not chargeable—before you even bid on the project.

24 LIMITING YOUR LIABILITY

"The art of being wise is the art of knowing what to overlook."
—*William James*, The Principles of Psychology, *1890*

As long as you provide the opportunity to negotiate a limitation of liability clause, and as long as your contract language is unambiguous, you can limit your acceptance of liability in a contract, regardless of whether or not you specifically discussed the term with the client.

California's superior court recently ruled in a landmark case (Markborough vs. Glenn) that as long as each party "is dealing in an arm's length transaction with an opportunity to accept, reject, or modify the terms of the agreement," the clause will be valid, even if the limitation of liability appears in the contract as standard boilerplate language and was not specifically discussed.

The client (Markborough) agreed, whether knowingly or simply because it failed to read the contract, to assume the risk of most of the economic loss that might result from Glenn's (the design professional's) negligence. "There is no justification for allowing Markborough to shift this loss to Glenn which neither agreed to assume it nor was compensated for such assumption."

While design professionals tow in a significant win, they must realize the implications of the decision: there must be an opportunity to negotiate the clause and the client must be in a position to delete or amend the clause.

It would also be prudent, according to Michael B. Murphy of Seversen & Werson (the law firm in San Francisco that filed the brief), for "Design professionals to keep records of instances where the proposed limitation of liability clause was challenged by a client and eliminated for an additional fee. These records could arguably be relied upon as evidence that the design professional is receptive to negotiating the clause as part of his or her business practice."

Here are some specific "To Do" solutions for professional liability:

1. Obtain per project insurance, and pass the cost on to the client.
2. Indemnify yourself in the contract from future liability by passing liability on to the seller/buyer.
3. Talk to clients about the issue in advance.
4. Evaluate stability of the carrier you choose.
5. Evaluate claims procedure of your carrier.
6. Find out qualifications of whoever will defend your claim.
7. Redo internal forms such as telecon memos.
8. Turn down work!
9. Have clients pay for all legal defense.
10. Have contractor review your drawings and specifications and sign off on them.
11. Go bare!
12. Don't switch carriers just because of the price!
13. Tighten the language of your contracts.
14. Hire only licensed project managers.
15. Go back to clients to find out about problems early.
16. Buy all firm's insurance from one carrier.
17. Group several firms under one policy.
18. Find out a carrier's capital base for supporting premiums.
19. Always address liability in negotiations.
20. Deal only with brokers who specialize in A/E insurance.
21. Raise deductible to three years' worth of profits.
22. Move firm away from pollution liability projects.
23. Devise and use a checklist for researching preexisting potential problems.
24. Assess a carrier's loss prevention program.
25. Ask for a list of A/E's insured by a carrier.
26. Put your details on CADD and secure them so they cannot be changed without your input.
27. Check out the track record of clients and their financial credit—how often have they sued? Do they have in-house counsel?

28. Avoid clients who use bidding for selection.
29. Avoid nontraditional approaches to design work.
30. Avoid equity positions in projects.
31. Be certain to operate legally in the state where the project is located.
32. Don't do projects outside your expertise.
33. Keep clients happy—happy clients don't sue.
34. Don't push contractors to make up schedule time.
35. Insist on construction phase services as part of every project.
36. Use standard form agreements.
37. Detail your specific scope of services for every job.
38. Detail a precise method to calculate the fee—avoids early dispute.
39. Always retain ownership and control of drawings and specifications!
40. Always delineate specific owner's responsibilities and schedule for delivery.
41. Never sign indemnification agreements, guarantees, and warranties.
42. Never be paid according to "upon completion of" clauses.
43. Keep objective project records—just facts, not opinions.
44. Keep current with billings and collections.
45. Do results-oriented billing detailing elaborately all effort.
46. Involve all of your people in loss prevention.
47. Minimize assets held in the corporation.
48. Spend more time with young staff to break down the adversarial environment.
49. Put an excess fee in if a client won't limit liability.
50. Have owners agree to pass on your limit of liability to others in contracts.
51. Institute a private statute of limitations on claims between you and your client.
52. Set up a separate corporation for high-risk work.
53. If you can go bare always use consultants who are insured.
54. Deal only with legal counsel who has specific A/E experience.

55. Refuse to indemnify anyone for their risks on their work.

56. Don't do work on a purchase order basis!

57. Structure a peer review program in your area.

58. Be sure to have signed contracts on all projects.

59. Run the firm so as to disperse most assets annually.

60. Have all subconsultants contract directly with owners.

61. Find out if your insurance is on the "claims made" or "occurrence" basis and understand the difference.

62. Beware of pollution exclusions for preexisting hazardous waste materials.

63. Make a list of potential hazardous materials such as vinyl asbestos tile, sandblasting residue, coal tar roofs, electric transformers, and teach your staff to be aware of them, especially with regard to renovation work.

64. Don't perform hazardous waste work without indemnification from the client. Even the Corps of Engineers provides indemnification.

65. Before working in other states investigate specific new liability laws that bind A/E's under certain circumstances.

66. Don't volunteer help on any issue not in your contract or you will be held accountable.

67. Consider hiring an attorney on your staff to negotiate all contracts.

68. Never start work until a contract is signed, and require that all staff working on the job read the contract.

69. Limit liability to the amount of your profit.

70. Resist politically motivated work.

71. Constantly review your firm's documentation procedures to improve them.

72. State all assumptions you are making on certifications.

The DPIC Companies have recently published two good books on the subject of limiting risk in providing architectural and engineering services. You should consider reading either one in order to better understand the intricacies of risk and liability in design. They are *The Contract Guide*, DPIC's Risk Management Handbook for Architects and Engineers, by Sheila Dixon and Richard Crowell, and *Lessons in Professional Liability*, A Notebook for Design Professionals (DPIC Companies, P.O. Box DPIC, Monetery, CA 93942).

25 NETWORKING, NETWORKING, NETWORKING

"Be ruthless, and don't get caught trying to do too much by going the extra mile unless you really understand what the extra mile is all about." —*Art Capstaff, President, The Endeavor Group*

What lessons have we learned from the years of economic turmoil that beset the early 1990s? The biggest lesson has been the need to return to basics, and the source of positive work flow is not just a marketing plan or marketing function, but a more basic precursor—and that is networking.

As a design firm owner, you should assess your networking skills and activities, and honestly put a plan together, whether formal or informal, on what kinds of networking activities you are most comfortable with, and which will allow you to make personal contacts with potential clients.

WHY NETWORK?

There are many opinions for and against networking but, honestly, the most successful design firm owners not only are organized and have structured marketing plans and financial tracking systems, but more importantly, they are tremendous networkers. You can hire good accountants and marketing specialists, but networking skills are partially inborn, partially cultivated, and they are 100% motivated by the need to make contacts and to get more work. The benefits are both personal and professional, and the results of networking can be astounding.

WHY NETWORKING IS NOT A CLICHÉ

Networking, as a term, certainly has become a cliché—but when you are well known in advance, and you are known as the single point of contact in your firm who will take care of all problems, when you are responsive, when you get down and have a good personal relationship with potential clients, it only follows that you get more work.

And I take it all the way. There are some consultants out there who feel you should get to know clients to a point; beyond a certain point, however, you should be reserved. I disagree. The clients who've trusted me over the years in design firm consultations are also great friends: they are the people I ski with, I vacation with, and who trust me for advice on the design industry. In nearly every major city I visit, I have friends who are also clients, who actually call my secretary in advance of my arrival to schedule to pick me up from the airport, just to talk with me for the hour ride to the hotel! I'm not saying this to pat myself on the back, but merely to illustrate that I've made myself available to my clients not just as their consultant, but as a trusted friend. There are ways in which you can do the same.

Obviously, everyone has their own style. My style is to live, sleep, eat, and breath management trends for design professionals. It's what has driven me beyond even my own goals for success. Only you can determine what style of networking best suits your personality, but you should identify the areas in which you have the opportunity to meet clients. Even if it makes you feel a little uncomfortable, just remember, a little pain, a little gain. Discomfort is good when it pushes you into a new realm.

NURTURING PRESS CONTACTS

Don't neglect the necessity of making friends with press contacts, whether that be local press or national magazine editors you may meet face to face at trade shows. Look for people who can help you further your career, and make sure they know who you are. Remember, no one is going to call you if they do not know who you are.

Here are a few tips on how to network with press contacts. To begin with, don't expect them to know who you are. They won't. You must do specific things to let them know that ABC

Architects is here, and that this is what you do. First, send them a press release once a month. Journalists are very busy people and they are always looking for a story. They are more than happy to read up on your latest design, as long as you put it down in terms as succinct as possible. Second, limit your press release to a one-page fact sheet, and provide the basic gist of the design accomplishment, along with names, addresses, degrees, and accomplishments of involved design professionals, and the name and address of the client. Third, make it as easy as possible for them to build a story around your design.

Don't expect glory, although you may get some. Expect that out of 12 press releases a year, you may get 1, 2, or 3 stories in the local press. This may not appear to be enough of a return on the investment, but it is. And if you do your homework, you'll probably get more.

Don't view the press as an intrusion. Even when they are critical of your work, they are still talking about you. And they can be a lot more forgiving when they know who you are.

Don't hound the press! There is nothing more annoying to an editor than a firm that calls continually, simply to ask for press. You must have a genuine story on your hands, or forget it.

Nurture press contacts as deliberately as you might nurture any other important contact. If there is an opportunity to meet press contacts, attend, shake their hands, and be friendly. Don't start talking about the greatness of your firm; just let them know who you are. Follow up that meeting with a note, at which time you can briefly describe that you may have some interesting ideas for articles. You may even want to provide a few ideas based on recent projects.

The important thing is that the editor knows who you are. There is nothing better than face-to-face contact.

WHY PEOPLE HATE TO NETWORK

There are several barriers we all put up against the concept of networking, and all of them are justified. Take a look at these barriers, categorized by Frank Sonnenberg, and then look at yourself. How do you compare?

1. *Selfishness/Stubborness.* You may refuse to believe you need anyone's help or advice. You've gotten this far on your own, so who could help you? And why should you spend the extra time when you can't see an immediate reward for networking?

2. *Myopia.* You may be short-sighted, and may not understand the need for networking. This not a fault: all of us are too busy today and will find time for everything tomorrow.

3. *Shyness.* Going out and meeting people face-to-face at a local political function may make you nervous or uncomfortable. That's understandable. It is difficult to approach those whom you do not know. You do not want to leave your "comfort zone" and deal with anything unfamiliar. There are ways around this. Networking doesn't necessarily mean you have to go out and meet strangers. In fact, networking really means becoming part of a group, becoming well known to your peers. You may choose to become a golf or tennis enthusiast, and cultivate a sport interest you'll share with many of your clients. You may volunteer your services to the community in a way that is comfortable to you. There are a million ways to network, and they don't have to make you uncomfortable.

4. *Lack of Know-How.* You may not know how, and you may not fully understand the benefits of networking. Read on!

NETWORKING TIPS

The following is a listing of activities that will not only bring in immediate business but will help your ongoing career. Take these actions steps immediately.

1. *Combine your interests with your career.* Sponsor a club or civic group activity at your office. Use company letterhead for all volunteer organization correspondence.

2. *Speak publicly about your project.* A civic club or a local school are venues for such presentations.

3. *Write an article.* Submit it to the local newspaper or a trade publication. If you cannot write, hire a ghostwriter to polish and/or write the material.

4. *Invite the local media.* Have them visit your offices or a local project. Get interviewed!

5. *Conduct a tour of your offices or unique projects for*

special interest groups. And don't forget potential client groups. Send out press releases and opening announcements to both the local press club and to local client groups.

6. *Keep in touch with past clients.* Pick one key success fact about a current project and write to tell them about how you are succeeding with your assignment.

EIGHT TIPS TO DEVELOPING A CLIENT NETWORK

You may or may not have time to try all of these, but choose two and pursue them over the next two months. You'd be surprised at how easy networking becomes:

1. *Send out a newsletter to clients.* Talk about your other clients, and how you have solved their problems. Don't go on and on about yourself, do not include photos of your staff and their latest job move, baby, or other news. Clients only care about information that relates to them. Provide them with useful information, checklists for pre-design conferences, advice for the client on choosing or working with a design firm, advice on anything that may be specific to their industry. A client newsletter should focus on the client and highlight the client. And be sure that your name and telephone number are included on each page.

2. *Join client associations, not peer associations.* Peer associations are great places to trade advice and to pat the backs of other design professionals. Don't expect, however, that these activities will get you more work. The best way to get more work is to apply for client sponsored design awards, to join client associations, and to be visible to the client population. If you are really daring, you'll cancel one of your professional association memberships today and use that money to join a client association.

3. *Get published.* Anywhere, anyhow. The point in this process is that clients should know who you are, even before you approach them. Be sure you contact, or are in some way visible, to your client population. Getting published is one of the earliest ways to become visible in this area.

4. *Get to know the clients, up front and personal.* Keep a running information file, whether on rolodex or on your computer, of all the personal data you can gather on each per-

son you meet. So and so has five children, they like to golf, they went to the University of Michigan, whatever. The next time they call you or vice versa, you can readily call up the information about them, and ask them—how're the kids? How's the golf game? Clients love to feel that they are the most important person to you, and this is one way to create that impression.

5. *Be genuine.* People who genuinely enjoy other people are the most successful business persons, because they come across as being human, and being real. None of the marketing activities presented here will go over, unless you are genuinely interested in these people, not just as job contacts, but as human beings.

6. *Develop a mailing list of clients.* And make it bigger than you think it should be. If you think you need 500 names, generate 1,000. Keep clients advised of your latest accomplishment, and do it in a friendly, one-page letter. The personalized approach is much more effective than the glossy brochure that gets tossed, within minutes, in the circular file. There is no greater way to waste money than to produce a brochure about yourself that costs a lot of money, and then send it out, without any other useful information, to the client. Unless you enjoy throwing money away, don't mail out your brochure. Keep it for your personal distribution, and mailing upon request. Direct mail efforts should be devoted to personalized, short letters or to information useful to the client.

7. *Chinese water torture the client.* But keep it simple. Send them a relevant article on a topic of interest to their profession, with a handwritten note. Send something once each quarter, if not once a month.

8. *Keep a preferred client short-list.* Write down the names of eight or ten clients you'd like to target, and get to know their decision-makers. Make a point, without being a nuisance, of getting them to know who you are. Go to functions they attend, get them to genuinely trust you. The higher the level of trust, the better your chances are of getting projects, and referrals for projects, from your preferred client short-list.

WHY SALES SHOULDN'T TAKE AN EFFORT

Believe it or not, your goal should be NO MORE MARKETING. You should not have to do any marketing at all in order to acquire sales. If your public relations activities and your networking abilities are strong, then everyone will know who you are, and your clients will come to you.

KNOW WHAT YOU'RE UP AGAINST

There are many sensible actions to take that will bring you results, and it's a shame that design firms too often simply do not know the simple ways to gain a competitive edge.

One of the simplest, and also one of the most commonly overlooked methods, is to assess the competition. The development of a competitive profile of comparable design firms in your region is one way in which you can identify their strengths and weaknesses, and learn how to play up your strengths. Following is a list of information to gather in order to develop a profile of your competitors:

1. Staff size and distribution among disciplines.
2. Technology currently in place.
3. Services offered and promoted.
4. Key staff members.
5. Office locations.
6. Major clients.
7. Recently completed projects (general).
8. Recently completed projects (specific market segments).
9. Fee structure.
10. Positioning strategy.
11. Relative market strength.
12. Interest in teaming opportunities.

You can obtain information using the following methodologies:

1. Contact past employees of identified firms.
2. Interview appropriate staff members.
3. Obtain and review the firm's literature.
4. Review and evaluate all published information.
5. Contact other related consultants and contractors.
6. Contact your clients and their clients.
7. Contact reviewing agency personnel.

MANAGING CLIENT CONTACTS

The most effective contacts can be made by yourself or your technical staff. Don't rely on "the marketing person" to network.

No offense meant to marketing people, who have great expertise in the appropriate area, but the client wants to talk with and identify with technical people who will understand their issues immediately.

Here is a step-by-step method for developing a program to support yours and your technical staff members' efforts in networking.

Step One. Create a short-list of your most desirable and profitable clients.

Step Two. Form client-contractor "teams" by assigning each member of your senior level technical staff an equivalently ranked "contact" from each client-firm on your list.

Step Three. List these teams on a sheet of paper with the teams in the far left column, and four adjacent blank columns corresponding to quarterly contacts. These will be checked off as contacts are made.

Step Four. Create a line item on the marketing budget for client maintenance. This should be generous enough to cover quarterly contacts.

Step Five. Learn as much as possible about your firm's current/previous performance.

Step Six. Document all client contacts in writing, with a copy to the marketing staff. Having marketing approve client maintenance expense reimbursements is another good checkpoint.

Step Seven. Give bonuses to each in-house member of the client maintenance team when a new project is awarded. The more immediate the reward, the more effective the system.

Step Eight. Aim for a 1–8 ratio of new to repeat work if you are an established firm. Younger, more aggressive firms should try for a 1–1.

A FINAL WORD

The fastest way around an obstacle has traditionally been to drive right through it—and in this competitive market, you have no other choice but to seriously assess and further develop your networking abilities. If you haven't done any networking activity, schedule some in, even if it takes an effort. After a while, networking will be so routine that clients will be friends and friends will be clients. In my book, there's no other way to go.

APPENDICES

PROPOSALS THAT GET WORK BY DAVID A. STONE

PART I—STRATEGIES

Focusing on Your Market

I recently had an opportunity to review four proposals from an architectural firm in the Midwest. The first was for a local low-income housing development, the second was an open contract for repairs and alterations with the U.S. Post Office. The third proposal was a joint venture on a new baggage handling facility at a regional airport, and the fourth was for the design of a new clubhouse at a private golf club. It would be difficult to find four more diverse project or client types.

Before you can sell anything, you have to know what it is that you are selling. Unfortunately, many design professionals are practicing this "shoot at anything that moves" school of marketing. Being everything to everyone not only gives mixed messages to a market in search of experts, it weakens your competitive position when aiming at a specific project.

Diversity like this detracts from a firm's ability to market and price its services based on the value it can bring to a project. It also encourages clients to use the firm for price samplings in a competitive bidding situation. Many firms have recently reported that long-established clients, with whom they have always been "wired" for jobs, have begun altering their policies to require competitive bidding from other design firms.

We're not suggesting you deny the reality of the market. Many firms could not survive focusing exclusively on a narrow market niche. But you may want to give consideration to refining your target markets. Continue to serve the project type and geographic area which you address, but reduce the number of client types that you aim for. The skill sets needed to effectively market to the U.S. Postal Service are not the same as those required for a nonprofit housing committee.

As much as it goes against the grain, turning down work establishes a sense of exclusivity among both clients and staff. Exclusivity creates value. Your firm should develop a detailed go/no go checklist that evaluates each project for appropriateness, profit potential, client "match," and desirability. And then practice saying "no" to jobs that you have no business doing.

Objectives of a Proposal

The objective in submitting a proposal is not to win the job, it is to be invited to make a presentation. In order to do that, the proposal has to:

1. Leave no doubt with the client about your ability to do the job.
2. Stand out from the other proposals.
3. Create a curiosity in the mind of the client about you.

Just about every firm that responds to a particular RFP or RFQ is capable of doing the work. Your proposal has to make you stand out as different and special. The client has to understand that they will get something different from you that they will not get from anyone else.

An effective proposal is a rifle shot, aimed precisely at the particular project you hope to get. It is short, simple, and to the point. If you write shorter proposals, it will cost you less and you will be able to produce more of them. If you are writing proposals that cost $10,000 to assemble, you are limited in the number that you can put on the street. If you streamline your proposals, getting your costs down to $2,000 per proposal, it makes sense that you can put out five times as many proposals, covering more clients and increasing the probability that you will be selected for more presentations.

The submissions that most architects and engineers make are not really "proposals" or "statements of qualification" at all. They are just collections of past projects and résumés.

Very few actually "propose" how they intend to deal with and execute the project at hand. Instead, the submissions are filled with "motherhood" statements such as:

We believe we can provide the District with an exceptional service,

or

We are well qualified to provide these services based on our experience, staff capability, and approach to this type of project.

Statements like these only set you up to be seen as identical to every other consultant bidding on the project. Can you imagine someone *not* saying they were qualified and sincerely interested? Let your proposal be characterized by *boldness* and *differentiation*. We will discuss the specifics of how you do this in this appendix.

Client Expectations

Different client types expect different things from your proposals. Perhaps the most obvious distinction in client types is between government and private sector clients. Many government requests ask for volumes of substantive data on your firm history and experience. On the other hand, many private sector clients only want the bottom line with as little "filler" as possible.

An RFP from a public sector client we saw recently included an elaborate questionnaire to be completed by every firm that responded. The client insisted that a specified format be followed precisely in order "to simplify the review process and to obtain the maximum degree of comparability."

Most private sector, and many lower level government clients, such as municipalities, prefer brevity. They usually make their expectations clear in the RFP. One municipal department wrote that "clarity and terse expression are essential and will form part of the assessment criteria."

Think about your client type very carefully when you are preparing your proposals. Every firm should have a predetermined set of criteria to assess what should be included in a proposal as determined by the client type. This should be one of the jobs of the marketing coordinator. And each proposal should be uniquely suited to the needs of the particular client.

Strategizing To Prepare Your Proposal

In order to determine the expectations of the client, you have to do client research. Who should do this research?

If step "A" in writing a proposal is determining the client's expectations through research, then step "A minus 1" is selecting the project team. The most qualified people to do the research and write the proposal are the team that will do the project. And the key person on that team is the project manager.

The project manager can be defined as the lead person on the project. It might be a principal or it might be a project engineer or architect. It may even be someone from outside the firm in the case of a joint venture. In any case the lead person is the one who will be expected to carry and represent the firm to the client. The lead person will stand up and make commitments on behalf of the firm and the project team, and will be responsible for ensuring that the project fulfils the expectations of the client in the end.

The most important decision prior to writing a proposal is the determination of who will lead the project. The second most important decision is who else will be on the team. This scenario implies a big project in a well organized firm that knows exactly who will do the work. But we all know it never happens this way. Most projects are small and require a fast response. Also, the nature of design work is that you never know which projects are going to go and which aren't. "Shoot from the hip" has to be the operative mode.

However, the earlier you can structure team the better your proposal, your presentation, and your chance of selection will be. At the very least, try to pick the principal and the project manager who will be part of the team.

Client Research

Step 1 in client research is to recognize that clients are people too. Look at the human characteristics of all your clients to try to determine the criteria they will use, as people, to make their decisions.

We recommend that you set up a client dossier. This could be a three ring binder in which you begin to collect information on each person within the client selection committee. Part of your research is to find out what makes your client tick as a person. What kind of car does she drive? Is he married or unmarried? Where is she from? Did he go to college? Was it Ivy League or west coast?

All this information is intended to help establish a rapport with the client as a person.

A 55 year old businessman from the Midwest, married for 30 years, who has worked his way up through the company to become president makes decisions in a very different way than a single, 30 year old female lawyer from New York who has recently been named to the board of directors.

Next, research to determine how the selection will be made. Will it be make by a board of directors or has the hospital administrator been given the authority? Will a municipal official decide on his own or does it have to go before the local council? Different strategies are required for different selection methods.

Consider the current situation in the market. Is it tight? Is government money available? Is the client substantial in this market? Is the market growing or diminishing? Every market has a cycle. If the market is in a downturn, understand the impact on this project as you prepare the proposal.

Then look at the particular company or institution that is sponsoring the project. What has been happening within this particular client's company or institution? Try to get the past five years' financial performance figures. Are they growing, stable, or shrinking? Has there been political turmoil? Is same leader in place as five years ago or have there been five leaders in five years?

Tap into your own network by calling other design professionals. How has this company dealt with architects and engineers on past projects?

Make a list of your findings. Discuss it, brainstorm it, strategize it with the project team or other managers. Don't allow your proposal to be written to a nonexistent nebulous, faceless "client."

Remember, clients are people too.

"Hot Buttons"

You must identify the "hot buttons" that are important to the client. Too many firms fill their proposals with boilerplate talk about all the jobs they've done, the education they have, and the CADD system they use. This approach misses the point that there is only one project in which your client is truly interested—his or her own.

We cannot emphasize this enough. Whether you are doing an introductory proposal or a full blown technical proposal, the most important thing to the client is *this particular* project. Not the fact that you have done 25 or 105 similar jobs, but what you are going to do on this project

Find out the main hot issues on the project. Then the entire proposal can be structured around them. Every project has them, whether they have been stated or not. Some of them will be written down in the RFP, which makes your life simpler. But be prepared to read between the lines to determine if what the RFP *says* is what the client *means*. If the issues have not been written down (and even if they have) you must do some digging into the background of the project and the client to find the true objectives and priorities on the job.

Spend an amount of time appropriate to the size and importance of the project investigating the specifics of how the project came about. Why is this project being done? Is it a hazardous waste project resulting from new federal legislation? If so, you may find that the client doesn't really want to do the project at all, but is being forced into it to comply with a law that has been imposed on the business. It represents an expenditure the client would rather not make.

Is it a municipal project that represents a significant feather in a political cap? Is it a community facility that has come about after years of volunteer committee labor? Each project has its own history and "soft spots."

It's useful to spend some time interviewing people in the area where the project will be built. Find out what the community issues are. What do they expect the project will be like? What relations do they have with the owners? Why is this project being done now? By spending this time you will find out many small pieces of information to make your proposal much more targeted to the people who will be making the selection.

Some RFP's request that you not interview certain people. These might include, for example, the members of the corporate board or a hospital committee. In a circumstance like this, we recommend that you try to make contact with them anyway. Because if you don't one of your competitors will. They may find that certain key hot button that makes the difference in the selection on this project.

At the very least, phone the board or committee members to introduce yourself. State that you will be submitting a proposal on the project and thank them for their attention to it. Don't ask specific questions, but leave them an opportunity to raise any issue that they may feel is important.

If you do go to interview anyone, don't bring brochures, business cards, or any other material that implies that you are "selling." The only reason you are going is to collect information that will be useful to you when you sit down to prepare your proposal.

Go through the RFP carefully. Often the key issues are written down but they don't always reflect the real concern of the client. Here are a few of the more common issues to appear in RFP's, along with what the client actually wants to know:

- *The Time Commitment and Availability of Project Personnel.* Clients don't want the disruption that comes with regular team personnel changes. They also want to know that the project team has a sense of urgency and personal commitment to the project.

- *Your Performance Record on Schedule (or Budget).* This is one where you have to read between the lines. What they mean is: "What methods and techniques will you use to keep this project on schedule/budget?"

- *Ability to Estimate Construction Cost.* This is another area where they don't care so much about "history" or "experience" as they do about the methods that you intend to use for controlling costs on this project.

- *Design and Conceptual Sensitivity.* This arises most often with architectural projects. What clients want to know is: "Are you able to listen and understand what we want? Do you have the ability to empathize and hear what we are saying?"

- *Litigation Record.* This one comes up when there is a lawyer on the selection committee. They want to know if you are about to lose your license or go bankrupt as a result of a claim. Either situation would cause them considerable aggravation.

- *Familiarity with Public Work.* This is a good one, which means, "Are you able to schmooze the funding and/or approvals process?" It can also mean: "Do you have the patience to deal with a building committee full of politicians and amateurs?"

- *Previous Performance.* In every case this means *proven* capability on projects that are identical to this one.
- *Qualifications of Key Personnel.* This *always* means the project manager. They also want to know about the level of personal interest that the project manager has in this job.

Make notes from any meetings or previous experience with the client to make sure your list is accurate and complete. Every item in the proposal has to relate directly to one of these hot buttons. In the absence of any obvious ones, it's safe to assume that every client is keenly interested in reduced construction costs, a schedule and budget that is maintained, and a firm grip on changes.

Certain RFP's are difficult to "read" when it comes to identifying the key issues. The most notorious is the "open contract" type, which will have you doing any number and type of projects for a fixed period of time with a ceiling on the overall contract amount. This type of RFP appears regularly from government sources such as the Post Office and the Corps of Engineers.

The utter lack of "hot buttons" makes an aggressive response to this type of request difficult. There is nothing about the client or the project which allows you to get a "hook" on the project and it's virtually impossible to establish yourself as uniquely qualified for work like this.

Proposal Length

Most proposals that design professionals write are far too thick and far too long. Forget any idea that your likelihood of getting a project is proportionate to the weight of the proposal. Nor should a large project automatically result in a thick proposal. Just about every proposal we have seen can be considerably shortened and still pack a lot more "substance" and "selling" into them.

Clients like short proposals. Many RFP's hint broadly or come out and state that they want short, concise documents that address specifically the project at hand. Clients react very favorably to the proposal that tells them everything in 10–15 pages and show them how to find what they are looking for. That is the kind of proposal you should be submitting.

Most design firm proposals can be reduced in volume by:

- Eliminating redundancy in the documents.
- Reducing the number of referenced projects.
- Taking the "motherhood" statements out of cover letters and project approach statements.
- Reducing the number of sections.
- Condensing and consolidating the material by cutting back on text.
- Reducing the formality of the document.
- Restricting résumés to a single page.
- Increasing the use of charts and diagrams.
- Keeping 254/255's and other forms out of the main body.

The Proposal Document

The project manager should write the entire first draft of any proposal. This is the person who has to do the client research, understand the issues, and stand up and defend the proposal statements in a presentation. Ultimately, this is the person who has to come through with the project.

A proposal written by marketing department, uninvolved principals, or other "writers" leaves an open opportunity for miscommunications to occur. A project manager making a presentation may not be aware of some of the statements made in the proposal. There is a built-in accountability when the person who has written the proposal must stand up and defend it.

Don't write a sophisticated proposal. Always use simple, basic English. Technical professionals often feel that their writing must reflect the sophistication of their work but this can turn a reader off. The Wall Street Journal is carefully edited so as to not exceed a sixth grade reading level.

A handy rule to keep your writing simple is the "3–7–11" rule. Have no paragraph more than 3 sentences, no sentence more than 7 words, and no word more than 11 letters. It's not an easy rule to stick to, but it will make your writing more accessible.

Another rule is to never let any paragraph go more than ten lines. If it is any longer, people will tend not to read it and will move on to the next heading. How can you make sure that you have written in simple language? Give the proposal to a sixth grader to read. Ask this young reader to circle or highlight any words that he or she doesn't understand. Then edit those words out and insert common language.

People like to read simple things. They resist reading long elaborate technical documents that they don't understand. And remember, clients are people first.

Proposal Organization

While many RFPs ask for specific items to be addressed in the proposals, there is a great benefit in providing the needed information in a format and order that suits *your* purposes. A proposal that is organized under headings that correspond precisely to the questions asked in the RFP shows a lack of innovation, decisiveness, and leadership.

Many clients allow you the discretion to stray from the format by stating in the RFP that they have the right to waive any "irregularities." Even seemingly rigid RFP instructions usually have some measure of flexibility. Some agencies provide a questionnaire to be completed. Don't take this to mean that the questionnaire has to form the body of your proposal. Take advantage of this flexibility by pushing the limits of the proposal "package." Let everyone else dutifully answer the questions asked. You want to go much further than that.

Most rigid RFP formats create a redundancy in the proposals that is tedious to the reader. By answering every question in the order that they were asked, you end up duplicating information. Clients certainly don't intend for this to happen. When you are faced with a rigid format or a questionnaire, include the completed form as an appendix. The committee then has the option of referring to their standard document but can be "sold" with your unique approach.

You can begin to set yourself apart from the competition by addressing all the required issues, but in a different order and different format than that asked. It is refreshing to clients as they read through the proposals, it lets you stand out as different, it wakes them up and causes them to think, and it shows you as a proactive firm that does not automatically take everything at face value.

Remember that the purpose of the proposal is not to get the job, but to get an interview. If your proposal creates sufficient curiosity in the mind of the client, you are sure to be invited.

PART II—TACTICS

Proposal Contents

There are seven key parts to every proposal:

1. Cover letter.
2. Executive summary.
3. Table of contents.
4. Body of proposal.
5. Ending summary.
6. Appendices.
7. Cover/binding.

We will review each of these items in turn.

COVER LETTER

Your cover letter is the client's introduction to you and your style. Use it to take a bold and aggressive stance about your capability to do the project.

Everyone uses the cover letter to either thank the client for the opportunity to propose or tell the client how pleased they are to be submitting this proposal. Set yourself apart by making your cover letter different. Most letters have far too much text. I suggest a less "prose-oriented" writing style because readers faced with a full sheet of text will tend to skim over it, searching out relevant data. Your letter should help them zero in on the things they want to hear.

Your letter should grab attention with information "headlines" and then help your readers to go straight to the key features that interest them in the body of the text. This method respects the readers' time by allowing each to choose the items that are important to him or her, and skim the aspects that don't matter as much.

Starting with the "Regards" line, set yourself apart. Choose one of the hot buttons and push it immediately:

> *Re: 10% reduction in construction costs on new school construction.*

This will get a reader's attention immediately. You don't need to reference the job; the client already knows which job it is.

Continue the letter by immediately relating the benefits the client will get by hiring you.

> *Over the past 30 years, the clients of Acme Engineering have saved over $2.5 million dollars in combined construction costs as a direct result of our commitment to budget reductions.*
>
> *More than four hundred clients have benefited from our rigorous attention to design excellence and dedication to schedule and budget.*
>
> *We continue this strong tradition on the School District #4 capital improvements program with:*

Here is where you hit the key items. Help the client by referencing each item to the page on which it is discussed in the proposal:

> • *Dedicated project personnel with exclusive responsibility and authority for the Polk Street School project.*
>   *(See page 5.)*
> • *Scheduling procedures to ensure strict adherence to client preferred deadlines.*
>   *(See page 8.)*
> • *Cost monitoring and control procedures to achieve our targeted 10% construction budget reductions.*
>   *(See page 7.)*
> • *Change order control processes that have resulted in an average change order tally of only 0.08% during the last ten years.*
>   *(See page 6.)*

Eliminate all trite statements. They waste valuable space and the client's time. You don't need any thank you's and it's obvious that you are pleased to have the opportunity to propose. The first sentence is the one that should grab your client. Start with the number one hot issue for this client and this project.

Use only present-tense, action-oriented verbs as you run down the hot buttons. Stay miles away from timid phrases like:

> Thank you for the opportunity. . . .
> We are very interested. . . .

We are confident the schedules can be met....
We are pleased to present our proposal....
This proposal is fully responsive to the RFP....
We look forward to your favorable consideration....

Always write as though you have the project already. Conclude the cover letter by stating that a complete design team kick-off meeting is scheduled for April 15th at 8:30 am in your boardroom and decks are clear to get rolling.

Always make use of a "P.S." This is the most-read part of any letter, and it provides an opportunity to reference or reinforce another important project issue.

> *P.S. Our design team has already begun a review of the files and design data that we prepared while designing modifications to your present installation in 1990.*

Your cover letter must be restricted to a single page. Anything longer than that does not get read.

The cover letter should hit the three or four key points that you have identified as the hot issues on the project. This is, of course, where it gets risky and most design professionals prefer not to take a chance. After all, how are you to know that you're hitting the right buttons? You reduce the risk through effective client research. Train yourself, your project managers, and the project teams to do proper client research so you can depend on them to pick the three or four items that are most important to the client.

The cover letter can also act as an executive summary. In many cases it can actually replace the executive summary and reduce the overall size of the document. Use it to lead the client through the proposal and to the specific locations where they can find the information they want.

The cover letter must always be signed by the project manager or other lead person who will be taking responsibility. Make it a bold, clear signature that reflects the pride you take in your services.

EXECUTIVE SUMMARY

When you receive a thick book the first thing you want to know is what's in the book. So, having identified the hot buttons, you must show the client the essence of the proposal and how they can find their way through it. You do not want to force the reader to start at the beginning and follow through to the end in a linear fashion.

The reason for this is that some clients are only interested in a single issue. There is always a board member with a particular personal interest. When that client is reading, he or she wants to go directly to that issue in proposal. Always put yourself in the position of the client who is faced with a stack of 30 proposals to go through. Make yours as easy to read and "user friendly" as possible.

Outline each of the key points made in your proposal, and then reference the page numbers where more detail can be found. Take each of the tabbed elements or each of your half-dozen major points and summarize them with a single paragraph on each. If you are describing the project team, describe exactly what is included in the proposal about project team. For example:

> *Acme Engineers has assembled a highly specialized team of recognized experts to focus on this project. The team has previously cooperated on six projects with the same high profile and delicate funding issues as those faced on this project. The team is led by John Doe, a veteran project manager who has recently won an award for his outstanding contributions to environmental remediation projects just like this one. (See pages 5–9.)*

As mentioned above, you can often use the cover letter as an executive summary to lead the client into and through the proposal. Only do this if it will not force the cover letter to exceed a single page. If you do have a separate executive summary, stick to two pages and treat three pages as an absolute maximum.

TABLE OF CONTENTS

Following the executive summary you must include a full Table of Contents. This is your opportunity to take apart and put in a graphic format a concise listing of the contents, which will allow even the most dubious of clients the opportunity to see each element within the proposal.

Depending on the size and complexity of the proposal, the Table of Contents can also be reinforced with an index at the back of the book, which allows clients to see other subjects. Together, the Table of Contents and the Index form a pair of items providing another feature to help the client get through proposal.

Restrict the Table of Contents to a single page. If there are more items than will fit comfortably on a page, you have too many and they should be consolidated. That is also a clue that you will need an index.

Don't use a confusing numbering system for your sections. Too many sections, subsections, and subsubsections will alienate the reader. Organize the material so that the logic of your approach is obvious. Then, in the body of the proposal, maintain the logic of your organization. Don't start a new section three-quarters of the way down a page. Give it a new page, with it's own heading.

Remember that the objective of a proposal is to get you interviewed. Therefore the objective of these tools is to get the client to read your proposal in the way you want it read.

THE MAIN BODY OF THE PROPOSAL

Writing Style. Most design professionals use too much text and the logic of their approach becomes lost. Think about it from the client's point of view. Who likes to be faced with a stack of proposals and have to read through all of them? The easier you can make this job, the more positively disposed the client will be toward your proposal.

Remember the "3–7–11 Rule" discussed earlier. That is, no more that 3 sentences in a paragraph, 7 words in a sentence or 11 letters in a word. Don't lose the thoughtful answers to the project approach questions, just describe what makes your approach different and better in a more succinct form.

Put Some Life Into It. The highly technical nature of many proposals tends to drain the "life" out of them. The writing style in most proposals is competent but dull. While it's important to address all the issues involved, it's also possible to reflect some of the enthusiasm and excellence that your firm brings to a project.

When writing a proposal remember that clients are people too and they will respond to other stimuli besides dry technical issues. They want to know that you *care* about their project and A/E's have to train themselves to think and write more in those terms. This is not to say that the selection is made based on emotion, but everyone could afford to put some more "sizzle" in their "sales." Clients want to look deeper than the raw numbers. Give your proposal life and make it clear why your firm is so special.

Don't be glorious with your language. Be succinct, tell the clients exactly what needs to be told, with no extras. But remember that part of the story is your enthusiasm and energy for the project.

What Goes into the Main Body of a Proposal. The main body of the proposal must contain these elements in this order:

1. The résumés of the project manager and key project team members. These should be written to stand out from the "filler" résumés that fatten most proposals.

2. Schedule and budget suggestions for this project, supported by four or five similar schedule and budget performances from your past.

3. Your team's capability, including any outside team of specialists whom you will hire for this particular project.

4. The approach you will take to the project, including the hot buttons for this particular project that you have identified through your research.

5. Five or six supporting projects from your past history, including references from those projects that show that you are the most capable and qualified firm for the project.

Once into the body of the proposal, you should walk the client through each element, showing how it relates to the project at hand. Whether it is a résumé, a project history, or an explanation of a particular technique that you use, take at least a short paragraph to explain how what you are about to show is directly applicable to this client's new project.

Key Project Personnel. In every image study we have seen there is one overriding element that clients want to see when selecting a design firm for a project. Today they are picking a firm based on the *capability*, not *experience*, of the project manager. The distinction is important.

They are less concerned with the case histories and years of experience in a particular project type than they are with the capability of the project manager as demonstrated in all that experience. When you stress "capability" rather than "experience" you write action words, as opposed to past tense.

> *Mr. Smith is a recognized expert in State and Federal housing codes and requirements. His personal involvement on both the Fairfield Apartments and Hillside development was instrumental in obtaining the same 20% density increases being sought on this project.*

The first step in rebuilding your proposals into winning documents is to get rid of the canned résumés. Take them apart and rebuild them to highlight the person and the capabilities. Frankly, the client is not interested in the fact that the project manager graduated from Yale in 1952. What they want to know is that the project manager, today, has just completed a project similar to the one you are proposing on and has not only saved a client $200,000 in cost but has brought it in ahead of schedule.

Rewrite your resumes to highlight the particular project capability that is *directly* relevant to the project at hand. Write a new résumé for each key team member on each new proposal so they become marketing statements for that project in and of themselves. There is no doubt this takes extra work but it targets the résumé to the proposal and the project and gives a much better chance of the client concluding that you are the best one to be interviewed.

When you describe relevant experience it should be addressing exactly the same problems as those which the client now has. For example: You are asked to propose on a hazardous waste study and the project manager has just completed another study. The first thing you want to talk about are the problems on the previous study. Describe them in a way that reinforces the client's confidence that your project manager can solve any current problems.

Although interested in you, the client is not four or five pages interested. Keep the résumés short and to the point. Restrict them to *one page only*. If there is more material than will fit on a page, edit it to keep only the most relevant material and fit it on a single sheet. This can be a very tough item to deal with because we love to tell clients about everything we have done in the past 15 years.

One of the most important criteria for the client is the capability of the project manager. This person's résumé must be the *first thing* the client encounters after the cover letter/ executive summary.

Sample resume:

Project Manager

Mr. John Doe, PE, is the project manager for the _____ *project.*

Notice the assertive, present-tense tone.

In a career that began after graduation from Rutgers University with a Master of Science in Civil Engineering in 1977, John has developed strong project and design leadership capabilities on projects focused in the wastewater and water treatment market. He has been a partner in Acme Engineers since 1984.

This is all you need by way of introduction and it gives all the background necessary. There is no need to provide state registration numbers or professional affiliations. If you say he is a PE, the client can assume he has a registration number and belongs to the appropriate associations. And the client is not interested in the fact that the person may be the president of the local Rotary club.

Now you can get on with the important material:

- *On the* _____ *municipal water treatment project in 1990, John successfully guided the project to completion four weeks ahead of schedule. The* _____ *project was identical in scope and size to the present project.*
- *Since 1988, 97% of Mr. Doe's projects have been constructed for less than the initial project budget.*
- *And so on.*

You should have five or six specific project "anecdotes" that relate directly to the hot buttons and to the issues of the project at hand. Use bulleted points only and keep the writing concise. State what this person is capable of doing that is *exactly the same* as that required on the current project, and then prove it with an example.

At the end of *each* résumé address the issue of schedule and availability for that individual.

Mr. Doe is currently assigned to the _____ project. His responsibilities will be completed on April 15th, at which time he will be assigned full time to the Scottsdale District wastewater project.

When you are working with subconsultants and associated firms, don't separate the résumés by firm. It gives an appearance of too much complexity and scares off potential clients. Rework *all* the résumés into a consistent graphic format and let the divisions between firms fade. Focus on the individuals as a "team." Look again at your joint venture proposals. Are the graphics all over the map with a variety of fonts, page layouts, and even types and colors of paper? If so, the proposal will look like what it is—a collection of preprinted résumés quickly bound together.

Stress Service through Schedule and Budget. High quality design is a feature that every client expects in a project today. While this may be a little hard for some designers to swallow, design has been reduced to the level of a nondescript, neutral, trite element in a proposal. In fact, surveys have shown that it is not the quality of design but the poor quality of the service that hurts the relationship on most projects.

Clients measure the quality of a project in terms of the success of schedule, budget, and the deliverables on the project. It is the promise not kept, the communication not delivered, the milestone date that was ignored that leads to the perception of poor quality in the mind of the client. Service is something that you can vividly demonstrate to a client in the words and diagrams of your proposal.

The project schedule and budget will be as follows. . . .

We stress these elements in our schedule and budget procedure. . . .

This is how we manage schedules and budgets in our firm. . . .

Even if the client does not ask for it specifically, you should address the issues of schedule and budget. This shows you to be forward thinking and proactive. You have taken a leadership role in the project by anticipating more than the client has asked for.

Many A/E's develop their schedules after they have been awarded a project. This is something you should do *in order* to be awarded the project. While it is not always possible to develop a detailed schedule, provide one labeled "preliminary" to serve as a point of departure in your discussions.

Always relate the schedule to calendar dates, not numbered days. When can you start? Which three months will be devoted to design? Are you going to touch base with the client during that time? What about approvals? Are there other consultants involved? If so, when do they get into the project? You have to show that you have more than a passing interest in the project.

Your schedule *must* be in graphic format. It should be a simple bar chart, which occupies one page only. Everyone understands the graphic and it communicates clearly.

The schedule should reflect the various tasks you have identified on the project, including those involving the client. It should show the significant milestone dates such as submittals and reviews, and should have the overall substance that the project deserves.

Stress the schedule and budget for the project at hand, and then support your estimates by showing the performance you achieved for your other clients on five similar projects.

Your Record on Schedule. Client RFP's are showing an increasing concern about schedule. In order to take an aggressive leadership position with a potential client, you must include a discussion regarding your record on keeping to schedules. Take advantage of the client's interest in schedule to say more than "we finish projects on schedule." How do you accomplish that? If you have finished the last five projects ahead of schedule, how much ahead were they? What techniques did you use?

Provide a brief explanation of your schedule tracking method. Do you use scheduling software? Do you employ bar charts, critical path or milestone tracking methods? Do you have weekly updates and team meetings?

The client wants the reassurance that comes from your confidence in your own system. It's far too easy to say "we finish on schedule."

It would even be a good idea to mention one project that fell behind schedule. Why did it fall behind and what specific actions did you take to recognize the situation and bring it back onto schedule? Anyone can handle a project that hums along. You want to demonstrate that you are reliable in bad weather too.

Budget Performance. It's hard to find a client who does not have project budget near the top of their priority list. Most RFPs state that the client is interested in your "experience" in sticking to budget. You have to read between the lines and realize that the client wants to know what specific techniques and methods you use to deal with the issue. One RFP we have seen recently came right out and asked the proposers to "comment briefly on the *methods* that their firms employ to maintain control of construction costs." As with schedule, a client's comfort is built on your level of confidence in your own methods and procedures.

Provide a bold, one paragraph introduction to this section. It might be something like:

> *In cooperation with current cost reduction efforts nationwide, Acme Engineers has established a firmwide policy of achieving construction cost objectives that are **10% below** those budgeted by the client. The following methods are used to achieve this goal:*

Then you can list, in bullet points, the specific techniques you use in cost control.

- *Use of XYZ, Inc. cost consultants.*
- *Strict substitution control procedures for contract bidding.*
- *Maintenance of a current and accurate database for our estimating software.*
- *Continuing education of project managers on cost-related issues.*
- *Review of cost estimates at these milestone dates:*
    - _____
    - _____
    - _____
- *Regular review with client of current construction cost estimates and presentation of cost reduction alternatives.*

Then you can back up your methods with specific, proven performance.

> *During the past three years, these five projects, which are similar in size and scope to the Northwest Middle School project, have achieved budget savings of at least _____%.*

- _____ $ _____ *below budget.*
- _____ $ _____ *below budget.*
- _____ $ _____ *below budget.*
- _____ $ _____ *below budget.*
- _____ $ _____ *below budget.*

When clients are concerned about costs, they are usually nervous about changes as well. Even though they may not specifically ask, this is another opportunity for you to take a leadership position. Take the matter aggressively under control by dealing with it directly.

In order to control the cost and schedule impact of change orders, Acme Engineers has recently revised its contemplated change order form to include:

- *The reason for the contemplated change.*
- *The impact on project schedule of the contemplated change.*
- *The impact on construction budget of the contemplated change.*

In order to minimize impact, each contemplated change will be reviewed with the client in light of these criteria.

In order to expedite the project, Acme Engineers is committed to a change order turnaround time not to exceed 48 hours.

During the last five years, cost increases due to changes on all Acme Engineers projects have averaged only 0.05%.

Extended Design Team. A high percentage of design firm proposals include the services of other consulting professionals as either subconsultants or joint venture partners. Under the heading of "Extended Design Team," you should highlight the firms that are going to be involved in the work, not the individuals. If there are key individuals within the consultant's firm, their résumés should be among the others in "Key Project Personnel."

It is very important to communicate, within the proposal, the nature of the overall association and the role of your firm within the group.

The only advantage to be gained by assembling a strategic alliance, joint venture, partnering relationship, or whatever other term we might want to use, is that it brings together parties who have complementary skills or resources. Together, they make up the ideal team, without redundancy or shortfall, to execute the work. Each has something positive and significant to offer the combined team, without which, the other is lost.

From the client's point of view, the job should be done with the least possible hassle. Quite frankly, the client could care less if there are one, two, or ten firms working together. The client wants a high quality project delivered on time, under budget, for a good fee. And—the client wants his or her life to be made simple. The more complexity that is *apparent*, the more nervous the client will be that you are going to make life difficult. You are there to *solve* problems, not create new ones.

To achieve this perceived simplicity, the associations you propose have to clearly show:

1. A cohesive, focused team.
2. A seamless organization that instills confidence in the client.
3. A clear sense of the complementary skills that the various firms contribute.

Many proposals do not make clear the strategic role that each participant plays. Clients are forced to ask themselves why they should be hiring you, instead of dealing exclusively with your joint venture partners.

There are three ways you can counteract this reaction, all of which are communicated in how you structure the proposal.

1. Have a truly distinct and valuable technical contribution that you, and only you, can make to the project.
2. Make the association appear so seamless, and the team so integrated, that it is the obvious solution to the client.
3. Set up your role as "master coordinator" of a group of talented, but disconnected "experts" who could not get themselves breakfast if you weren't there.

To accomplish the first, you have to focus the proposal much more on your particular capabilities with respect to the specific requirements of the project at hand. Your generic capabilities will not do in this situation.

The second point is made by presenting the team as a cohesive unit. This means all résumés look the same and the project organizational chart does not mention firms, just individuals.

The third goal is reached by focusing on your project management capabilities. Here the project organizational chart would reflect the various firms, all working through you to connect with the client, approval agencies, funding sources, and so on.

If local presence is the only capability you can bring to the table, the client will resent the fees they are paying you and contract negotiations will be much more difficult.

In order to ease the client's concerns about logistics and coordination in an extended design team, take advantage of your "extensive experience" to highlight the smooth nature of the working relationships you have with your consultants:

> *Acme Engineers has been designing, constructing, and providing expert opinion on waste treatment projects in the state of Delaware for over 30 years. During this time the firm has evolved a cohesive team of experts that enjoys a cooperative, synergistic working method. This long-term consistency provides for optimal working relationships and efficient design solutions.*

Give each firm a *single page* profile, similar to those you developed for the key team members:

> *ABC Architects:*
>
> - *Use bullet points to highlight capabilities.*
> - *List achievements.*
> - *Show specific project solutions (innovative and cost cutting).*
> - *How will this consultant make a difference on **this** project with **this** client?*
> - *Address this consultant's availability with regard to the schedule.*

List other consultants in a similar manner.

Project Approach. Have you ever lost a project to a firm that had never handled that particular project type in your marketplace? Of course you wondered what you did wrong. This will happen when a young firm comes along with little or no experience with the job or client type, but with the ability to tell the client precisely what they will do on this project instead of what they have done on others.

Design clients will base their selection more on what you will do for them than on what you have done for someone else. And while we can't tell you exactly what to write in your proposal, we can tell you to be very particular with regard to the project at hand and tell the client what you will do. The project approach statement is your opportunity to explain the specific tactics you will employ on the project. Here is where you can reinforce the hot buttons that you have identified through your research.

Begin by outlining the scope of the work to be done. Make this a very simple listing of tasks. Use bullet points, not numbers, as numbers may communicate a priority of items that is not consistent with that of the client.

The engineering/architectural services covered by this proposal include these 15 items:

-
-
-

This proposal does not include:

-
-
-

Don't let yourself make "motherhood" statements about project approach issues. These are statements to which no one can object but which cannot be backed up. A recent one we have seen is: "Preliminary design concepts will be developed to confirm the program." How is this translated into the specific project at hand? Always do a "reality check" on all your proposals to weed these out.

Give your approach strength by taking an aggressive leadership stance and assuming you have the project already.

We have determined that these projects fall into three basic categories. . . .
Our immediate focus upon starting the Happy Valley project is. . . .

And demonstrate your knowledge of the pertinent issues.

The project team will review the overall project program to ensure that ISTEA funding is not jeopardized by incorporating additional pavement rehabilitation.

Describe what makes your approach different and better. Give substance to the proposal by outlining a bulleted list of specific steps in the project including deliverables, milestones, schedules, and responsibilities in each phase.

Too many design professionals put a lot of "experience" related language in the body of their proposals. You should have no "experience" language in the meat of proposal. Your discussion should deal exclusively with your capability and your tactical approach to this job. Clearly outline step by step exactly how you intend to do this client's project.

Make your project approach statement a "work plan." An effective work plan is not made up of extensive text, it is a collection of lists, diagrams, budgets, schedules, and comments that detail your approach.

A good work plan will show:

- **What** needs to be done through the project definition and a task list.
- **When** it needs to be done through the schedule.
- **Who** is responsible through a project organization chart.
- **How** much it will cost through a project budget.
- How **quality** will be assured through a quality control plan.
- How the **client** will be kept happy through a client management plan.

Within the proposal you can use pictures, drawings, and graphics. In fact use lots of them with the body of your proposals. If they are used appropriately graphics and pictures provide a great deal of assistance to the reader of a proposal as well as enhancing the text. But every picture or graphic *must* have a caption. A nice long caption too. The caption has to be a description of exactly what the picture is of, what the diagram represents, or how to interpret and use this particular graph. Without effective captions, graphics can cause more frustration than they relieve.

There is a danger in the design professions of overweighting the graphics and pictures. Find a balance for the client who wants a clearly written, delineated, graphic presentation that is easy to read.

Before you leave this section, review your list of "hot buttons" to make sure you have addressed all of them, including the ones the client may not even be aware of.

When You Don't Know Enough. There are times (in fact fairly often) when you may not know enough about the project to make an aggressive, coordinated proposal. This is a frequent occurrence for consulting engineers who work through a prime consultant.

If you do not have enough information from the client to properly propose on the project, then you must make assumptions. And clearly state to the client the assumptions you have made.

Not long ago, a midwestern firm was proposing on a project in Chicago. They had interviewed the client, but the client was still not entirely sure what was wanted. Rather than make an assumption, the firm chose to state in their proposal that the first task on the project would be to interview the client further to determine exactly what was needed.

However, a competitor chose to approach the client with a more aggressive stance. This firm's proposal stated that, "Assuming that this is what you need, here is how we will do the project." And then the proposal proceeded to outline, in detail, the tactics and methods the firm would use on the project. This technique worked to instill a high level of confidence in a client who was being indecisive, and the competitor was awarded the project.

To make use of this approach you must:

1. Make assumptions about the project.

2. Describe the assumptions you have made very clearly.

3. Follow the assumptions with the step-by-step procedures you will use on the project based on your assumption.

This will show the client how your firm and your project team would work under a particular set of circumstances. It will give the client more meat on which to base the decision. It does expose you to a degree of risk, but it just may wipe out competitors who have not been bold enough to make assumptions.

Representative Projects. Don't succumb to the temptation of your history. Most architects and engineers include page after page of endless projects, none of which have any meaning for the client. You would do much better to limit the number of projects you reference in the proposal and focus on those that are directly relevant.

Don't show business park master plans, walkway bridges, and state administrative headquarters to church committees. Don't tell the low-income housing group about a luxury apartment complex you've just finished. By doing so, you communicate to the committee that you have missed, or aren't concerned about, their culture and their priorities.

Including too many diverse project types can work against you in a proposal. One firm in the west recently responded to RFP's for two projects. One was for indefinite contract work for the U.S. Postal Service and the other was for the design of a new clubhouse for the local golf course. These two projects represent the polar opposite of high volume, low margin work and high margin, low volume work. Neither is good or bad, just different.

But from the client's point of view, there is a great difference between being "highly qualified" to do the U.S.P.S. work and being "highly qualified" to design the golf course clubhouse. If you were on the selection committee for the golf course and knew that one of the firms did the Post Office work, would you be interested in them? Likewise, if you were on the committee for the Post Office and found out that one of the firms did golf club facilities, would you have confidence in their ability to maintain your priorities for post office repairs and alterations?

Five Projects Only. The best tactic is to pick out five or six projects that are as close as possible in scope to the current project, and then list six or seven key elements of those projects that reinforce the hot buttons. What made those projects similar to this one? How were the technical solutions applicable? How were the "hot buttons" on this project dealt with on previous jobs?

You want to relate the scope of a past project to the current one and then go deeper. These elements will show that you have acquired substantial capability while doing identical jobs for other clients.

If a client is concerned about local experience, make sure all the projects you list are local projects to comply with that requirement. Don't make a list of representative projects and then repeat another list showing local jobs. Fulfil both requirements simultaneously. This will eliminate redundancy and shorten your proposal.

If you are including projects done by associated firms or consultants, don't reinforce the different sources of the work by including them in different sections. It confuses the reader and it causes the client to ask why they should hire you instead of going straight to the other firm.

References. Always include your references along with the specific project with which the referee is associated. Don't list them all in a separate category entitled "References." List the reference, or several references, from another project that support a particular element of the project at hand. Give some background on the relationship you have with the individual, the difficulties you worked through together, and the achievements you made on this person's behalf. Make it clear that you and your references are real people.

Have each reference directly connected with the representative project. That way you can direct your client as to what to look for with each reference—quality of work, timeliness, cost control, or any other critical aspect.

Perhaps the most effective reference is a letter from a previous client that relates to the particular project you have at hand. To build up a supply, make it a practice to ask for reference letters at the end of each job.

But don't put all your reference letters in a section of their own or in an appendix. Instead, extract appropriate sentences and phrases from the letters and include them in the body of the proposal. Then, in parentheses, give the name, company, and phone number of the person who made the statement.

By using this tactic, you can also include verbal statements that have been made about your firm but that you may not have in writing. Look inside the dust cover of any best-selling book by one of the management gurus to see this technique in use.

It is also a good practice to send a copy of the proposal to each reference, letting each one know that you have used his or her name and thanking each for assisting you. This way you make sure these individuals are willing and are at least primed about the job.

Don't make the fatal mistake of including a standard boilerplate reference list that is several years old. If the client calls and the person listed is no longer with that firm, it can really hurt you. You may even lose the interview because of a small quality item like this.

Litigation Record. We are detecting a growing concern on the part of clients with regard to design professionals' litigation record. Several RFP's we have recently viewed have specifically asked for the detailed litigation record of the respondent.

If you have not been involved in any claims, you should use the opportunity provided by this excellent performance to say more than, "We don't have any outstanding or pending litigation."

Acme Engineers has absolutely no experience in project-related litigation. The firm maintains this policy of naiveté through a strict program of:

- *Fastidious attention to quality.*
- *Rigorous review procedures.*
- *Continuous open communications.*
- *Cooperative, team-oriented attitudes.*

Acme Engineers has no intention of gaining experience in this area. The client, contractor, and consultants will be briefed during the project kick-off meeting regarding the specific tactics to be used by all parties including:

- *Meeting schedules.*
- *Review and acceptance procedures.*
- *Project communications.*
-
-
-

254/255. One of the best ways to be seen as being different from every other consultant who has submitted a proposal is to avoid using any kind of standard form. As much as possible, try to leave your 254/255 forms out of the main body of the proposals, as they only serve to reinforce your similarity with all the other submittals. While you cannot exclude the 254/255, inserting it in as an appendix will give the greatest emphasis to the body of your own proposal. Ideally, you want to convince the client to interview your firm before they ever get to the 254/255. The attitude should be "Here are all the important things about Acme Engineers. And, by the way, here is our 254/255."

SUMMARY

A good proposal is like a good speech. First, you tell them what you are going to tell them. That's the cover letter. Then you tell them why it's important. That's the executive summary. Then you tell them. That's the body of the proposal. And finally you tell them what you told them.

But never put the words "summary" or "conclusion" in the proposal. Instead, call it "Key Points Reiterated."

The key points of our proposal are:

1. . . . .
2. . . . .
3. . . . .

At this time you go back to the executive summary and reiterate the key points you have made in a different way. This will "tie the ribbon" on the proposal.

Anyone who has taken the time to read all the way through will have the items nicely summarized, but not in a summary. If a reader has only skimmed through, you will reinforce any key issues he or she may have missed. If the reader is right-handed and flip through books from back to front, you have provided an executive summary at that reader's "start" of the document.

This "summary" is a reinforcement of the key points you have made throughout the proposal. It's important to jog the reader's memory on the key points, especially if it has been a long proposal.

APPENDICES

An appendix should include optional material that will reinforce the points you made in the proposal, but like all the other proposal elements, it should be short and succinct. Consider the client who reads through your very voluminous proposal only to find an appendix that is even more voluminous. It's unlikely it will ever be read.

Some of the elements that find their way into appendices are:

Résumés. The only reason you would include résumés in an appendix would be if there were additional team members for which the client wanted information beyond those included in the main body. Do not, as one engineering firm did, have well-written, one page résumés in the body, and then have what they called "complete" résumés for the same individuals in the appendix.

Standard Forms or Questionnaires. Some clients insist that each firm complete a standard form or questionnaire. This has the effect of making all the firms appear as similar as possible to aid in comparing "apples with apples." Of course you want to achieve the opposite effect and be incomparable with anyone. All standard forms should be relegated to the appendix unless the client has specifically stated otherwise. This gives the committee the option of referring to their standard document but they can still be "sold" with your unique approach.

SF 254/255's. Everything previously stated about standardized comparisons applies to the SF 254 and 255 forms. Never let these documents form the body of your proposal unless the client has specifically stated that your submission with be rejected without them. Push the limits of the proposal package as far as you can to create a differentiation between yourself and your competition.

References. Never have a separate listing of references. Each reference must be included with the project to which it refers. Standard reference lists run the dual risk of being too generic for the project at hand and going out of date without your being aware.

Firm History. Include a history of your firm only if the client has specifically asked for it. If it has been requested, restrict it to one page because you don't want it playing an important role. The client is more interested in whether you can do today's project than yesterday's. The firm history should state the age, how many projects you have done, what type of projects you have done, and the relevant experience of your firm. Don't include a firm organization chart as it can be a liability. It changes all the time and may not suit what client has in mind. It's far too easy for a client to wrongly interpret your organization as being too big, too small, or the wrong setup. Clients are more interested in your project organization than that of your firm. Only include a firm organization chart if you are specifically asked, and then put it at the very back of the appendix.

Philosophical Commentary. Some clients are in the habit of asking for your comments and philosophical approach to their project. This happens regularly in the education market. If you are asked to comment on "Architecture and the Middle School Environment," restrict your views to four paragraphs maximum. Keep the comments restricted to architecture, not general teaching philosophies. While the question seems important, it's a bit of a throw-away. In the same way that the Miss America contestants are asked their views on world politics, the judges only want to see how articulate you are and if you have thought about the issue. The best way to handle this would be if your firm has published any articles or given any presentations on the topic. If so, the documents should be appended to the proposal. Make sure that any documents included are of the highest quality. Don't photocopy an old piece—retype it to make it look first class. Be sure to included the publication or event in which the piece was presented.

Index. The last page in your proposal should be an index. It will serve as a reinforcement to the Table of Contents, show you to be thoroughly organized, and help your client find any specific item that cannot easily be located.

The index should be a single page listing 20–40 items that are relevant to client hot buttons. Be sure to include the names of the key project participants in the index, particularly those on the client's team. There is something seductive about finding your name in print that can make the client soften to your proposal.

PHYSICAL APPEARANCE

Binding. The binding system you use should be simple, attractive, and easy to use. And it should *not* be the standard, spiral bound system everyone uses. The world of proposals has been spiral bound to death. Other than the fact that it is an inexpensive system, spiral bound proposals are hard to deal with, hard to file, hard to add to or subtract from without tearing pages, and every one of your competitors uses them.

Make the last proposal you sent be the last one you will spiral bind.

Consider using a one-half inch or one inch 3-ring binder instead of spiral binding for your next proposal. A binder offers several advantages. It increases the visibility of your proposal in the pile of others and it allows both you and the client to easily insert additional material or notes. By using the type of binder that has the clear "view panel" in front, you can customize the proposal with your own cover. If you go to the trouble of making a spine insert as well, your firm name will be looking at the client from the spine of the binder on their bookcase every day.

Some firms have binders made up with their firm name silk-screened on the cover and spine. It's not expensive and it has a long-term benefit. Even if your firm is not chosen on this project, the client will likely throw the contents of the binder away and use it for something else. The binder will then serve as a continual marketing piece.

Your proposal should always look as professional as possible. If the project warrants, have a cover page printed that is unique to this client. Let the client know that the proposal was uniquely prepared for this project and this project alone.

Dividers. You *must* have some type of tab dividers to separate the sections of the proposal. If you can have tabs preprinted with section titles on them, that is best. If not, use a lettering system such as Kroy or Letraset. In either case, don't number the sections, forcing the reader to refer to the table of contents. Instead, put the actual section name on each tab.

Always think of your proposal sitting in a stack along with 50 others. Then imagine yourself as a committee member who must go through them all. The smallest conveniences in navigating through the document becomes significant to the reader. Make your proposals as "user friendly" as possible.

Headings and Page Numbering. Make sure your page numbering system is consistent. Don't just number text pages; the schedules, diagrams, and appendices need numbers too. Your table of contents must list page numbers as well as section headings where the information can be found.

Use many headings and a consistent type face, size, and style to distinguish between sections, subsections, headings, or any other organizing principles. If new sections are titled in 14-point Helvetica bold, do this consistently throughout the document. Then make subsections in 12-point Helvetica bold, and topic headings in 12-point Helvetica plain (or some other consistent style).

Start each section with a clear heading at the top of a new page. Never begin a heading or subsection three-quarters of the way down a page. Instead, leave some white space as a visual rest stop and start fresh at the top of the next page.

Make your document graphically simple to read. Start with a big letter at the beginning of a section, and visually draw the reader's eye to that paragraph. Don't split paragraphs or sentences between pages, especially a right page to left page paragraph. Instead of the long paragraphs of prose that we see in most proposals we review, make yours visually interesting and easy to read.

Collect copies of several newsletters or other professionally written media and copy elements of their graphic style that you find attractive and effective.

Visual Layout. Don't emphasize the content of your proposal at the expense of the visual design of the pages. Have key headlines on each page. Have question marks. Ask your client rhetorical questions in bold letters. Use graphics that are different. Make your document visually interesting for readers. Make them want to turn and find out what's on the next page.

Prepare a checklist of these basic physical features and review it before each proposal goes out the door. It's easy to forget some of the more basic things in the heat of the moment.

Color. Avoid the use of color in your proposals. The quality of color produced by xerographic technology is still not adequate. This poor quality is severely compounded when clients, as they inevitably do, make additional photocopies of the proposal on a black and white copier.

An additional reason to avoid color is that most proposals don't have it throughout. The color pages tend to stand out as "standard proposal sheets" that go into everyone's submittal. As much as possible, the finished document should look like it was prepared, cover to cover, specifically for *this* job and this job alone.

Delivering Your Proposal

As much as possible, all your proposals should have a consistent physical format. It raises the perception of the quality of your work and imposes a discipline within the firm. Have a checklist that is used on all projects to review the physical attributes of your proposals.

- ☐ Spelling and grammar checked
- ☐ Page numbers checked
- ☐ Cover letter signed
- ☐ Everything in right side up
- ☐ Business card included
- ☐ Correct number of copies
- ☐ _____
- ☐ _____

Never mail your proposal. The Post Office will destroy or lose it.

Box or package the proposal securely and express mail or courier it to the client to guarantee it will arrive intact and on time. If you are close enough or if the proposal is sufficiently important, hand deliver the package personally. Hand delivery has the additional advantage of an opportunity to enhance the personal relationship you have with the client. It may also allow you to find out more regarding the hot points on the project, which could be helpful in the presentation.

Under no circumstance should your proposal arrive late. First, it's highly likely you will be disqualified. Second, if the client does decide to accept the proposal, your first action on the project is deliver a submission late. The client is bound to wonder how the remainder of the job will go.

Always call the client after the proposal deadline. Has your proposal been received? Are there any questions you can resolve to help make the decision easier? Is everything absolutely clear?

Review of Key Proposal Pointers

- Write a cover letter that is succinct, covers the hot points, and refers to the body of the proposal.
- Include an executive summary that reinforces the cover letter, covers all the hot buttons in more specific detail, and again refers to the body of the proposal.
- Have a table of contents and have sections that are divided with labeled tabs.

- Make the body of the proposal graphically interesting and simple to read, using graphs, charts, diagrams, photographs, and less text.
- Ensure that your proposal relates specifically to how you will do this project for this particular client.
- If you don't know enough of the specifics about the project, make some assumptions but describe those assumptions clearly.
- Summarize your proposal with a summary that is not a summary.
- Only use an appendix if it's absolutely necessary and then keep it short.
- End with an index that includes the client's name.
- Deliver the proposal in a graphically interesting and easy to use binding system.
- Deliver it on time.

Imagine yourself as the person who has to read through 20, 50, or 100 proposals. What would you like to see? Respond to your own proposal: Is it easy to read? Bound in an easy to use fashion? Does it address the specific needs of this project?

We began this report by suggesting that the objective of a proposal is not to get the job, but to be invited to the interview. If your proposals are sufficiently different than those of your competition, they will make the client curious about you. Maintain a bold, aggressive attitude. It instills confidence in the client. And never apologize for being the best.

B PSMJ LIST OF MARKETING AND MANAGEMENT CONSULTANTS

1993 Management and Marketing Consultant List

For the past 18 years, **PSMJ** has compiled a list of management and marketing consultants who specialize in serving architects, consulting engineers, interior designers, planners and other design professionals. This year, for the first time, we have included our own consultants on the list in response to an increasing demand from our clients to raise the profile of our services.

To be included on the list, a firm must demonstrate to us that they have broad and significant experience in solving the unique management problems of design firms.

If you need assistance in selecting a consultant, contact **PSMJ** at: Ten Midland Avenue, Newton, MA 02158 USA, (617) 965-0055, FAX (617) 965-5152.

A. ALL PHASES OF MANAGEMENT

Barlow Associates, Inc. - 25 years consulting exclusively to design professionals. More than 500 clients in North America. Services include: organization/operations/profit improvement/mergers/acquisitions/internal transfer to ownership/ management seminars, etc. Contact Ken Barlow, Barlow Associates, Inc., 1155 North Service Road West, Suite 11, Oakville, Ontario, Canada L6M 3E3. 416/827-3500, FAX 416/827-1099.

Compass Consulting Group Inc. - assists A/E/P firms in Total Quality and Process Improvement implementation; Organizational, Cultural and Team Development; Needs Assessment and Vision-based Strategic Planning. Contact N. Boyce Appel, Compass Consulting Group, Inc., 86 Allen Road, Atlanta, GA 30328. 404/255-4925, FAX 404/851-9545.

The Coxe Group, Inc. - enters its 27th year and provides a full range of consulting services—strategic planning, ownership expansion/succession, marketing, financial management, personnel development/motivation/ compensation, key personnel search, training, total quality management, partnering, project process, mergers/acquisitions—to the evolving needs of the A/E/P community. Contact Hugh Hochberg, The Coxe Group, Inc., Seattle Tower, Suite 1700, 1218 Third Avenue, Seattle, WA 98101-3021. 206/467-4040, FAX 206/467-4038.

Edgar, Dunn & Company - provides general management consulting assistance in the areas of organization; business planning; profit improvement; management succession; ownership transition; marketing; finance/accounting; mergers/acquisitions; and ESOPs. Contact James M. Edgar, Edgar, Dunn & Company, 847 Sansome St., San Francisco, CA 94111. 415/397-5858, FAX 415/394-7629.

Enion Associates, Inc. - 34 years serving architects & engineers. Organization studies emphasize key man assessment, financial systems, marketing, matrix project management. ownership transition, mergers & acquisitions, strategic planning. executive recruiting. Contact Dick Enion, Enion Associates, Inc., P.O. Box 185, Swarthmore, PA 19081. 215/566-7550, FAX 215/544-7083.

Everett & Douglas Thompson Associates, Inc. - consultants to management of architectural and consulting engineering firms. Organization Studies, Long Range Planning, Human Resources Management, Training Programs, Client Perception Surveys and Acquisition Searches. Contact Everett S. Thompson, Everett & Douglas Thompson Associates, 1501 Briarcliff Drive S.E., Grand Rapids, MI 49546. 616/949-1309.

Flynn Heapes Kogan, L.C. - specializing in forceful strategy development through strategic business planning and future trend analysis. Specialty in the ownership transition process. Focus on our industry's five strategic systems: marketing, project operations, human resources, finance and leadership structure. Contact Ellen Flynn-Heapes and Raymond F. Kogan, Flynn Heapes Kogan, L.C., 218 N. Lee Street, #301, Alexandria, VA 22314. 703/838-8080, FAX 703/838-8082.

Hensey Associates - serving engineering and technical organizations since 1974. Services include strategic planning, organization re-design, management team development, and total quality management, among others. Contact Mel or Carol Hensey, Hensey Associates, 8776 Long Lane, Cincinnati, OH 45231. 513/931-0414.

Brian J. Lewis Company - has assisted over 100 U.S. and overseas A/E clients since 1980, preceded by 26 years hands-on engineering/managerial/owner experience. Specialize in ownership transfer, mergers/acquisitions. Contact Brian J. Lewis, P.E., Brian J. Lewis Company, 241 Chimney Lane, Wilmington, NC 28409-4911. 910/799-2367, FAX 910/791-7756.

Management Design - provides full-range business consulting services, including long-range and strategic planning, assessments, retreats. Experience includes 500+ A/E/D/P firms, all sizes & phases of growth, over 23 years. Contact George Schrohe, Management Design, 100 Bush St., Suite 650, San Francisco, CA 94104. 415/989-4338.

Martin-Simonds Associates, Inc. - is a consultant to engineering and architectural firms and offers over 17 years of expertise in the areas of strategic planning, marketing, human resources, employee surveys, client satisfaction surveys, management development and acquisitions/mergers. Contact John M. Simonds, Martin-Simonds Associates, Inc., 506 Second Avenue, Suite 3100, Seattle, WA 98104. 206/623-2562, FAX 206/682-8256.

Parkhill & Company - The mission of Parkhill & Company is to assist A/E firms in elevating the quality of management practices to the level demanded in project delivery. Contact Charles A. Parkhill, Parkhill & Company, 2900 West Maple - Suite 107, Troy, MI 48084. 313/649-1211.

Practice Management Associates, Ltd. - The publishers and editors of PSMJ/AEMJ/PM newsletters and PSMJ surveys offer complete consulting services to the design community. Services include strategic planning, ownership/management transition, operations, project management, training, marketing, compensation, and financial management. Clients served throughout the U.S., Canada, Australia and New Zealand. Consultants include Frank Stasiowski, David Rinderer and David Stone. Contact Judy Clausen, Practice Management Associates, 8850 Villa La Jolla Dr. #106, La Jolla, CA 92037. 619/450-6685, FAX 619/450-2968.

Roenker Bates Group - serving consulting needs of technical organizations since 1986; services include strategic planning, ownership transition, management team building, financial analysis and project management training programs; also facilitate partnering workshops. Contact Gary D. Bates, Roenker Bates Group, 11231 Cornell Park Drive, Cincinnati, OH 45242. 513/489-6663, FAX 513/489-2533.

Don Thompson Management Consultant - services include retreat facilitation, strategic planning, management audits, ownership transition, organizational development, human resource training in communications and other in-house seminars. Contact Don Thompson, 3247 Embry Hills Drive, Atlanta, GA 30341. 404/455-8414.

Warner Raboy Associates - specializes in consulting with A/E/P firms on competitive strategic planning; marketing professional services; written/verbal communication techniques; financial management; and project management information systems. Contact Suzanne Warner Raboy, Warner Raboy Associates, 521 Fifth Ave., Suite 1740, New York, NY 10175. 800/487-9302, FAX 800/488-7471.

B. COMPREHENSIVE MARKETING

Building Development Counsel, Inc. - provides professional services for A/E firms nationwide in pursuit of Federal Government Design awards. Identify projects, agency contacts, 254/255 critiques and contract negotiating assistance. Contact John Filice, Building Development Counsel, Inc., 1717 K Street, NW, Suite 502, Washington, DC 20036. 202/429-2575, FAX 202/429-2806.

Coyne Associates - national firm since 1975, consults in evaluating/organizing marketing and PR programs, mar-

keting plans, workshops/sales training, presentation interviews, staff evaluation, corporate identity. Contact John Coyne, Coyne Associates, 4010 East Lake Street, Minneapolis, MN 55406. 612/724-1188, FAX 612/722-1379.

Flynn Heapes Kogan, L.C. - market research, market planning, sales and communications. Typical projects include image and competitive positioning research studies, market assessments identifying and penetrating new markets, market audits, sales & communications training, and strategic planning. Contact Ellen Flynn-Heapes and Raymond F. Kogan, Flynn Heapes Kogan, L.C., 218 N. Lee Street, #301, Alexandria, VA 22314. 703/838-8080, FAX 703/838-8082.

Kenney and Associates - Comprehensive services. Planning through implementation: marketplace positioning, competitive strategies, marketing program evaluation, marketing plans, research, direct client contact, customized training sessions/seminars, proposal preparation, presentation strategy/training, and communications. Contact Carolyn E. Kenney, Kenney and Associates, 8201 Edgewater Drive, #205, Oakland, CA 94621. 510/653-8808.

Lawson Research International - provides comprehensive marketing research and consulting. Conducts training workshops and keynote presentations in A/E sales, marketing and business development. Contact John W. Lawson, Lawson Research International, 902 Sugarloaf Road - Clarke #50, Colorado Springs, CO 80829. 800/386-9377.

The Lentz Group, Inc. - Marketing strategy and plans, proposals and presentations, research, public relations, direct mail, canned data, award submittals (including FAIA), seminars and presentation training. Contact Kay Lentz, 2600 Citadel Plaza Drive, Suite 510, Houston, TX 77008. 713/864-2623, FAX 713/864-7430.

Brian J. Lewis Company - see listing under "A - All Phases of Management"

Marketing Research Consultants - specializes in marketing research services, including image surveys, client satisfaction surveys, market studies, and other customized research studies dealing with better understanding markets and clients. Contact Tina McGurk, MRC, 752 Glenview Road, Glendale, CA 91202. 818/244-4870.

Martin-Simonds Associates, Inc. - see listing under "A - All Phases of Management"

Parkhill & Company - see listing under "A - All Phases of Management"

Practice Management Associates, Ltd. - see listing under "A - All Phases of Management"

Frank H. Smith III, AIA - over 12 year's experience in marketing program audits, market plan development, image studies, new client/market identification, qualifications statement/ presentation preparation, market research, brochure development. Contact Frank Smith, 4222 Conway Valley Road NW, Atlanta, GA 30327. 404/237-7750.

Warner Raboy Associates - see listing under "A - All Phases of Management"

C. Public Relations/Marketing Communications

BA Communications, Inc. - assists clients in reaching their clients through targeted marketing communications, public relations and media placement. Reprints of published materials are used for marketing. Contact Lois E. Boemer, BA Communications, 797 Washington Street, Suite 5, Newtonville, MA 02160. 617/527-2080, FAX 617/527-6329.

Capelin Communications, Inc. - the first PR office to work exclusively with the design professions, still the standard of measure. Strategy, writing, publicity, events, crisis management, training, counsel. National clientele. Contact Joan Capelin, Capelin Communications, Inc., 257 Park Ave. S., New York, NY 10010. 212/353-8800, FAX 212/353-8499.

Coyne Associates - since 1975, conducts PR audits; helps organize PR/marketing communications/identity programs; writes and designs brochures, logos, advertising, direct mail, client newsletters, publicity, articles. Contact John Coyne, Coyne Associates, 4010 East Lake Street, Minneapolis, MN 55406. 612/724-1188, FAX 612/722-1379.

Fuessler Group Inc. - is a nine-year old full-service marketing communications firm that has helped nearly 90 professional service firms nationwide attract attention, change perceptions, build image, and broadcast accomplishments. Contact Rolf Fuessler, Fuessler Group Inc., 324 Shawmut Ave., Boston, MA 02118. 617/262-3964, FAX 617/266-1068.

Hardeman Communications - specialists in communications programs for professional services firms. We develop and implement public relations, community information, and publications programs that support your business development goals. Contact Ann Hardeman, Hardeman Communications, 70A Greenwich Avenue/285, New York, NY 10011. 212/620-3028.

Kenney and Associates - Planning through production and implementation of communications materials for the design professional. Writing and presentation training seminars, special events, brochures, newsletters, articles, and direct mail. Contact Carolyn E. Kenney, Kenney and Assoc., 8201 Edgewater Drive, #205, Oakland, CA 94621. 510/653-8808 .

John R. Kubasek & Associates, Inc. - serves construction industry clients exclusively; development of total marketing strategies and implementation of plan(s); full public relations and in-house graphics services; accredited advertising agency. Contact John Kubasek, John R. Kubasek & Associates, Inc., 407 Manor Road, Staten Island, NY 10314.

718/727-4366, FAX 718/720-7918.

The Lentz Group, Inc. - see listing under "B - Comprehensive Marketing"

Practice Management Associates, Ltd. - see listing under "A - All Phases of Management"

D. Financial Management

AE Resources - firmwide and project related financial management including budgeting and reporting, needs analysis and implementation of financial management software systems, operations management, tax planning and ownership expansion/transition plans. Contact Richard Pipkin, A/E Resources, 116 New Montgomery Street, Suite 506, San Francisco, CA 94105. 415/957-1956, FAX 415/957-0786.

Arthur Andersen & Co. - provides assistance to architectural and engineering firms in solving government contracting, cost accounting, and other financial and accounting issues. Contact Dean Fischer, Arthur Andersen & Co., 33 West Monroe Street, Chicago, IL 60603. 312/507-6079.

Design Management Consulting, Inc. - comprehensive advice on financial issues, including firm valuation, ownership transition, incentive compensation, profit planning, government contracting and financial reporting systems. Contact Bill Fanning, Design Management Consulting, Inc., 271 Cross Gate Dr., Marietta, GA 30068. 404/971-7586, FAX 404/977-3679.

Management Design - provides financial & profit planning profitability analysis/implementation plans, computerized accounting systems integrated with project cost control/ project management training programs and government contracting. Contact Steve Quiggle or George Schrohe, Management Design, 100 Bush Street, Suite 650, San Francisco, CA 94104. 415/989-4338.

Richard Nanni, CPA - CPAs/Management Consultants providing financial management expertise to A/E firms for 17 years. Specialized Time-Shared Financial Management provides broad experience on call. Contact Richard Nanni, Business Consulting and Management Group, 740 Hickory Drive, Geneseo, IL 61254. 309/786-9872, 309/944-6663, FAX 309/786-9994.

Practice Management Associates, Ltd. - see listing under "A - All Phases of Management"

Repole Associates - part time controller, financial manager, specialize in business plans and cash forecasts. Also do overhead audits, company valuations and ownership transitions. Contact Joe Repole, Repole Associates, 15 Gryzboska Circle, Framingham, MA 01701. 508/879-6340.

Roenker Bates Group - see listing under "A - All Phases of Management"

Tofias Fleishman Shapiro & Co., P.C. - We service over 40 architectural/engineering firms of all sizes, providing tax planning, strategic and business planning, and accounting and auditing services. Contact David Wexler (ext. 107) or Jeffrey Mead (ext. 235), Tofias Fleishman Shapiro & Co., P.C., 205 Broadway, Cambridge, MA 02139. 617/547-5900.

Warner Raboy Associates - see listing under "A - All Phases of Management"

E. HUMAN RESOURCES

Compass Consulting Group, Inc. - see listing under "A - All Phases of Management"

Edgar, Dunn & Company - see listing under "A - All Phases of Management"

Brian J. Lewis Company - see listing under "A - All Phases of Management"

Management Design - conducts compensation surveys and provides human resources consulting and planning services, including performance evaluation programs, personnel manuals, employee recruitment, development and retention plans. Contact Rose Anthony, Management Design, 100 Bush Street, Suite 650, San Francisco, CA 94104. 415/989-4338.

Martin-Simonds Associates, Inc. - see listing under "A - All Phases of Management"

Charles M. McReynolds - 32 years experience in all aspects of human resources as applied to consulting engineers and architects. Author of book Human Resource Management for Design Firms published by ACEC. Contact C.M. McReynolds, 19 Suffolk, Suite A, Sierra Madre, CA 91024. 818/798-4287.

Practice Management Associates, Ltd. - see listing under "A - All Phases of Management"

F. EXECUTIVE RECRUITING

Claremont-Branan, Inc. - recruiting consultants with more than nine years of specialized A/E experience throughout the U.S. International experience. Contact Phil Collins, 2302 Parklake Drive NE, Suite 460, Atlanta, GA 30345. 404/491-1292, FAX 404/939-9747.

Brian J. Lewis Company - see listing under "A - All Phases of Management"

McNichol Associates - Over 17 years' experience as executive recruitment specialists solving the management needs of architectural, engineering and construction firms nationally and internationally. Contact John McNichol, McNichol

Associates, 600 Chestnut Street, Suite 1031, Philadelphia, PA 19106. 215/922-4142, FAX 215/922-0178.

Charles M. McReynolds - we specialize in locating partners, regional office managers, department chiefs and technical gurus. Our searches are conducted on an hourly rate basis with a guaranteed maximum. We don't conduct contingency or advance fee searches. Contact Chuck McReynolds, Charles M. McReynolds, 19 Suffolk, Suite A, Sierra Madre, CA 91024. 818/798-4287.

Marjanne Pearson Associates - established national practice for proactive recruiting and selection services. We specialize in working with high-profile architectural and related design firms for principal-level design, technical, management, and marketing positions. Contact Marjanne Pearson, Marjanne Pearson Associates, 1174 Holman Road, Oakland, CA 94611. 510/452-1460, FAX 510/452-1411.

Powers Consultants, Inc. - serves planning/design firms - architects, consulting engineers, A/Es, geo-environmental engineering, interior design - on a national basis, providing clients with search services on a retained basis. Contact William D. Powers, Powers Consultants, Inc., 2241A South Brentwood Blvd., Ste. IV, St. Louis, MO 63144. 314/961-8787.

Practice Management Associates, Ltd. - see listing under "A - All Phases of Management"

G. QUALITY MANAGEMENT/QA/QC SERVICES

Compass Consulting Group, Inc. - see listing under "A - All Phases of Management"

William M. Hayden, Jr. Consultants, Inc. - offers TQM consulting services and Partnering for Project Quality™ workshops exclusively for consulting engineers, architects and environmental services firms worldwide. Co-founder of both the Design & Construction Quality Institute and the A/E & C Division of ASQC. Contact Bill Hayden, William M. Hayden Jr. Consultants, Inc. P.O. Box 56022, Jacksonville, FL 32241-6022. 904/260-7700, FAX 904/260-7701.

Martin-Simonds Associates, Inc. - see listing under "A - All Phases of Management"

Practice Management Associates, Ltd. - see listing under "A - All Phases of Management"

Copyright 1993
PSMJ
Ten Midland Avenue
Newton, MA 02158 USA
(617) 965-0055
FAX (617) 965-5152

INDEX